Kayte Harrier

Astute and accessible, comprehensive and compelling, here's an outstanding introduction to classical apologetics. You'll find yourself going back time after time to this invaluable reservoir of insights and wisdom. Read it with a highlighter in hand!

—**Lee Strobel,** founding director of the Lee Strobel
Center for Evangelism and Applied Apologetics
at Colorado Christian University

Groothuis and Shepardson have written a brilliant defense of classical apologetics. They've ably shown, with incredible lucidity, impressive research, and tightly given arguments, that God exists and that Christianity is the true religion founded by God. And they've mounted a sophisticated and comprehensive defense of the need, importance, and validity of defending and commending these beliefs to others. *The Knowledge of God in the World and the Word* is an outstanding one-stop resource to equip believers to share powerful arguments for Christianity. Read it. Study it. Then go and tell of this God revealed in the world and in the Word.

—**Paul M. Gould,** associate professor of philosophy of religion,
director of the MA in philosophy of religion program,
Palm Beach Atlantic University

I heartily recommend this valuable volume by Doug Groothuis and Andrew Shepardson. Their book serves as an excellent guide about reasons for God's existence and the Christian faith. In addition to clearly laying out these arguments, the authors place them in their proper theological and philosophical context. What's more, the authors include examples from their own academic and ministry experiences, helping bring these arguments into a clearer light and make them more accessible and relevant.

—**Paul Copan,** Pledger Family Chair of Philosophy and Ethics,
Palm Beach Atlantic University, and author of *Is God a Moral Monster?* and *Is God a Vindictive Bully?*

If there's anything our world needs today, it's the knowledge of God—and this book delivers! It is academically astute but also highly accessible to readers who are new to the topic. And in the end it shows how we can apply what we've read to our everyday conversations with friends and colleagues who desperately need the information we've learned. This book is a winner!

—**Mark Mittelberg,** executive director of the Lee Strobel Center for Evangelism and Applied Apologetics at Colorado Christian University, and author of *Contagious Faith* and *The Questions Christians Hope No One Will Ask (With Answers)*

THE
KNOWLEDGE
OF GOD
IN THE WORLD
AND
THE WORD

THE
KNOWLEDGE
OF GOD
IN THE WORLD
AND
THE WORD

• • •

An Introduction to
CLASSICAL APOLOGETICS

DOUGLAS GROOTHUIS and
ANDREW I. SHEPARDSON

ZONDERVAN
ACADEMIC

ZONDERVAN ACADEMIC

The Knowledge of God in the World and the Word
Copyright © 2022 by Douglas Groothuis and Andrew I. Shepardson

Requests for information should be addressed to:
Zondervan, *3900 Sparks Dr. SE, Grand Rapids, Michigan 49546*

Zondervan titles may be purchased in bulk for educational, business, fundraising, or sales promotional use. For information, please email SpecialMarkets@Zondervan.com.

ISBN 978-0-310-15440-2 (audio)

Library of Congress Cataloging-in-Publication Data

Names: Groothuis, Douglas R., 1957- author. | Shepardson, Andrew I., author.
Title: The knowledge of God in the world and the word : an introduction to classical
    apologetics / Douglas Groothuis, Andrew I. Shepardson.
Description: Grand Rapids : Zondervan, 2022. | Includes index.
Identifiers: LCCN 2022025157 (print) | LCCN 2022025158 (ebook) | ISBN 9780310113072
    (hardcover) | ISBN 9780310113089 (ebook)
Subjects: LCSH: Apologetics. | Natural theology. | God (Christianity)--Knowableness.
Classification: LCC BT1103 .G7625 2022 (print) | LCC BT1103 (ebook) | DDC
    239--dc23/eng/20220725
LC record available at https://lccn.loc.gov/2022025157
LC ebook record available at https://lccn.loc.gov/2022025158

Cover design: Bruce Gore | Gore Studio, Inc.
Cover photo: © Tanawat Thipmontha / Getty Images
Interior design: Kait Lamphere

Printed in the United States of America

22 23 24 25 26 27 28 29 30 31 32 /LSC/ 15 14 13 12 11 10 9 8 7 6 5 4 3 2 1

To my wife, Kathleen, whose patience, kindness,
prayers, and love helped make this book possible
—Doug

● ● ●

To my beautiful wife, Kelsey Rae
—Ike

CONTENTS

PART 1:

OBJECTIONS TO CLASSICAL APOLOGETICS

PART 2:

GOD EXISTS

PART 3:

THE CHRISTIAN STORY IS TRUE

INTRODUCTION

Do you know that Christianity is true? Do you even think about it this way? You may know that 3 +3 = 6 or that Mars is the next furthest planet from the Sun after Earth. You may know your best friend or know that you like pizza. But what do you know about Christianity? As Christians, we rightly think that placing one's faith in Jesus means that we *know Jesus*. Of course, this is of utmost importance: "Here I am! I stand at the door and knock. If anyone hears my voice and opens the door, I will come in and eat with that person, and they with me" (Rev. 3:20). Jesus does not simply want us to know things about him, but he wants us to know him as Savior, Lord, and friend. But it is possible that you haven't really thought of your faith in terms of *knowing that Christianity is true*. This is important because whether or not you have thought about it this way, you would claim that you know a number of important things because of your faith in Jesus: (1) God exists, (2) Jesus is God, (3) Jesus lived a perfect life, (4) Jesus died on the cross for your sins and rose again, (5) the Holy Spirit is God and lives in you now, and so on. These items of knowledge logically follow from your faith in Jesus.

Is it possible to share your knowledge of God with those who are outside of God's family? Could they ever come to share in your knowledge? Is there hope that they, too, could come to faith in God? We think that the answer to all these questions is yes, and we are eager to show you how *apologetics* is an important tool as you think about sharing your faith with others. Apologetics is the ministry of defending and commending the knowledge of God that is revealed in the Bible and in the world around us. Coming from the Greek word *apologia*, meaning an account or a defense of the truth of one's position, apologetics helps you to explain to others what you know to be true about the Christian faith.[1]

THE STAKES ARE HIGH

I (Ike) have many friends who grew up in the Christian faith but left it behind. People leave the faith for various reasons. Some have suffered spiritual, emotional, or sexual abuse. Some have found various Christian subcultures to be unaccommodating to LGBTQ persons. Some are appalled at the moral failings of Christians or their willingness to sellout to political candidates and causes that are deemed objectionable. When I've seen a loved one deconstruct their faith this way and ultimately leave it behind, it grieves me. Of course, I grieve for the friend who I believe now misses out on participating in God's redemption of the world through the church, flawed as it is. But I grieve as well for the ways unanswered or poorly answered questions can factor into someone rejecting Christianity. For example, many people believe that Christianity is antiscience. While we do not think this is the case (in fact, you'll see in the pages that follow that we find in the natural world some key evidences for the existence of God), some Christians give the strong impression that scientists are not to be trusted. Some Christians are antiscience. This creates a conflict between the scientifically minded person and his or her faith. What is at stake in studying apologetics is the ability to answer the questions of people who struggle with intellectual and existential questions where they perceive a conflict between their Christian faith and some other important issue such as their love of science, their reverence for reason, or their personal identity. Apologetics can do just that.

Think also about the person who has a sense of longing in her life for something deeper. Perhaps this person has no heritage of Christian faith but seems like a spiritual seeker. In our experience, we have seen these people be open to having spiritual conversations or to attending a church

---

1. See Gerhard Kittel, ed., *Theological Dictionary of the New Testament*, trans and ed. Geoffrey W. Bromiley (Grand Rapids: Eerdmans, 1967), 4:103; see also Colin Brown, ed., *The New International Dictionary of New Testament Theology* (Grand Rapids: Zondervan, 1986), 1:51.

service. They often read religious books or express reverence for various religious traditions. There is a long tradition in Christian thought for what is happening in such a person. These people are showing that they have eternity in their hearts (Eccl. 3:11), they have restless hearts that cannot rest until they rest in God (Augustine), they have an infinite spiritual hole that can only be filled with an infinite object (Blaise Pascal), or they have a desire that nothing in this world can satisfy (C. S. Lewis).[2] What would happen today if such a person came to your church and asked a member of the congregation a question about why God would allow so much suffering in the world? What would happen if such a soul showed up at your small group and asked about why you think we can trust the Bible when it is filled with legends and myths? What would you say if one of these for whom Jesus died asked you, "How can I know that Jesus really is God?" We see apologetics as a key way to address questions that can help people to find their way closer to Jesus.

Finally, consider our broader culture in the West today. Christianity seems as if it is on the retreat, and the traditional explanations from the Christian worldview are increasingly implausible for many Westerners. When my wife and I (Ike) moved onto a new street, we started getting to know our neighbors and inviting them into our lives in various ways. We formed a quick connection with a dear couple who we invited to church. After politely declining to join us at church a couple of times, they offered an explanation: "We're committed atheists." They were eager to be our friends, but they did not want to join us at church. Moreover, they seemed to try to limit future conversations about spiritual matters by letting us know that their atheism was serious. What if, by showing that Christianity is true and rational and pertinent to every aspect of life, you were able to help people like this to see that the answers that the Christian worldview offers are worth considering? What if you could help awaken a desire to look at the Bible as a source of knowledge? What if you could help point people who would otherwise continue in their search for money, adventure, and pleasure to start searching for Jesus? This is what apologetics can help you to do.

---

2. See respectively, Augustine, *The Confessions of Saint Augustine*, trans. Rex Warner (New York: Signet, 2001), 1:1; Blaise Pascal, *Pensées*, trans. A. J. Krailsheimer (New York: Penguin, 1966), 148/428; C. S. Lewis, *Mere Christianity*, rev. ed (New York: HarperOne, 1980), 136–37.

WHY THIS BOOK IS DIFFERENT

While there are many great books out there about the subject, this book will introduce you to a helpful way to think about apologetics without assuming that you have previous knowledge in the subject. The method that we discuss is the *classical* method. This helpful way to think about apologetics first shows that God exists by appealing to evidence of his existence outside of the Bible. Second, the classical method shows that certain features of the biblical worldview are true by appealing to evidence in philosophy, history, archaeology, science, and biblical studies. Classical apologetics helps you to frame in your mind the two steps most helpful for engaging those who are skeptical about the truth of Christianity. However, we are not dogmatists about the method. Throughout the book, we will give you tips and reflections to encourage you to meet your friends, neighbors, and loved ones *where they are*, considering what questions they have and what objections they bring up. The method is helpful for you to remember the contours of Christian apologetics but flexible enough for you to develop great skills in how you sensitively speak the truth in love to others.

Another way this book is different is that we do not assume you have previous knowledge about apologetics in order to get something out of the book. In fact, we have written the book with church small groups, introductory level college and seminary classes, and lay leaders in mind. There will be times when you will see some academic jargon, but we have diligently attempted to explain and define the jargon without watering down the material. This is because we believe that apologetics should not be the sole domain of scholars. We believe everyday Christians can and should do apologetics without feeling like they must develop expertise first. To that end, we talk about apologetics as people who actually do apologetics in our day-to-day lives. While we have serious academic backgrounds, Ike has spent a considerable amount of his professional career working in the software industry, and Doug has a lengthy background in campus ministry. We do not just lecture on these things. Because of this, you'll hear our firsthand accounts from the field and be able to see through our eyes how to engage everyday folks with the truth and rationality of Christianity. We have friends and family members who have come to know Jesus with the aid of apologetics, and we have seen many of our Christian brothers and sisters greatly strengthened in their faith by the material in this book.

WHAT'S TO COME

The first chapter will give you an introduction to the topic of apologetics and some key terms such as general revelation, special revelation, and natural theology that apologists use to explain our task. It will also walk you through the biblical basis for apologetics and the kind of Christian character needed to do apologetics. Chapters two and three will address some serious objections to Christian apologetics including those made by Christians who think that faith should not appeal to reason and those made by skeptics who think that religion is inherently illogical. Chapter 4 will look at the nature of the universe and discuss some philosophical and scientific reasons why God must exist to explain the universe's existence and why anything exists at all (Cosmological Arguments). Chapter 5 investigates the very idea of a Perfect Being like the God of the Bible and why the existence of God is required to even have a coherent thought about God (Ontological Arguments). Chapter 6 will examine our moral knowledge and intuitions and show that moral values and duties such as the evilness of murder or the goodness of generosity require a divine foundation (the Moral Argument). It will also discuss the problem of evil. Chapter 7 will explore how the cosmos is filled with evidence that it has been designed by a wise and powerful being who is outside the universe. This chapter will introduce readers to the arguments from physics and biology for the intelligent design of the universe (Design Arguments).

In chapter 8, we will shift our attention away from showing that God exists to discussing God's revelation in the Bible. We will show how the Bible is a reliable and accurate historical document that can show us the truth about God's revelation. Chapter 9 will take this line of thinking deeper by showing that Jesus of Nazareth is God and deserves our attention for his claims, credentials, and works in history. Chapter 10 will then provide proof of Jesus' resurrection in history and show how you can explain this key truth to others who have questions about Jesus. The book will then conclude with some considerations about how you can actually use apologetics in your life and ministry, especially in evangelism and discipleship.

• • •

What you're about to study is powerful and serious, but there is also great encouragement in the Bible as you do apologetics. In the spring of 1977, when I (Doug) was in college, I wrote an apologetic letter to the editor of the University of Oregon newspaper. One of my professors, an embittered religious studies scholar, wrote a letter in response saying I didn't know what I was talking about. I then realized that my Christian witness would be contested by people in authority. I responded in writing to my professor's critique in a subsequent letter to the editor, but the exchange helped me to realize that I was in a battle for ideas. As Paul reminds us,

> For though we live in the world, we do not wage war as the world does. The weapons we fight with are not the weapons of the world. On the contrary, they have divine power to demolish strongholds. We demolish arguments and every pretension that sets itself up against the knowledge of God, and we take captive every thought to make it obedient to Christ (2 Cor. 10:3–5).

In beginning your journey in Christian apologetics, it is helpful to step back and to take stock of the fact that we are not talking about merely intellectual things, but we are dealing with arguments and pretensions that are against the knowledge of God. Yet we must also gratefully acknowledge that God has given us weapons in this spiritual war that have real power to accomplish his will. Our part is to take our thoughts captive in obedience to Jesus. In doing so, think again about how God might use you to speak the truth in love to those around you. What opportunities might he open up for you to confidently share your knowledge about God? Who in your life needs to hear about the hope that you have in Jesus? Which Christians in your life need strengthening in their walk with Jesus with solid answers about the truth? We invite you to join us on this exciting opportunity to discover the knowledge of God in the world and in God's word.

CHAPTER 1

WHAT IS CLASSICAL APOLOGETICS?

We are so pleased that you have joined us in the quest to discover the knowledge of God in the world and the Word. Whether you are reading this book in a small group, for a class, or for personal enrichment, the effort is worth it as you prepare to share with others why you have hope in Jesus. This is, after all, what apologetics is all about. We care about showing others what God has done in the world around us, showing others who God is, and helping them to see that they, too, can know God. What you will learn in this book is important for a number of reasons. First, this book is written to help you learn how to be a better witness for Jesus in a world where people do not already understand the basic Christian message. Apologetics is a way of carrying out the Great Commission. Remember how Jesus sent out his earliest followers:

> Then Jesus came to them and said, "All authority in heaven and on earth has been given to me. Therefore go and make disciples of all nations, baptizing them in the name of the Father and of the Son and of the Holy Spirit, and teaching them to obey everything I have commanded you. And surely I am with you always, to the very end of the age." (Matt. 28:18–20)

Followers of Jesus today rightly read this passage as a command to participate in the Lord's mission to bless the nations through the establishment of his kingdom and as an encouragement that Jesus' authoritative presence remains with his followers as they partner with him in that mission. In the pages that follow, you will learn how to point others to Jesus by helping them see that the Christian message is true and not just a matter of personal taste or cultural upbringing. One of the best ways to lead someone to embrace Christ is to help them to see that Christ is real and that he is who the Bible says he is. Apologetics helps you to lead people to Jesus by showing them that he is God.

Second, this book is written to help you respond in a loving and knowledgeable way to those who ask the important questions in life. If you interact with people around you who are not Christians, then you probably have heard questions that people have about faith. Why do Christians believe that an ancient document is true? Doesn't science disprove God? If God is all-powerful and all-good, then why is there so much evil in the world? Isn't it arrogant to believe that Christianity is true and everyone else is wrong? Now there are certainly times when questions such as these do not require a response. Sometimes these are spoken rhetorically by someone who is suffering. Sometimes these are spoken not out of genuine seeking but out of condemnation and skeptical gamesmanship. However, in our experience, these questions are more often genuinely asked. We recommend that the most loving, Christlike thing to do is to provide answers to people's questions. Francis Schaeffer offered this encouragement on this subject:

> Paul went to the Jews, and what happened as he talked to them? They asked Paul questions, and he answered. He went to the non-Jews, the Gentiles, and they asked him questions, and he answered. He went into the marketplace, and there his ministry was a ministry of discussion, of giving honest answers to honest questions. . . . Consider the ministry of our Lord Jesus himself. What was his ministry like? He was constantly answering questions.[1]

---

1. Francis A. Schaeffer, "Form and Freedom in the Church," in *Let the Earth Hear His Voice: Official Reference Volume, Papers, and Responses*, International Conference on World Evangelization: Lausanne, Switzerland, ed. J. D. Douglas (Minneapolis: World Wide Publications, 1975), 372.

"Honest answers to honest questions" is an important value for apologists, and we are grateful that God has seen fit to provide solid answers to life's biggest questions. This book represents our desire to share those answers with you in prayerful hope that they will help you to respond lovingly with the truth to those around you who have honest questions.

Third, we recognize that intellectual doubts are common among Christians.[2] These are not things to be shoved aside or addressed with simple platitudes. Christians should be able to assuage their intellectual doubts with reason and evidence. Think about the much maligned apostle Thomas, who said, "Unless I see the nail marks in his hands and put my finger where the nails were, and put my hand into his side, I will not believe" (John 20:25). Jesus did not pronounce judgment on Thomas for his desire for evidence. Instead, Jesus appealed to the evidence on his resurrected body and welcomed Thomas to examine it himself. "Put your finger here; see my hands. Reach out your hand and put it into my side. Stop doubting and believe" (v. 27). Some people may never struggle through doubt, but for many of us, intellectual doubts can trip us up and cause us to stagnate in our faith. They can be discouraging, and for some, intellectual doubts about the truth of Christianity can be a factor in rejecting Christian faith altogether. Some of those who will read this book may never struggle with intellectual doubt, and that's great. But we all likely have people in our families and churches who have real questions about the truth of Christianity. Just as it is loving to be able to respond to the questions of those who are outside the family of faith, so we must embody Christ's love in learning how to help Christians with their doubts and questions.

Finally, apologetics is worth our attention simply because it helps us to receive the knowledge of God. Knowing God and knowing about God are ends in themselves; they don't need to be justified by some other utilitarian goal. Learning about God should be one of the ambitions of a Christian life. Consider a close friend or a loved one. The genuineness of your affection and the sincerity of your commitment to that person can largely be seen in how well you know them. What do they like to talk about? What important things have they done? What do they love and hate? Why are

---

2. Of course, not all doubt is intellectual. We address this in chapter 11.

they the way they are? When you know these things about a loved one, it represents your genuine love for them. Your knowledge of your loved one is beautiful in and of itself. This is exactly the kind of knowledge on which apologetics focuses our attention. How did God create the world? What are God's commands? What do we read about Jesus that is so arresting and beautiful? How can we know that he really did what the Bible says he did? When we learn these things through apologetics, we are learning to love and know God better, and that is a lofty goal.

KNOWLEDGE STARTS WITH REVELATION

We have called this book *The Knowledge of God in the World and the Word* because we think that part of what makes Christianity so beautiful is that God has revealed God's self to us. This is amazing because God is under no external compulsion to do so. God could have remained silent or aloof, yet by his love he has seen fit to speak to us. Classical apologetics begins, then, with the presupposition that God has revealed God's self in some key ways. First, God has spoken through the Bible. The Bible itself, along with the person and work of Jesus Christ and the Holy Spirit, is part of a class of God's self-revelation known as special revelation. We take this to be the definitive revelation of God. It forms the primary material from which we understand the truth about God, humanity, the good life, the world, and any other topic it addresses. In this text, we will explore why the Bible is historically reliable, why Jesus is rightly received as God in human form, and why it is correct to believe that Jesus died and rose from the dead. The Bible is the primary way we understand these truths.

But God is not only known through the Bible. God has also revealed God's self more universally in the world, and this is known as general revelation. All people have access to knowledge of God's existence, some of God's attributes, and the moral law provided through this type of God's revelation in the world. Think about these words of David:

> The heavens declare the glory of God;
>> the skies proclaim the work of his hands.

Day after day they pour forth speech;
     night after night they reveal knowledge.
They have no speech, they use no words;
     no sound is heard from them.
Yet their voice goes out into all the earth,
     their words to the ends of the world. (Ps. 19:1–4)

Apologetics cares deeply about the knowledge of God that we learn about from looking at the world around us. While the Bible remains the definitive authority on life and doctrine, the Bible itself claims that God has also spoken in other ways, particularly in what you see in the natural world, in logic, and in the human conscience. The kinds of arguments you will see in the first half of the book are related to God's general revelation. We will learn how the very concept of God logically entails God's existence, how the origin of the universe and the design of certain features of the creation are evidence for God, and how the moral law requires the existence of a divine lawgiver.

The two categories of God's revelation explained above, special and general revelation, have often been poorly explained and misrepresented. We should first note that these are not simply sources of knowledge that can be used and interpreted however one wants. These are modes of God's own revelation. In that sense, God is the giver of his revelation, and the proper interpretation is God's.[3] We should also understand that some people have mistakenly understood that general revelation is only about what has been revealed in the natural world. Indeed, some have mislabeled this category as "natural revelation," but this is mistaken. In fact, the Bible (usually) takes place in the natural world. Jesus was born as a natural man, just as much as he is the eternal, spiritual, and nonnatural Son. So special revelation is often about the natural world and about natural events.[4] Moreover, arguments that refer to our

---

3. This is a further reason to hold the Bible as the definitive source of revelation. It provides the proper interpretation of general revelation.

4. N. T. Wright makes this point about the Bible, and for this reason he rejects the natural/special distinction. He is correct to reject the insinuation that the Bible does not relate to the natural world, but in making the point, he misses out on the theological benefits of the general/special distinction that is used by most apologists. See N. T. Wright, *History and Eschatology: Jesus and the Promise of Natural Theology*, The 2018 Gifford Lectures (Waco, TX: Baylor University Press, 2019), esp. ch. 1.

conceptions of God and the moral law relate to aspects of our minds, which are nonnatural and mental. When you think about an argument that shows God's existence, you are doing a mental activity, not simply a natural one.[5] So it would be a mistake to say that there is a spiritual, biblical revelation on the one hand and a natural revelation on the other. We say *general* revelation because it is revelation that is given generally or universally to all humanity, whereas the Bible is *specially* given to God's people at specific times in history. This is why it is important to refer to God's *special* revelation (the Bible, Jesus, the Holy Spirit) and God's *general* revelation (nature, logic, the human conscience).

CLASSICAL APOLOGETICS DEFENDS AND COMMENDS THE KNOWLEDGE OF GOD

Classical apologetics is the ministry of defending and commending the knowledge of God that is revealed in the Bible and in the world around us. Apologetics shows how Christianity is true, rational, and pertinent to every area of life. The classical strategy begins by first establishing the existence of God as revealed in the world around us, showing how the picture of God as revealed apart from the Bible actually corresponds in some important respects to the God we see in the pages of the Bible. The way apologists do this is called *natural theology*, which is rational reflection on God's general revelation. While natural theology may corroborate special revelation, its source material is the data of general revelation, and it is more explicitly philosophical than special revelation. Natural theology employs deductive and inductive argumentation and inferences to the best explanation. In particular, natural theology develops arguments for God's existence, including, but not limited to, ontological arguments, moral arguments, design arguments, and cosmological arguments. You will learn these arguments in the first half of this book and see how helpful they are in showing others that God actually exists. While arguments cannot compel someone to believe, they are important in demonstrating

---

5. Mental states are, of course, often related to brain states, but mental states are not reducible to brain states. It is beyond the scope of this book to defend substance dualism, but see J. P. Moreland, *The Soul: How We Know It's Real and Why It Matters* (Chicago: Moody, 2014).

the truth of theism. However, the classical approach does not just stop there. Apologetics examines the life and ministry of Jesus of Nazareth, showing that he is God through his claims, credentials, and deeds. This is accomplished by showing the historical reliability of the Bible and by explaining that the Bible's conclusions about Jesus are true. The second half of the book will examine these topics.

The method is not the most important thing here. For example, many people already believe in one God, so while natural theology may be helpful in providing them rational grounds for their belief, they may need to learn more about some of Christianity's truth claims about Jesus. For some, their interest in speaking with you about these most important issues may begin with an objection, a prayer request, or an honest question. We recommend using the right evidence for the right person at the right time with the Holy Spirit leading you as to how best to live out the ministry of apologetics in your context. For example, someone in your life may be fascinated by the life and teachings of Jesus. For that person, it may be wise to start to explore Jesus' claims, his death, and resurrection. Then, as questions and objections arise, you may offer some natural theology to establish the existence of God and the supernatural worldview that sits behind Jesus' life and ministry. Even so, the classical approach is helpful for establishing that God exists and then showing that Jesus is God.

THE BIBLICAL BASIS FOR APOLOGETICS

The approach to Christian apologetics that we describe here is not simply a modern approach to answering skeptical questions and explaining that Christianity is true and rational. In fact, the approach that we commend here is deeply informed by the Bible. Of course, the cultures of the biblical world and the questions that ancient peoples had about God were different from our culture and its questions. But even so, apologetics is commanded and modeled throughout the Bible. The Old Testament establishes the importance of rational thinking and the value of historical evidence in how one looks at God and God's work. We see this in Deuteronomy 13, where the children of Israel were warned about false prophets who did miracles to incite others to worship other gods. "If you hear it said about one of the towns the LORD your God is giving you to live in that troublemakers have arisen among you and have led the people of their town astray, saying, 'Let us go and worship other gods' (gods you have not known), then you must inquire, probe and investigate it thoroughly" (vv. 12–14). Spiritual claims deserve to be investigated, and God wants his people to seriously examine the truth.

God appealed to reason and history often in the book of Isaiah, showing that his plans and promises are true. For example, as God pronounced judgment and offered hope to his people, he invited them, "Come now, let us reason together" (Isa. 1:18 ESV). God does not hesitate to engage us this way. When God was explaining the judgment and his ability to restore his people, he appealed to historical evidence:

> But now thus says the LORD,
>   he who created you, O Jacob,
>   he who formed you, O Israel:
> "Fear not, for I have redeemed you;
>   I have called you by name, you are mine.
> When you pass through the waters, I will be with you;
>   and through the rivers, they shall not
>   overwhelm you;
> when you walk through fire you shall not be burned,
>   and the flame shall not consume you."
>   (Isa. 43:1–2 ESV)

God was saying that his past actions in creating and forming his people were the basis for his ability and desire to care for them in their ordeals ahead. God's actions in history are the kinds of things we can reflect on to give us knowledge that is pertinent for our lives today. This is vital for the apologetic task, for classical apologetics uses historical evidence to show that the Bible is reliable and that Jesus' life can be examined historically to show that he is who the Bible says he is.

Jeremiah's prophecies against the religious practices of the nations surrounding the people of Israel show the logical absurdities of worshiping idols.

Thus says the LORD:

> "Learn not the way of the nations,
>   nor be dismayed at the signs of the heavens
>   because the nations are dismayed at them,
> for the customs of the peoples are vanity.
> A tree from the forest is cut down
>   and worked with an axe by the hands of
>   a craftsman.
> They decorate it with silver and gold;
>   they fasten it with hammer and nails
>   so that it cannot move.
> Their idols are like scarecrows in a cucumber field,
>   and they cannot speak;
> they have to be carried,
>   for they cannot walk.
> Do not be afraid of them,
>   for they cannot do evil,
>   neither is it in them to do good." (Jer. 10:2–5 ESV)

Do you see the logical flow of the argument? God could simply have said that his people should worship God alone and left it at that, but instead he showed them that it is logically absurd to worship or fear other gods. Here is God's argument: (1) The religions of the nations are vanity. (2) They make their gods from common materials. (3) They fasten their gods in the places where they worship them. (4) Further, their gods cannot speak or move. (5) Therefore, (2), (3), and (4) show that (1) it is absurd to be afraid of gods that cannot speak or move and have to be made by human hands.

In the New Testament, we see the biblical basis for apologetics come into closer focus. Though Christians do not usually talk about him this way, Jesus is the apologist *par excellence*. For example, when John the Baptist's followers asked Jesus if he was the one to come, Jesus made an appeal to evidence as his reply, "Go back and report to John what you hear and see: The blind receive sight, the lame walk, those who have leprosy are cleansed, the deaf hear, the dead are raised, and the good news is proclaimed to the poor" (Matt. 11:4–5). Of course, Jesus could have appealed to his divine authority and simply said, "Yes," but instead he was willing to reveal himself via evidence that supported his authority and mission. In another instance, Jesus used careful argumentation to respond to the charge that he was casting out demons by the power of Satan.

> "Every kingdom divided against itself will be ruined, and every city or household divided against itself will not stand. If Satan drives out Satan, he is divided against himself. How then can his kingdom stand? And if I drive out demons by Beelzebul, by whom do your people drive them out? So then, they will be your judges. But if it is by the Spirit of God that I drive out demons, then the kingdom of God has come upon you." (Matt. 12:25–28)

This is a *reductio ad absurdum* (reduction to absurdity), and we will discuss this particular example more in chapter 2. But the point is that Jesus defends his own identity by appeal to logical argumentation. He provides for us an example that reasoned arguments have a place in how we tell others about the Christian faith.

Paul taught and modeled an apologetic ministry as well. He found common ground with the Athenians while showing them what was missing in their concept of an "unknown god" (Acts 17:16–34). He instructed that spiritual warfare includes showing how errant points of view are false: "We demolish arguments and every pretension that sets itself up against the knowledge of God, and we take captive every thought to make it obedient to Christ" (2 Cor. 10:5). In fact, Paul saw it as a key part of his personal mission that he was "defending and confirming the gospel" (Phil. 1:7). A few verses later, he stated it more plainly about his time in prison: "I am put here for the defense of the gospel" (v. 16). Paul's ministry was marked by him making a case for the truth of the gospel, whether it was through reasoning from the Scriptures, pointing to God's revelation in nature and the human conscience, or exposing the lies of faulty worldviews. His warning to the Colossians was characteristic of his concern to expose and defend against false perspectives: "See to it that no one takes you captive through hollow and deceptive philosophy, which depends on human tradition and the elemental spiritual forces of this world rather than on Christ" (Col. 2:8). Paul was saying that it is possible to fall prey to bad philosophy, and this kind of philosophy "is contrasted against another philosophy, one that is based on Christ."[6] We know that this contrast exists, because Paul had already detailed to his readers what the philosophical principles based on Christ are in Colossians 1 (esp. vv. 9–23). Namely, he wanted his readers to be filled by God "with the knowledge of his will through all the wisdom and understanding that the Spirit gives" (1:9). It is this kind of knowledge, revealed by God through the Spirit, to which apologetics points.

A couple of other New Testament passages deserve attention, as well, in how they teach us about the ministry of apologetics. First Peter 3:15 shows us part of what it means to live in a culture where Christians suffer persecution: "But in your hearts revere Christ as Lord. Always be prepared to give an answer to everyone who asks you to give the reason for the hope that you have. But do this with gentleness and respect." Apologetics begins with genuine love and reverence for Jesus, and the goal of apologetics is that Christ would be revered as Lord in our lives and in the lives of those with whom we share the knowledge of God. Part of the means by which we share that knowledge is through giving the reason for the hope that we have in Jesus. These reasons can include your personal experiences with God and his people, but they can and should also include the kinds of reasons that we will show you in this book. We should be able to show why it is rational to believe that God exists and why Jesus is God. Why do we think a resurrection is possible? Why do we believe that our trust in the Bible is reasonable? When we start to answer these questions, we are able "to contend for the faith that was once for all entrusted to God's holy people," as Jude 3 commands us. And when we can defend and commend the Christian faith as true and rational and pertinent to every aspect of life, then we may even be able to "be merciful to those who doubt" (Jude 22), by helping them to see that faith in Jesus is intellectually credible and existentially safe.

---

6. Mark W. Foreman, *Prelude to Philosophy: An Introduction for Christians* (Downers Grove, IL: InterVarsity, 2014), 80.

CHRISTIAN CHARACTER IN APOLOGETICS

Just as the Bible gives us motivation for our apologetic ministry, it also gives guidelines for how we engage in that ministry. Apologetics uses intellectually sound arguments for the truth of Christianity, but it should be done in a spiritually wise manner. As you begin this journey of defending the knowledge of God in the world and the Word, you must take note of the state of your own soul and your character. Start asking God to reveal to you how you might not just grow intellectually through learning apologetics, but also how he might help you to avoid some of the pitfalls that are common to us all. We trust that God, in his grace, will guide you in two key ways: avoiding the sin of arrogance and developing the virtue of studiousness.

The besetting sin of apologists is arrogance. Once a woman or man begins to understand the rational power of apologetics, it is all too easy to become cocky in the defense of the faith. We all love to win arguments and hate to lose them. What could be better than winning an apologetics argument for the existence of God or for the resurrection of Jesus? After all, these are matters of eternal importance, and people need to see the truth of what the Bible teaches about God and salvation. There is also a thrill in giving a sound argument when so many Christians fail at this task.

I (Doug) well remember the sense of intellectual confidence and meaning I experienced when I began to study the work of apologist Francis Schaeffer (1912–84) in the middle 1970s. After reading his groundbreaking book, *The God Who Is There,*[7] I realized that Christianity offered rational and existentially compelling answers to life's greatest questions, and that the brightest and most influential non-Christian philosophers and artists had failed to find truth and meaning. These were heady thoughts for a new convert who was a sophomore attending a secular university. Although I could get cocky in my apologetic endeavors, I was always reminded by Schaeffer that apologetics is not an intellectual game that can be won or lost. Schaeffer wrote,

---

7. Francis A. Schaeffer, *The God Who Is There: Speaking Christianity into the Twentieth Century.* IVP Signature ed. (Downers Grove, IL: InterVarsity, 2020), Kindle.

If I begin to enjoy [apologetics] as a kind of intellectual exercise, then I am cruel and can expect no real spiritual results. As I push the man off his false balance, he must be able to feel that I care for him. Otherwise I will only end up destroying him, and the cruelty and ugliness of it all will destroy me as well. Merely to be abstract and cold is to show that I do not really believe this person to be created in God's image and therefore one of my kind.[8]

Schaeffer was speaking of doing negative apologetics, wherein we show the non-Christian that their worldview is illogical or does not fit the facts (see 2 Cor. 10:3–5). But the point stands for any apologetic endeavor. Apologetics engages an unbeliever who is made in God's image, loved by God, and therefore worthy of respect and love, however much they may be denying God's truth. The apologist should always depend on the Holy Spirit, moment by moment while listening and responding to the unbeliever.[9] We "should be quick to listen, slow to speak and slow to become angry" (James 1:19) and filled with the fruit of the Holy Spirit: "love, joy, peace, forbearance, kindness, goodness, faithfulness, gentleness and self-control" (Gal. 5:22–23). The apologist should never shrink back from explaining the offense of the cross (1 Cor. 1:18–25), but in so doing, should never be offensive in tone or manner.

Apologists should be both kind and smart; that is, they need to develop the virtue of studiousness while they grow in love and kindness. This entails learning to discern the spirit of the times, unmask its falsehoods, and confront it with biblical truth, which is living and active (Heb. 4:12). Consider the tribe of Issachar, who were armed for battle under the leadership of David: "From Issachar, men who understood the times and knew what Israel should do—200 chiefs, with all their relatives under their command" (1 Chron. 12:32).

"Understanding the times" requires an understanding of the basic worldviews that oppose Christianity, where they came from, their intellectual weaknesses, and how the Christian worldview better explains the world than its pertinent rivals. We return to the classic example of

---

8. Schaeffer, 154

9. On the Christian life, see Francis A. Schaeffer, *True Spirituality* (Wheaton, IL: Crossway, 2020).

this skill found in Acts 17 when Paul addressed the Greek philosophers at Athens. He was conversant with their philosophies and even quoted their own thinkers to make one of his points. His deep learning was well used in apologetics. Yet Paul exposed the illogic of their worldview and offered a Christian alternative. As a result of his brilliant message, "When they heard about the resurrection of the dead, some of them sneered, but others said, 'We want to hear you again on this subject.' At that, Paul left the Council. Some of the people became followers of Paul and believed. Among them was Dionysius, a member of the Areopagus, also a woman named Damaris, and a number of others" (Acts 17:32–34).[10]

To emulate Paul, apologists should come to terms with the basic philosophical ideas that control the culture in which God has placed them. Today in North America these ideas include moral relativism, postmodernism, critical theory,[11] scientific materialism, pantheism, Buddhism, and Islam, among others. A modern classic that explains the intellectual drift of Western culture is *The Universe Next Door* by James W. Sire.[12] How the Christian message and the Christian life challenge postmodernism and scientific materialism is trenchantly presented in *Kingdom Triangle* by J. P. Moreland.[13]

This kind of apologetic study cannot be done on the cheap, and no one should try to cut corners. While every Christian should be able to give a reason for the hope that is within them (1 Peter 3:15), God calls some Christians to develop the intellectual rigor to outthink the world for Christ. Consider the kind of discipline Paul advocated in relation to apologetics:

> Do you not know that in a race all the runners run, but only one gets the prize? Run in such a way as to get the prize. Everyone who competes in the games goes into strict training. They do it to get a

---

10. For excellent exposition on this passage, see Paul Copan and Kenneth T. Litwak, *The Gospel in the Marketplace of Ideas* (Downers Grove, IL: IVP Academic, 2014).

11. See Douglas Groothuis, "America, Critical Theory, and Social Crisis," Centennial Institute, September 2020, https://centennial.ccu.edu/america-critical-theory-and-social-crisis/.

12. James W. Sire, *The Universe Next Door: A Basic Worldview Catalog*, 6th ed. (Downers Grove, IL: IVP Academic, 2020).

13. J. P. Moreland, *Kingdom Triangle: Recover the Christian Mind, Renovate the Soul, Restore the Spirit's Power* (Grand Rapids: Zondervan, 2007).

crown that will not last, but we do it to get a crown that will last forever. Therefore I do not run like someone running aimlessly; I do not fight like a boxer beating the air. No, I strike a blow to my body and make it my slave so that after I have preached to others, I myself will not be disqualified for the prize. (1 Cor. 9:24–27)

Any Christian in a position of intellectual leadership, such as a pastor, any kind of teacher or writer, evangelist, and so on, should be able to flex some apologetic muscles when needed. Since Paul said that "the church of the living God" is "the pillar and foundation of the truth" (1 Tim 3:15), so those who shape the teaching ministry of the church should be able to defend that truth and teach others to defend it as well.

And so we begin this study in the knowledge of God. Engage in it wholeheartedly, and pray that God will use this to bear fruit in your life and in your ministry through what you learn in the pages that follow.

STUDY QUESTIONS

1. What is apologetics and what Scriptures support it?
2. What is distinctive about classical apologetics?
3. What is natural theology?
4. What are the biblical texts that support natural theology?

SUGGESTED READING

Fesko, J. V. *Reforming Apologetics: Retrieving the Classic Reformed Approach to Defending the Faith.* Grand Rapids: Baker Academic, 2019.

Forest, Benjamin, Josh Chatraw, Alister McGrath, eds. *The History of Apologetics: A Biographical and Methodological Introduction.* Grand Rapids: Zondervan Academic, 2020.

Gerstner, John H., Arthur W. Lindsley, and R. C. Sproul. *Classical Apologetics.* Grand Rapids: Zondervan Academic, 1984.

Groothuis, Douglas. *Christian Apologetics: A Comprehensive Case for Biblical Faith.* 2nd ed. Downers Grove, IL: IVP Academic, 2022.

Holmes, Arthur. *Contours of a Worldview.* Grand Rapids: Eerdmans, 1983.

Moreland, J. P. *Kingdom Triangle: Recover the Christian Mind, Renovate the Soul, Restore the Spirit's Power.* Grand Rapids: Zondervan, 2007.

Schaeffer, Francis. *The God Who Is There.* Downers Grove, IL: InterVarsity, 2020.

_____. *True Spirituality.* Carol Stream, IL: Tyndale House, 2001.

Sire, James. *The Universe Next Door: A Basic Worldview Catalog.* 6th ed. Downers Grove, IL: InterVarsity, 2020.

Wright, N. T. *History and Eschatology: Jesus and the Promise of Natural Theology.* The 2018 Gifford Lectures. Waco, TX: Baylor University Press, 2019.

PART 1

OBJECTIONS TO CLASSICAL APOLOGETICS

CHAPTER 2

THEOLOGICAL OBJECTIONS
TO APOLOGETICS

When I (Ike) was an undergraduate student, I took a wonderful course on New Testament interpretation from a theologically conservative Catholic priest at my Jesuit university. While I was (and remain) an evangelical, I loved opening the Bible for the first time with scholarly eyes. My classmates were from all over the world and from various confessional traditions, and we all eagerly studied the New Testament documents together, diving into form criticism, redaction criticism, and the various other challenges that come with studying ancient literature. With this kind of scholarly investigation into the New Testament came some skeptical questions from time to time. While our professor always wanted to uphold an orthodox confession regarding the person and work of Jesus Christ, he wasn't really concerned with combating every skeptical objection to the traditional picture of Jesus. In response to one particularly skeptical question posed by a student about the Bible, our professor claimed something to the effect of, "Well, the Bible is a faith document. We accept what it says on faith." As a well-intentioned young Christian, I nodded in agreement. After all, the Christian faith is something to be lived, not a set of scientific claims to be investigated and defended. Christianity is about knowing Jesus and obeying his commands. Christianity is about experiencing the Holy

Spirit's presence and bringing the message of the gospel to the whole world. It isn't about answering skeptical claims with historical evidence. It isn't about trying to prove that the Bible is true or to show people that some ancient way of life makes perfect sense. People just need to respond to Jesus in faith, not have all of their questions answered. Or so I thought.

Many well-meaning Christians dismiss apologetics with a reaction similar to my agreement with my professor's statement about faith. "We don't need to do apologetics. These things just cause arguments and strife." "Following God means taking a leap of faith." "If it makes sense, it's not God!" "You don't need to defend God." Well-meaning Christians may even appeal to the Bible itself to dismiss apologetic strategies for defending the Christian worldview. Here are some of the passages they may quote:

- "'Blessed are those who have not seen and yet have believed'" (John 20:29).
- "Where is the wise person? Where is the teacher of the law? Where is the philosopher of this age? Has not God made foolish the wisdom of the world?" (1 Cor. 1:20).
- "And so it was with me, brothers and sisters. When I came to you, I did not come with eloquence or human wisdom as I proclaimed to you the testimony about God. For I resolved to know nothing while I was with you except Jesus Christ and him crucified. I came to you in weakness with great fear and trembling. My message and my preaching were not with wise and persuasive words, but with a demonstration of the Spirit's power, so that your faith might not rest on human wisdom, but on God's power" (1 Cor. 2:1–5).
- "For we live by faith, not by sight" (2 Cor. 5:7).
- "And without faith it is impossible to please God, because anyone who comes to him must believe that he exists and that he rewards those who earnestly seek him" (Heb. 11:6).

If those who reject apologetics are applying these verses correctly, then a book like the one you're reading now shouldn't exist! The Christian faith doesn't need defenders; it simply needs people willing to take a leap of faith. Skeptics don't need their questions answered; they need only to accept the gospel and be saved. Christians don't need apologetics to strengthen their faith; they just need to walk by faith.

However, our investigation of the issue has led us to a different conclusion, and this is why we have developed a lifelong commitment to the ministry of apologetics. Not only is apologetics a ministry commanded in Scripture, but it was practiced by the earliest Christians and by Jesus himself. Even so, if one is to do apologetics, one must consider the objections to apologetics made by well-meaning Christians who reject apologetics. This chapter focuses on theological objections to apologetics made by Christians who think that apologetics is irrelevant or perhaps even dangerous to Christian faith. Here we address these common objections:

1. Apologetics is contrary to authentic Christian faith.
2. Apologetics, namely, the natural theology needed for classical apologetics, is impossible prior to Christian faith.
3. Apologetics misunderstands the nature of religious truth and is therefore offensive toward other religions.
4. Apologetics turns reason into an idol and produces a "god" who is nothing like the God of Abraham, Isaac, and Jacob.
5. Apologetics tries to usurp the role of the Holy Spirit in bringing someone to faith.

We will address each of these objections in turn, showing that they misunderstand the purpose and biblical basis of apologetics.

1. APOLOGETICS IS CONTRARY TO AUTHENTIC CHRISTIAN FAITH

Children are so beautiful in their simple trust. When a trusted person tells a child something, the child immediately believes and trusts that they are getting the straight facts. If you tell kids that they have won a trip to Disneyland, they're likely to believe you. And young children who grow up in Christian homes typically don't doubt God's existence or his goodness.[1] This natural ability to trust is something the Lord commends in children: "Truly I tell you, unless you change and become like little children, you will never enter the kingdom of heaven. Therefore, whoever takes the lowly position of this child is the greatest in the kingdom of heaven" (Matt. 18:3–4). Indeed, we should seek to emulate children in how they trust God, ready to believe that what God says is true and willing to follow him as he leads us.

Yet some argue that apologetics, with its complex arguments and careful use of reason and evidence, is decidedly unlike the childlike attitude that Jesus commends. Some argue that apologetics is dangerous. Some argue, quite contrary to evangelical advocates of apologetics, that either Paul was not doing apologetics during his encounter with the philosophers in Athens (see Acts 17:16–34) or that he later repudiated his attempt to do apologetics in Athens.[2] So then, whatever apologetics produces will not be real faith at all, but a kind of counterfeit for the authentic faith that true Christians ought to have. Let's take a look at these challenges.

Fideism

First, many Christians hold that true faith is contrary to or, in the least, makes no reference to reason. This is called *fideism*, and it is perhaps most famously expounded by the Danish philosopher Søren Kierkegaard: "If I am able to apprehend God objectively, I do not have faith; but because I cannot do this, I must have faith. If I want to keep myself in faith, I must continually see to it that I hold fast the objective uncertainty, see to it that in the objective uncertainty I am 'out on 70,000 fathoms of water' and still have faith."[3]

More recently, philosopher of religion Carl A. Raschke has explained the issue this way, appealing to Paul's explanation of the cross in 1 Corinthians 1:21–24:

---

1. There is even significant evidence that children are born with a propensity to believe in God. See Justin L. Barrett, *Born Believers: The Science of Children's Religious Belief* (New York: Free Press, 2012).

2. This important apologetic encounter will be explained in detail below.

3. Søren Kierkegaard, *Kierkegaard's Writings, Volume 12.1: Concluding Unscientific Postscript to Philosophical Fragments*, trans. Howard V. Hong and Edna H. Hong (Princeton, NJ: Princeton University Press, 1992), 204.

One can never be convinced of the truth of faith. . . . Christ cannot be proved, only apprehended. He is apprehended not as human wisdom, but as *God's wisdom,* a wisdom that amounts to God taking on the most wretched guise of a crucified criminal in contrast with his infinite majesty in order to overcome once and for all the purely "dialectical" opposition of finite and infinite, human language and the divine, redemptive mystery for all creation. There is no way that reason can reconcile this opposition. The cross requires simply a personal surrender in faith to God's mysterious workings in time and history.[4]

Raschke is saying that Christianity is not about attempting to understand God's wisdom by using the human capacity to reason. In fact, trying to understand or explain God using human reason is impossible. One can only "surrender in faith." This would seem to rule out apologetics altogether. If one cannot use reason to understand or explain God, then one cannot defend the Christian faith by using reason. The only thing to do would be for individuals to surrender in faith. The first problem one may notice about this is a practical one. Some people outside of the Christian faith have questions about the possibility of God's existence, the problem of evil, or the truth of the Bible. Simply claiming that their only intellectual option is to surrender in faith seems to fail to take their questions seriously.

Fideism fails for reasons more central to the nature of Christian faith as well. First, knowledge is impossible without having good reasons for one's beliefs. Consider your belief that you are reading English words. This belief is true only if you are meeting certain conditions. (1) *You must, in fact, be reading English words.* That is, the truth of the matter is that there is a being (you) who is actually reading words in English. This truth would rule out other possible explanations, such as dreaming about reading, being tricked into thinking you're reading by an evil scientist, and so on. This is the *truth* criterion for knowledge. But (2) *you must also have good reasons for your belief to be considered knowledge.* This is

---

4. Carl A. Raschke, "Faith and Philosophy in Tension," in *Faith and Reason: Three Views,* ed. Steve Wilkins, Spectrum Multiview Books (Downers Grove, IL: IVP Academic, 2014), 42.

the *justification* criterion. If I were to flip a coin and catch it without revealing if it landed heads or tails, and you were to form the belief that the coin landed heads up and the coin actually did land heads up, you couldn't claim to have *known* that the coin was heads up. You were accidentally correct. However, if you had seen beforehand that it was a trick coin with heads on both sides, then your belief that the coin landed heads up would have been *reasonable*, and you rightly would have been able to claim that you *knew* the coin was heads up. All of knowledge works like this, and if one has beliefs that God exists or that Jesus has provided salvation from sin, then one only has knowledge if those beliefs meet the truth criterion and the justification criterion.[5] Knowledge about God is no different from any other kind of knowledge in this regard. If someone knows that God exists or that Jesus has provided for salvation, then that person only has knowledge if he or she has some kind of reason for believing as he or she does. Jonah Haddad argues that if this were not the case, then "we would have nothing by which to evaluate knowledge-claims and would be subsequently led right back into the insanity of skepticism."[6]

If faith were against or contrary to reason, then we could not evaluate other religions' beliefs from the outside.[7] Fideism maintains that a person can have religious knowledge only if they respond personally in faith. But think about how absurd this is. Suppose your friend is a skeptic who believes that Jesus of Nazareth is a myth and never existed. You want to introduce your friend to Jesus, but the roadblock standing in his way is his belief that Jesus never existed. You lovingly show your friend evidence that Jesus existed in history and that many of the Bible's claims about Jesus' life are corroborated by contemporary non-Christian historians and writers. Through this kind of rational investigation, your

---

5. For more on the idea that knowledge is justified, true belief, see J. P. Moreland and Garrett DeWeese, *Philosophy Made Slightly Less Difficult: A Beginner's Guide to Life's Big Questions*, 2nd ed. (Downers Grove, IL: IVP Academic, 2021), 50–68. For the sake of this discussion, we are assuming that someone with a religious belief indeed *has* a belief, which is the third criterion for knowledge.

6. Jonah Haddad, *Insanity: God and the Theory of Knowledge* (Eugene, OR: Wipf and Stock, 2013), 91.

7. Haddad, 91. For the role that reason plays in evaluating religions from the outside, see Paul J. Griffiths, *An Apology for Apologetics: A Study in the Logic of Interreligious Dialogue* (Maryknoll, NY: Orbis, 1991).

friend forms the belief that Jesus existed. Though he doesn't have true faith, this friend has nevertheless rationally evaluated some aspects of Christianity and developed some actual religious knowledge. However, on fideism, this rational exercise actually stands in the way of your friend coming to true faith. The rationality of the historical investigation is opposed to the development of true faith. This is absurd because belief that Jesus actually exists is obviously a prerequisite to Christian faith. You cannot have faith in Jesus if you do not think he exists. It is obvious that the rational investigation into the historicity of Jesus would be necessary, though not sufficient, for faith to develop in this particular person.

In fact, fideism actually seems to provide some reasons for belief. Consider what is necessary for fideism to be true. A fideist has beliefs that they can profess. These beliefs are about God, requiring that belief in God is possible. These beliefs are the result of some kind of personal encounter with God. Against their intentions, these beliefs that the fideist holds require them to have some good reasons in the form of evidence. Jonah Haddad claims that the fideist is giving evidence that "people are capable of holding beliefs, and it is possible to believe that God truly exists. Moreover, I [the fideist] am claiming that by acting in faith, I have encountered God, proving my blind leap to be grounded in reality that I have personally subjected to an empirical test."[8]

Fideism further misunderstands the nature of Christian faith. Christian faith need not be total certainty, but they have always held that evidence is an significant part of believing in God. Consider John's authorial note after describing Jesus' resurrection, John's and Peter's view of the empty tomb, Jesus' post-resurrection appearances to Mary Magdalene, Thomas, and other disciples: "Jesus performed many other signs in the presence of his disciples, which are not recorded in this book. But these are written that you may believe that Jesus is the Messiah, the Son of God, and that by believing you may have life in his name" (John 20:30–31). John's hope is that readers will consider the evidence he provided as a foundation for faith. Consider also the writer of Hebrews, speaking about Abraham's faith in God when he was

---

8. Haddad, 92.

called to sacrifice Isaac: "Abraham reasoned that God could even raise the dead" (Heb. 11:19).

Indeed, many Christians have historically understood Christian faith as being comprised of three elements: *noticia* (knowledge), *assensus* (assent), and *fiducia* (trust).[9] Think about what it means to have faith that Jesus rose from the dead. You have *noticia* (knowledge) that the event took place. This could be gained any number of ways: through testimony, historical research, or a vision of the risen Christ. You have *assensus* (conviction or assent) that the truth of the resurrection applies in a significant way to your own life. But you must also have *fiducia* (the willingness to step out and trust) in the one who has resurrected, that is, Jesus. Faith includes all three of these elements, which means that Christians shouldn't neglect the *noticia* element to favor one of the other two. Indeed, *assensus* and *fiducia* logically depend on *noticia*. How could someone have true faith in Jesus if they didn't even have knowledge that Jesus exists?

Probably most significant for Christians, the notion that reason and faith have nothing to do with one another is not actually supported by 1 Corinthians. Let's take a closer look at the text:

> Where is the wise person? Where is the teacher of the law? Where is the philosopher of this age? Has not God made foolish the wisdom of the world? For since in the wisdom of God the world through its wisdom did not know him, God was pleased through the foolishness of what was preached to save those who believe. Jews demand signs and Greeks look for wisdom, but we preach Christ crucified: a stumbling block to Jews and foolishness to Gentiles, but to those whom God has called, both Jews and Greeks, Christ the power of God and the wisdom of God. (1 Cor. 1:20–24)

Fideists claim that this passage demonstrates that apologetics, with its attempted use of reason to defend and commend the faith, is not biblical.

---

9. The great Reformed pastor and theologian Louis Berkhof, for example, taught that faith has an intellectual element, an emotional or existential element, and a volitional (that is, relating to the will) element. See Louis Berkhof, *Systematic Theology*, 4th rev. and enlarged ed. (Grand Rapids: Eerdmans, 1941), 503–6.

However, is that what is really happening in this passage? The immediate context of the passage does not seem to have anything to do with the kinds of things apologetics does, such as showing that God exists, the Bible is reliable, and Jesus rose from the dead. The passage is about the way to salvation, "God was pleased through the foolishness of what was preached to save those who believe" (v. 21). Even so, a fideist might reply, the passage calls the Christian message "foolishness" to Greeks and a "stumbling block" (Gk., *skandalon*) to Jews.

So then, we shouldn't try to use worldly standards of intelligence to show that Christianity is true. But this misses the significance of Paul's message here. Paul was saying that it is foolish, by Greek philosophical standards, to start with first principles like a First Mover (a Greek concept of a divine cause of the universe coming into its present form) and then proceed to use reason alone to come to the conclusion that a Jewish God-man would have to provide an atoning death on a cross.[10] For Jews, the idea that the Messiah would be crucified would have indeed seemed scandalous. Gordon Fee explains as much in his commentary on 1 Corinthians: "Although in Roman times the Jews did not crucify, they did afterward hang those who had been stoned, especially blasphemers and idolaters. They saw hanging therefore as the ultimate fulfillment of the law ('because anyone who is hung on a tree is under God's curse,' Deut. 21:23)."[11] Paul was saying that this message of the cross is not one that you would conjure up using Greek philosophical wisdom or Jewish messianic hope. However, this does nothing to show that reason itself is off-limits. It merely shows that God's plans are counterintuitive to what reason alone might conclude.

In fact, Paul used reason to make arguments in his writings, particularly in 1 Corinthians. In chapter 15, Paul confronted some who were denying that the dead in Christ would be raised. He said, "If there is no resurrection of the dead, then not even Christ has been raised" (v. 13). The problem with this is that if Christ hasn't been raised, then

---

10. In this spirit, the Roman historian Tacitus called Christianity "a most mischievous superstition" in *The Annals*, trans. Alfred John Church and William Jackson Brodribb, Internet Classics Archive, 15.44, http://classics.mit.edu/Tacitus/annals.11.xv.html.

11. Gordon D. Fee, *The First Epistle to the Corinthians*, rev. ed., NICNT (Grand Rapids: Eerdmans, 2014), 79.

Christians have no way out of their sin. "Then those also who have fallen asleep in Christ are lost. If only for this life we have hope in Christ, we are of all people most to be pitied" (vv. 18–19). But, of course, Christ did indeed rise from the dead. One may formalize Paul's argument this way:

1. If there is no resurrection, then Christ has not been raised. This means that there is no way out of sin, and therefore no eternal hope, for believers living or dead.
2. But Christ has been raised.
3. Therefore, there is a resurrection.

This is a *modus tollens* argument, a logical argument form well known to the Greeks and to philosophers and apologists today. If premises 1 and 2 are true, then the conclusion (3) follows necessarily. How ironic it would be for Paul to reject reason in his explanation of the message of the cross in chapter 1 only to rely on reason for his argument regarding the resurrection in chapter 15! Paul's defense of the faith, in fact, relies on reasoning, and this is something we see in Paul's message to philosophers in Athens as well.

Apologetics and Paul at Mars Hill

Apologists love the story of Paul at Mars Hill (or the Areopagus), recounted by Luke in Acts 17:16–34. This story shows Paul going into hostile intellectual territory with real spiritual concern for those who do not know Jesus, and he appeals to their altar "TO AN UNKNOWN GOD" (v. 23) and to a couple of philosophers whose words could be read as pointing to a loving "God who made the world and everything in it" (v. 24). Paul seems to be doing apologetics by trying to find common ground between the God of the Bible and previous Athenian understandings about God.

That said, some Christians deny that Paul was doing apologetics in this story. C. Kavin Rowe, for example, claims that Luke's telling of the story is not to show the common ground between Christianity and Greek philosophical theology, but to show that Greek thinking led only to idolatry. The Greeks' belief in a god led them to make idols, and this is precisely why Paul "was greatly distressed to see that the city was full of idols" (v. 16). Paul thought that the Greeks were not doing natural theology, but that they were guilty of "natural idolatry."[12] Myron Bradley Penner agrees with this interpretation by arguing that natural theology (such as used by classical apologists) "is anathema to Paul because, rather than pointing in the direction of the One True God, such efforts point *away* from this God (which is shown to us in Jesus)."[13] Rowe is correct in arguing that Paul was indeed distressed about the Athenians' idolatry, and it is true that we are not to make images of God (see Ex. 20:4–6). But this does not undermine Paul's apologetic strategy of finding common ground with one key element of Greek philosophical theology: the belief in some kind of high god. Does the Greek conception of this god correspond completely to the ways in which Christians know God (i.e., the God of Abraham, Isaac, and Jacob; the Trinity)? Of course not, but that does nothing to minimize the fact that there was a true notion of God in Greek thinking that Paul wanted to use to point to the "God who made the world and everything in it" (v. 24) who is revealed in Jesus Christ.[14] Classical apologetics can clearly account for this by attributing the origin of this concept in God's general revelation, the idea that God has shown something of his existence and nature to the world apart from revelation in the Bible, in Jesus, and in the Holy Spirit.

Some respond to this interpretation by affirming that Paul was indeed doing apologetics in Athens, but that his approach was a failure. After all, these interpreters argue, Luke recounted that people "sneered" (v. 32) when Paul mentioned the resurrection, and only a small number believed the message: "Dionysius, a member of the Areopagus, also a woman named Damaris, and a number of others" (v. 34). They contend that shortly after, by the time Paul visited Corinth, he had renounced the practice. Paul later recounted,

---

12. C. Kavin Rowe, *World Upside Down* (Oxford: Oxford University Press, 2010), 38. Rowe footnotes C. K. Barrett, *Acts*, ICC (London: T&T Clark, 1994), 2:850–51.

13. Myron Bradley Penner, "The Unknown Mover (or, How to Do 'Natural' Theology in a Postmodern Context)" *Philosophia Christi* 21, no. 1 (2019): 205.

14. For a more thorough rebuttal of Penner on this score, see Andrew I. Shepardson, "General Revelation and the God of Natural Theology: A Response to Myron Bradley Penner," *Philosophia Christi* 21, no. 1 (2019): 207–13.

When I came to you, I did not come with eloquence or human wisdom as I proclaimed to you the testimony about God. For I resolved to know nothing while I was with you except Jesus Christ and him crucified. I came to you in weakness with great fear and trembling. My message and my preaching were not with wise and persuasive words, but with a demonstration of the Spirit's power, so that your faith might not rest on human wisdom, but on God's power. (1 Cor. 2:1–5)

Instead of using the same approach that he used in Athens, Paul looked only to the Holy Spirit's power. Instead of using rational persuasion, he presented the simple truth of the gospel.

But did Paul initially embrace but later reject apologetics because he deemed the strategy a failure? We have already shown that Paul continued to use logical argumentation in his writings to the Corinthians, so it doesn't seem that he rejected the practice. In addition, the idea that Paul *failed* in Athens would certainly be odd to the many evangelists and preachers throughout the age of the church who have offered the opportunity to confess faith to their hearers with only limited results. This argument essentially claims that apologetics was deemed a failure by Paul because only a few people converted. By that same logic, we ought to deem each of our evangelistic encounters a failure when only a few convert. The truth is that we do not always know how God will use results that seem small.[15] We never know the significance of the small acts of charity we perform, the few that we lead to the Lord, and the prayers that we pray on this side of eternity. It is better to avoid minimizing "results" and thereby avoid the risk of minimizing the work of the sovereign Lord over history (Ps. 31:15).

---

15. In fact, it may be that Dionysius, one of the few whom Paul converted, became a key figure in the early Athenian church. The fourth-century church historian Eusebius noted, "That member of the Areopagus, Dionysius by name, whom Luke records in the Acts as having received the faith for the first time after Paul's public address to the Athenians in the Areopagus, is described by one of the ancients . . . as having been the first Bishop of the Church at Athens." See Eusebius, *Pamphili, Ecclesiastical History: Books 1–5*, in *The Fathers of the Church: A New Translation*, vol. 19, trans. Roy J. DeFerrari (Washington, DC: Catholic University of America Press, 1953), 143–44. If this historical note is true, then someone who was briefly mentioned in Acts became an important patriarch in a historically significant church. But even if this note by Eusebius is not accurate, it doesn't really matter, because obeying God is still the right thing to do even if the results are not easily detectable.

But there is not really a reason to look negatively on Paul's interaction with the Athenians anyway. Kenneth E. Bailey helps us in the modern world to see the significance of Paul getting a hearing at the Areopagus in the first place. "The philosophical guild at Athens was the intellectual center of the entire Greco-Roman world. Leading Roman families often sent their children to Athens for advanced education. To have received a hearing in that bastion of Greek learning was a huge victory in itself."[16] This is why Luke dedicated so much space to it and why he omitted any hint of negative tone in his presentation of the historical episode.[17]

The reason Paul changed his message for the Corinthians is most likely to do with the fact that Corinth was a different context than Athens.[18] The great biblical scholar F. F. Bruce concurs. "Paul by this time was no novice in Gentile evangelization, experimenting with this approach and that to discover which was most effective. It is probable that Paul's decision at Corinth was based on his assessment of the situation there."[19] This is why Paul claimed in 1 Corinthians 9, "To the Jews I became like a Jew, to win the Jews. . . . To those not having the law I became like one not having the law . . . so as to win those not having the law" (vv. 20–21). Paul simply knew how to contextualize his message![20] We commend an apologetics that does no less than to, in the example of Paul, lovingly assess the worldview of one's audience in light of the Christian worldview and to tailor the message to that audience. For example, if you're speaking with atheists, then consider offering some arguments for the existence of God. If you're conversing with Latter-day Saints, then perhaps rely more heavily on arguments for the reliability

---

16. Kenneth E. Bailey, *Paul through Mediterranean Eyes: Cultural Studies in 1 Corinthians* (Downers Grove, IL: IVP Academic, 2011), 104.

17. Paul Copan and Kevin D. Litwak, *The Gospel in the Marketplace of Ideas: Paul's Mars Hill Experience for Our Pluralistic World* (Downers Grove, IL: IVP Academic, 2014), 22.

18. Reasons for this are manifold. As Copan and Litwak argue, "Paul was chiding the Corinthians for their spiritual pride and puffed-up, misguided wisdom. . . . The word of the cross is not folly because it is irrational or illogical, but it strikes at the heart of human pride and boasting in this-worldly achievements." Copan and Litwak, 23.

19. F. F. Bruce, *Paul: Apostle of the Heart Set Free* (Grand Rapids: Eerdmans, 1977), 246. Bruce thought that Paul would have been discouraged with the results in Athens but would not have blamed his methodology. Copan and Litwak argue that Paul was actually using a similar style of argumentation "bridge-building" "before and after Athens," in *The Gospel in the Marketplace of Ideas*, 23.

20. Copan and Litwak, *Gospel in the Marketplace*, 25.

of the Bible and the uniqueness and divinity of Christ given his claims. In all situations, ask good questions and be a good listener just like our hero in the faith, Paul.

Karl Barth's Critique of Natural Theology

The last contention to consider is the broader notion that apologetics is contrary to authentic Christian faith is that from the Swiss neoorthodox theologian Karl Barth. For the Christian, Barth argues, natural theology is off-limits because its subject, the knowledge of God revealed apart from Scripture, "differs fundamentally from the revelation in Jesus Christ and whose *method* therefore differs equally from the exposition of Holy Scripture."[21] This means that natural theology leads to idolatry, the conjuring and worshiping of a god who is nothing like the Jesus Christ of the Bible. The method of natural theology, "the intrinsically godless reason of man . . . is inimical to belief."[22] This is because reason is corrupted by sin. Sin's effects go deeper, too, destroying the image of God in humanity and making impossible any point of contact for receiving knowledge about God outside of Scripture.[23]

Barth's contention that sin has destroyed the image of God in humanity will be addressed below; however, his wholesale rejection of natural theology requires some examination. First, it is helpful to understand Barth's context. A theological liberalism that denied the truth and sufficiency of the Bible and the uniqueness and divinity of Jesus Christ was rampant in Europe prior to and during Barth's life. This meant that the discipline of natural theology had gone in some strange directions. For example, National Socialism, which Barth firmly opposed, attempted to see the work of God in the historical rise of the German people, the Nazi Party, and Adolf Hitler. A prominent theologian of the time named Paul Althaus advocated for this depraved natural theology. "Our Protestant Churches have greeted the turning

---

21. Karl Barth, "No!," in Emil Brunner and Karl Barth, *Natural Theology: Comprising "Nature and Grace" by Professor Dr. Emil Brunner and the Reply "No!" by Dr. Karl Barth*, trans. Peter Fraenkel (London: Centenary, 1946), 74–75, emphasis in original.

22. Karl Barth, *Church Dogmatics 1.1 [sec. 1–7]: The Doctrine of the Word of God*, study ed., ed. G. W. Bromiley and T. F. Torrance (London: T&T Clark: 2009), 26.

23. See Barth, "No!," 106.

point of 1933 as a gift and miracle of God."[24] Althaus was specifically (and correctly) named by Barth as a propagator of a natural theology that led to idolatry, the idolatry of the German *Volk* and their führer.[25]

But is Barth's context anything like ours today?[26] Perhaps, in certain ways, people tend to make gods in their own image or look to worship something in the natural world itself, but there is a whole tradition of natural theology that attempts to see God's revelation as the key to any further investigation into the knowledge of God. This is exactly the tradition you see represented in this book. Indeed, we reject creating a god in our own image through our own autonomous investigations into the natural world. Instead, we commend a natural theology that recognizes that God has revealed God's "eternal power and divine nature . . . being understood from what has been made" (Rom. 1:20). If God has shown God's self, then our attempts to see God are not idolatry, but worship! Additionally, Christians doing natural theology need not look to the self or to their ethnic or national group for the foundation for God's revelation in the natural world. God is the foundation for God's own revelation and for reason itself. That is, humanity does not discover God; God speaks to humanity. Humanity doesn't conjure up logical systems; rather, God's rationality is the foundation for any (lesser) human rationality.

---

24. Paul Althaus, *Die deutsche Stunde der Kirche*, 3rd ed. (Göttingen: Vandenhoeck & Ruprecht, 1934), 5; quoted in Robert P. Erickson, *Theologians under Hitler: Gerhard Kittel, Paul Althaus and Emanuel Hirsch* (New Haven, CT: Yale University Press, 1985), 85.

25. Barth, *"No!,"* 104. "What Calvin wrote in those first chapters of the *Institutes* has to be written again and this time in such a way that no Przywara [a Jesuit] and no Althaus can find in it material for their fatal ends" (104). He was against any influence of Roman Catholic theology upon Protestantism as well.

26. Alister E. McGrath argues that Barth may have approved of a natural theology that was grounded in the context of the Christian community. "It is clear that a number of factors shape Barth's anxieties concerning natural theology, including his belief in the theological destructiveness of the reassertion of human autonomy and his perennial fear that theology might be reduced to anthropology. . . . Barth's concerns about natural theology can be met by reconceptualizing natural theology as an intellectual undertaking within the community of faith, on the basis of its doctrinal commitments." See Alister E. McGrath, *The Order of Things: Explorations in Scientific Theology* (Oxford: Blackwell, 2006), 87–88. This means that Christians can do natural theology with other Christians. While this is an improvement on Barth's *"No!"* to natural theology, it fails to do what natural theology can meaningfully (and biblically) do, namely, show someone who is *outside* the Christian community that a good and powerful Creator exists. However, we agree that the conversation on the methods and legitimacy of natural theology and apologetics should take place within the Christian community, which is why we ground the possibility of doing natural theology and apologetics in the *Logos* and the *imago Dei* (see below).

This is why the doctrine of Christ as *Logos* (Word) is vital for natural theology. In Jesus, we experience the point of contact between God's revelation and human minds. "In the beginning was the Word (*Logos*), and the Word was with God, and the Word was God. . . . In him was life, and that life was the light of all mankind. . . . The true light that gives light to everyone was coming into the world" (John 1:1, 4, 9). When we reason correctly about God's revelation to infer the existence and nature of God, we are doing so not by exercising "godless human reason," but by reflecting on God showing God's self to the world and by reason accessible to humanity via the *Logos* who has become human and has come into the world.

The idea that doing apologetics is contrary to Christian faith is a powerful objection, but we have shown that (1) genuine Christian faith can be rational, (2) the example of Paul at Mars Hill is an example of good contextual apologetics, and (3) we need not fear that natural theology will lead us to conjure up and worship a false god if God's own revelation is the standard for success. However, we need to consider a slightly different position, that of some Christians who argue that doing apologetics requires one to become a Christian prior to reasoning rightly about God.

2. APOLOGETICS, NAMELY, THE NATURAL THEOLOGY NEEDED FOR CLASSICAL APOLOGETICS, IS IMPOSSIBLE PRIOR TO CHRISTIAN FAITH

In an old *Peanuts* comic strip, Linus is telling Lucy that he wants to become a doctor when he grows up. Lucy, ever the one to take the wind out of someone else's sails, rebukes Linus by saying, "You could never be a doctor! You know why? Because you don't love mankind, that's why!" Linus shouts back as Lucy flees the scene, "I love mankind. . . . It's *people* I can't stand." If there's anything that life will teach you, it is that people can let you down. People will fail you, and sometimes you may even feel similarly to Linus. The biblical worldview sheds some light on the fact that humanity is often a great disappointment. The problem of sin and the fall is central to Christian anthropology. As James W. Sire says,

"Human beings were created good, but through the fall the image of God became defaced."[27] Humans, it seems, have the capability to do wonderful and beautiful things, but this capability, under sin, entails the ability to do awful and terrible things. According to some Christians, the effects of the fall are deemed so significant that there remains no point of contact in the *imago Dei* (image of God) for humanity to receive God's revelation, particularly God's revelation apart from Scripture. In his interpretation of Calvin's views on sin's impact on revelation, Herman Bavinck states, "Man no longer has an eye to see God; to do so he needs faith."[28] Barth and many other Protestant theologians agree with this basic argument: humanity is unable to see God's revelation in the Word or in the world because humanity is traumatically altered by sin. "One might call [receiving God's revelation prior to salvation] an objective possibility, created by God, but not a subjective possibility, open to man. Between what is possible in principle and what is possible in fact inexorably lies the fall."[29] Thus, after exploring various philosophical arguments for the existence of God, Bavinck concludes, "The proofs . . . are not *sources* but rather *products* of faith."[30] This position is called the *Reformed objection to natural theology*, and if this objection holds, then it means that the Bible does not support doing natural theology for those outside the household of faith because of sin's devastating effects on the non-Christian's ability to receive God's revelation prior to faith.

There are two chief reasons to reject the Reformed objection. First, the Bible seems to highly esteem general revelation, reason, and the ability to find common ground with those who do not have faith in God. Consider David's hymn of God's revelation in the natural world:

> The heavens declare the glory of God;
> the skies proclaim the work of his hands.

---

27. James W. Sire, *The Universe Next Door: A Basic Worldview Catalog*, 6th ed. (Downers Grove, IL: IVP Academic, 2020), 26.

28. Herman Bavinck, *The Doctrine of God* (Grand Rapids: Baker, 1985), 66.

29. Barth, *"No!,"* 106. See also Michael Sudduth, *The Reformed Objection to Natural Theology*, Ashgate Philosophy of Religion Series (New York: Routledge, 2009); Alvin Plantinga, "The Reformed Objection to Natural Theology," Proceedings and Addresses of the American Philosophical Association 54:49 (1980), https://www.pdcnet.org/acpaproc/content/acpaproc_1980_0054_0000_0049_0062.

30. Bavinck, *Doctrine of God*, 79.

> Day after day they pour forth speech;
>> night after night they reveal knowledge.
> They have no speech, they use no words;
>> no sound is heard from them.
> Yet their voice goes out into all the earth,
>> their words to the ends of the world. (Ps. 19:1–4)

A few things are worth mentioning about this passage. To begin, one sees the natural world revealing God's glory. That is, God has revealed God's self through nature. Now the kind of revelation that is contained in the natural world includes "speech" and "knowledge," though what is revealed is not encoded in a natural human language. Yet this revelation is available everywhere in the world. Common ground exists between those who already have God's definitive revelation in the Bible (for David, the law of Moses) and those who "hear" the declarations of the glory of God in the natural world. Later David shifts his focus to "the law of the LORD," or as John Goldingay translates it, "Yhwh's teaching."[31] "Yhwh's 'teaching' can refer to the world of the prophets and thinkers as well as to *the* Torah . . . and to oral as well as written teaching, while its application to Genesis—Deuteronomy as a whole indicates that in principle it could refer to the story of Yhwh's acts with Israel."[32] This means that the teaching mentioned in Psalm 19 may even refer to God's revelation in the course of history, something that the children of Israel's Gentile contemporaries who were experiencing the events of Genesis through Deuteronomy could have known simply by hearing about the children of Israel, rather than from special revelation.[33] Regardless of whether "Yhwh's teaching" includes Israel's history, this psalm is significant in that David was claiming that knowledge about God is available everywhere in the natural world. How strange it would be for

---

31. John Goldingay, *Psalms: Volume 1: Psalms 1–41*, BCOTWP (Grand Rapids: Baker Academic, 2006), 290.

32. Goldingay, 290–91.

33. This seems to be exactly what happened to Rahab, who told the spies, "We have heard how the LORD dried up the water of the Red Sea for you when you came out of Egypt, and what you did to Sihon and Og, the two kings of the Amorites east of the Jordan, whom you completely destroyed. When we heard of it, our hearts melted in fear and everyone's courage failed because of you, for the LORD your God is God in heaven above and on the earth below" (Josh. 2:10–11).

a theologian to tack on the proviso that this knowledge is only available to the redeemed!

Reason is something, in particular, that is called upon, employed, and approved of throughout the Bible.[34] We have already seen this in Jesus' identity as the *Logos* and Paul's argument about the resurrection in 1 Corinthians 15. But consider, as well, God's word to Israel in Isaiah 1. God spoke in various ways about the covenant relationship he had with Israel and how Israel had rebelled: "I reared children and brought them up, but they have rebelled against me" (v. 2). He identified himself as "the Holy One of Israel" (v. 4) and "the LORD Almighty" (v. 9), and yet Israel persisted in their rebellion. That is, God was not at fault. God had been an attentive parent, a blameless God in covenant relationship with Israel, and the God with all of the power to carry out his promises, but Israel still failed to meet God's moral standards. God's perfection and power logically entailed that God did not need Israel's sacrifices. "The multitude of your sacrifices—what are they to me?" (v. 11), and that Israel needed to "learn to do right" (v. 17). So God summarized the situation:

> "Come now, and let us reason together,"
> Says the LORD,
> "Though your sins are as scarlet,
> They will be as white as snow;
> Though they are red like crimson,
> They will be like wool.
> "If you consent and obey,
> You will eat the best of the land;
> "But if you refuse and rebel,
> You will be devoured by the sword." (Isa. 1:18–20 NASB)

God was making a legal case against Israel in this chapter, using reason to draw attention to their failure to fulfill the covenant.[35] Never is the

---

34. See Douglas Groothuis, *Christian Apologetics: A Comprehensive Case for Biblical Faith*, 2nd ed. (Downers Grove, IL: IVP Academic, 2022), 174–79; and Shepardson, "General Revelation and the God of Natural Theology," 210.

35. See Walter Brueggemann, *Isaiah 1–39*, Westminster Bible Companion (Louisville, KY: Westminster John Knox, 1998), 19–20. "This summons is in the language of adjudication."

tone simply "Because I say so." Though great significance is attached to the fact that God is the one speaking, the significance of God's speech is that God was rightly judging Israel and pronouncing upon them the logical consequences of their sin. As one can see, God employs and never impugns the use of reason, and the Bible is complementary to general revelation and to finding conceptual common ground with those who are outside of the family of God.

The second reason to reject the Reformed objection is its misunderstanding of the *imago Dei*. According to the Reformed objection, sin has destroyed the point of contact in the *imago Dei* for the non-Christian to receive general revelation. This is not the case, however. When the Bible talks about humans being made in the image of God, this means a number of things, including the ability to reason.[36] So if the image of God is destroyed through sin, then the sinner would be incapable of reason. Moreover, the change brought about in a person by salvation does not cause them to cease being a sinner. Yes, the person saved by grace through faith is justified before God, but it is not as if the saved person has become perfect enough through the Holy Spirit to avoid moral or intellectual errors. B. B. Warfield argued as much when he contended that if salvation is what makes knowledge possible, then no knowledge would be attainable by the unregenerate person at all.[37] This, of course, is absurd. Those who are not yet part of God's family can and do know many things. This is not to say that salvation lends no epistemic (that is, relating to knowledge) advantage to the saved person; it is merely saying that knowledge is possible for the one who is not saved. In fact, knowledge of God is a necessary precondition to give intellectual assent (*assensus*) to the idea that God raised Jesus Christ from the dead. The person who agrees that God raised Jesus from the dead, but lacks the willingness (*fiducia*) to entrust himself to God, still has knowledge that God exists. As Carl F. H. Henry argued, "Scripture

---

36. For a helpful view of the nature of the *imago Dei*, see Millard Erickson, *Christian Theology*, 2nd ed. (Grand Rapids: Baker, 1998), ch. 24.

37. B. B. Warfield, "Introduction to Francis R. Beattie's *Apologetics*," in *Christian Apologetics Past and Present: A Primary Source Reader*, vol. 2: *From 1500*, ed. William K. Edgar and K. Scott Oliphint (Wheaton, IL: Crossway, 2011), 400. Warfield referred to any kind of knowledge as a "science," an intellectual inquiry that requires at least some contact with the truth of how things really are.

refutes the view that men have no knowledge of God. . . . Had man's rational competence not survived the fall, he could neither know nor communicate intelligible truth, nor could intelligible revelation be appropriated by him or meaningfully addressed to him."[38] All of this means that though sin has catastrophically wounded the *imago Dei*, sin has not annihilated the *imago Dei*. The image of God remains in the one who is not a Christian and is a precondition for any knowledge about God or anything else.

Since we have addressed the Reformed objection, we proceed to consider three more objections to apologetics, one from theologically liberal Christians who deny the uniqueness of Christianity, one regarding the propriety of reasoning about God, and one regarding the relationship of apologetics and the Holy Spirit.

3. APOLOGETICS MISUNDERSTANDS THE NATURE OF RELIGIOUS TRUTH AND IS THEREFORE OFFENSIVE TOWARD OTHER RELIGIONS

One of the hallmarks of evangelicalism in particular, and theologically conservative Protestantism generally, is the idea that Christianity is uniquely true among the world's religions. This point of view does not deny the possibility of some truth in other religions, but it does highlight the claims of the Christian worldview as true, rational, and pertinent to every area of life while denying the truth claims of other religions insofar as they contradict Christian truth claims. This position is called *particularism*. Harold Netland explains,

> (1) The Bible is God's distinctive written revelation; it is true and fully authoritative; and thus, where the claims of Scripture are incompatible with those of other faiths, the latter are to be rejected. (2) Jesus Christ is the unique incarnation of God, fully God and fully man, and only through the person and work of Jesus is there

---

38. Carl F. H. Henry, *God, Revelation and Authority, Volume II: God Who Speaks and Shows* (Wheaton, IL: Crossway, 1999), 136.

the possibility of salvation. (3) God's saving grace is not mediated through the teachings, practices or institutions of other religions.[39]

This position is consistent with the Bible's teaching and of the tradition of the church (broadly) through the centuries. Of course, not all Christians have held this position, and to those who deny particularism, apologetics poses a unique challenge. In particular, religious pluralism affirms that "salvation (or enlightenment or liberation) should be acknowledged as present and effective in its own way in each religion."[40] If Christianity is not uniquely true, then why care about defending its truth or rationality? If other religions provide access to salvation of some kind, then why be concerned with explaining to those of other religions how the Christian worldview is pertinent to their lives? For pluralists, apologetics mistakenly presupposes that Christianity alone is true, so apologetics is offensive to other religions and should be rejected.[41]

Proponents of this position have used a couple of arguments to support their position against apologetics. The first comes from the Scottish arch-skeptic David Hume who argued that natural theology does not lead in the direction of a singular deity. "A great number of men join in building a house or a ship, in rearing a city, in framing a commonwealth: Why may not several Deities combine in contriving and framing a world?"[42] While Hume did not tease out the implications of this point of view to the extent of saying that there may actually be many gods or

39. Harold Netland, *Encountering Religious Pluralism: The Challenge to Christian Faith and Mission* (Downers Grove, IL: IVP Academic, 2001), 48.

40. Netland, 53.

41. The chief positions that Netland employs in his analysis of the nature of religious truth are the particularist, the universalist (who claims that Jesus is necessary for salvation but provides salvific provision for those outside the Christian faith), and the pluralist (who regards all religions as equally true and efficacious ways of providing salvation/liberation/enlightenment). See Netland, 48–54.

42. David Hume, "Dialogues concerning Natural Religion, Part V," in *Dialogues and Natural History of Religion*, ed. J. C. A. Gaskin, Oxford World's Classics (Oxford: Oxford University Press, 1998), 69. William James took this line of reasoning further, "The warring gods and formulas of the various religions do indeed cancel each other, but there is a certain uniform deliverance in which religions appear to meet." William James, *The Varieties of Religious Experience: A Study in Human Nature* (New York: Simon & Schuster, 1997), 393, quoted in Larry Witham, *The Measure of God: Our Century-Long Struggle to Reconcile Science & Religion: The Story of the Gifford Lectures* (San Francisco: HarperSanFrancisco, 2005), 87. The religions all delivered people from a kind of psychological uneasiness. Hume's "many gods" objection is addressed in the next chapter.

many equally valid religions, religious pluralists have used this kind of reasoning to conclude, as John Hick did, that "the universe is religiously ambiguous . . . our environment is capable of being construed—in sense perception as well as ethically and religiously—in a range of ways."[43] The result of this kind of skepticism about religious truth is that many or all religions may be true at the same time. Therefore, apologetics misses the mark epistemologically; if multiple interpretations about religious reality are correct, then the Christian apologist is simply mistaken in claiming that Christianity is uniquely true, rational, and pertinent to all areas of life.

A second argument for religious pluralism attempts to appeal to specifically Christian sympathies about the nature and character of God. The argument centers around the idea that God is just and loving. That is, God is just and would not let so many different religions with so many dedicated followers develop if God did not intend for there to be truth to find in those religions. Plus, God is love, and a loving God would not want so many people to be deceived.[44] Paul Knitter says it this way: "Why, if Jesus is the only saviour and Christianity the only really true religion, has God allowed so many other religions to continue to prosper? And instead of competing and fighting with each other, can the religions dialogue and co-operate together toward a world of greater peace and well-being?"[45] We see in this set of questions the arguments that (1) it is incoherent to believe that Christianity is the only true religion while acknowledging that God has allowed so many religions to prosper; and (2) we should stop arguing and fighting and start cooperating to solve problems instead. For Knitter then, apologetics is misguided about religious truth and distracts from the greater opportunity of cooperation

---

43. John Hick, *An Interpretation of Religion: Human Responses to the Transcendent*, 2nd ed. (New York: Palgrave Macmillan, 2004), 12. Hick included atheism as a live option as well.

44. One should note how this is slightly different from the Christian inclusivist position, which holds that Christianity is uniquely true, but that God provides universal salvation to people regardless of their faith. See Netland, *Encountering Religious Pluralism*, 51–52. One might encounter a Christian who says, "If God is love, then why would God condemn people to hell?" who would opt for inclusivism. However, this same statement could be uttered by a skeptic who is either honestly questioning or potentially trying to undermine the Christian worldview. For more on this question, see Groothuis, *Christian Apologetics*, 653–61.

45. Paul Knitter, "The Meeting of Religions: A Christian Debate," in Gavin D'Costa, Paul Knitter, and Daniel Strange, *Only One Way? Three Christian Responses on the Uniqueness of Christ in a Religiously Plural World* (London: SCM Press, 2001), 50–51.

and dialogue. This argument can be taken a step further to simply say that apologetics is dangerous and is offensive to others who rightly trust the truths found in their religions. "Exclusive claims isolate the community of faith from neighbors of other faiths, creating tensions and disturbing relationships within the larger community."[46] Thinking that you are right and others who don't think like you are wrong is likely to decrease social cohesion and cause violence.

Pluralism holds some appeal for many in the West because it seems to value the dignity and goodness of the billions of people throughout history who, to our knowledge, have not embraced Christian faith. However, deep philosophical and theological problems are associated with the position that all religions are equally true. Philosophically, Hick begged the question against Christian apologetics to say that the universe is religiously ambiguous. The ministry of Christian apologetics exists to show the truth of Christianity, and it amasses many arguments for the existence of God (ontological, cosmological, design, and moral) and for distinctively Christian truth claims (such as the divinity of Jesus, the reliability of the Bible, and the resurrection of Jesus from the dead). To dismiss all of these arguments out of hand is intellectually irresponsible. Evaluating a large body of evidence requires time and care, and this attention is not allotted to Christian apologetics in the work of Hick and other pluralists.

Moreover, the notion that all religions are equally true ignores the fact that the religions make contradictory truth claims. Consider Christianity's claim that Jesus is Lord. By "Lord," Christians mean that Jesus is the ultimate authority as God. Islam, on the other hand, claims that Jesus is merely a prophet, albeit an important one. Islam diminishes the authority of Jesus and denies his deity. These two claims cannot both be true at the same time and in the same respect because of the law of noncontradiction ($A \neq$ non-A). As a consequence, this kind of confusion about the nature of truth might actually lead to offense and violence.

---

46. Stanley J. Samartha, "The Cross and the Rainbow," in John Hick and Paul F. Knitter, *The Myth of Christian Uniqueness: Toward a Pluralistic Theology of Religions* (Maryknoll, NY: Orbis, 1987), 81. Samartha goes on to say that "sterile apologetics" detract from the cultural beauty that can result from interreligious affirmation and interfaith experiences. He has in mind the work of Hindu artists who paint on Christian topics. See Samartha, 82–83.

For example, a Muslim may be offended by hearing a pluralist affirm that Islam's teaching that Jesus is merely a prophet is true *while at the same time* affirming that Christianity's teaching that Jesus is Lord is true. The Muslim may protest that Islam has been misunderstood and, perhaps, mocked by giving equal weight to a Christian belief that Islam has specifically ruled out.[47]

Theologically, pluralism is incredibly problematic for Christians given all of the individual statements regarding Jesus' uniqueness and the overarching narrative of Jesus' importance in the Bible. For example, Jesus claimed about himself, "I am the way and the truth and the life. No one comes to the Father except through me" (John 14:6). The context of this is Jesus' farewell address to his disciples, where he claimed to be going to the Father, about whom he said, "I am in the Father and the Father is in me" (v. 11). He also promised that the Father would send the Holy Spirit in Jesus' name (v. 26)! Jesus' disciples eventually understood the significance of Jesus' identity by claiming him to be the fulfillment of Jewish prophecy and the key figure in God's story of salvation. "Salvation is found in no one else, for there is no other name under heaven given to mankind by which we must be saved" (Acts 4:12; see also 1 Tim. 2:5). These passages are just representative of the ways in which the Bible singles out Jesus for divinity, worship, uniqueness, sufficiency, and superiority. Christianity simply makes exclusive claims about the person and work of Jesus Christ that, by definition, rule out other religions' claims about ultimate reality and salvation/enlightenment/liberation. This fact does not entail that Christianity is true, but simply shows that Christianity's claims about Jesus cannot be interpreted to allow for the possibility of the truth about what matters most being found in other religions.

That said, Christianity does have room for the notion that *some* truths may be found in other religions. The doctrine of general revelation shows how this can be. Consider again Paul at Mars Hill, who quoted approvingly the Greek poets Epimenides and Aratus, respectively, when he claimed that God "is not far from any one of us. 'For in him we live

---

47. "The Messiah, Jesus, son of Mary, was nothing more than a messenger of God" (Surah 4:171), *The Qur'an*, Oxford World's Classics, trans. M. A. S. Abdel Haleem (Oxford: Oxford University Press, 2004), 66.

and move and have our being.' As some of your own poets have said, 'We are his offspring'"(Acts 17:27–28).[48] More specifically for our pluralistic context, Gerald McDermott shows that the Buddhist doctrine of "dependent origination" rightly affirms that "no phenomenon in the cosmos is isolated and without cause but every phenomenon is linked with every other phenomenon."[49] This corroborates the contingency and interdependency of elements within the cosmos and coheres with the idea that Christ holds everything together (see Col. 1:17). Of course, a Buddhist would interpret the doctrine of "dependent origination" differently within the Buddhist worldview (one that excludes God), but the doctrine on its own contains some truth. This is where the manner in which Christians disagree with the truth claims of other religions is so important. Most of what is offensive about how people view religious differences is found in how people disagree about religious reality. If a person's attitude is *I'm going to tell you heathens how you're wrong about your religious beliefs and why you need to convert to Christianity*, then that person can rightly expect interreligious dialogue to be fraught with relational strife. However, if one seeks to explain one's beliefs with a genuine willingness to listen to one's counterpart from another religion, then perhaps the interchange will remain respectful and peaceful.

We ought not take this too far, though. "Everyone getting along nicely" isn't necessarily the goal. Christianity, after all, makes truth claims that deny the truth claims of other religions and the claims of those who deny the truth of all religions (religious pluralists). Christianity claims that humans are sinners in need of a Savior, and this may be tough to swallow. Christianity invites us to lay down our pride and to become like children to enter the kingdom of God. This may cause some offense. Yet the manner in which we explain these truths of Christianity makes all the difference. When we as apologists show the fruit of the Spirit in our lives, the Spirit himself will empower us to "give an answer to everyone who asks [us] to give the reason for the hope that [we] have" and to do it "with gentleness and respect" (1 Peter 3:15).

---

48. See F. F. Bruce, *The Book of Acts*, NICNT (Grand Rapids: Eerdmans, 1977), 359–60.
49. Gerald R. McDermott, *Can Evangelicals Learn from World Religions? Jesus, Revelation & Religious Traditions* (Downers Grove, IL: InterVarsity, 2000), 141.

4. APOLOGETICS TURNS REASON INTO AN IDOL AND PRODUCES A "GOD" WHO IS NOTHING LIKE THE GOD OF ABRAHAM, ISAAC, AND JACOB

The pluralists considered above say that apologetics is inherently disrespectful. But some Christians affirm the uniqueness of Jesus and Christianity and make the claim that Christian apologetics is disrespectful to God by identifying the idolatrous god of natural theology with the God of the Bible. This objection claims that apologetics in general, and natural theology in particular, is guilty of ontotheology, the sin of using philosophy to attempt to control and manipulate the concept of God. This means that any concept of "god" that results from philosophical or apologetic discourse will be an idol. Christians who hold to the ontotheology objection claim that the god of natural theology is not the God of Abraham, Isaac, and Jacob. For example, they argue that the God of the Bible is relational but not logical. God in the Bible is dynamic and mysterious, not someone who can be reduced to propositions such as "The cause of the universe is God." Carl A. Raschke argues, "To talk about God as an ultimate *fact* . . . is to finitize the One who is, and who was, and who is to come."[50] This means that using philosophy to talk about God attempts to control and manipulate the concept of God, but the God of the Bible resists all control. Myron Bradley Penner agrees, claiming that apologetics buys into the use of secular philosophical reason, producing something "tantamount to conceptual idolatry and methodological blasphemy."[51] He is saying that God reveals God's self on God's terms. It is a sin to try to use reason to discover God. If one uses reason this way, then reason actually takes the place of ultimacy over God. Another way of thinking about the ontotheological objection is to think about its fruit. Merold Westphal argues that when the apologist uses philosophy to talk about God, this results in a god that is not really worthy of worship. "Our philosophical theologies . . . can easily lapse, both in appearance and in fact, into trying

---

50. Carl A. Raschke, *The Next Reformation: Why Evangelicals Must Embrace Postmodernity* (Grand Rapids: Baker Academic, 2004), 81–82.

51. Myron Bradley Penner, *The End of Apologetics: Christian Witness in a Postmodern Context* (Grand Rapids: Baker Academic, 2013), 62.

to make everything clear, thereby producing a God not obviously related to prayer, worship, and witness."[52]

These claims are potentially devastating to the apologetic enterprise, and they deserve some attention.[53] First, the claim that the philosophers' god is logical and that the God of the Bible is relational is a false dichotomy. Indeed, God presents us with mysteries and paradoxes, but that does not entail that God is illogical. Remember that God is the one who bids, "Come now, and let us reason together" (Isa. 1:18 NASB). Even when God seems to defy our expectations ("You thought I was exactly like you," Ps. 50:21), God doesn't contradict God's self or deny God's nature. In fact, God stays consistent to his word and is dependable. "Jesus Christ is the same yesterday and today and forever" (Heb. 13:8). And Jesus actually employed logic on many occasions. For example, he used the argument form of *reductio ad absurdum* (reduction to absurdity), when he was charged with casting out demons by the power of Satan:

> Every kingdom divided against itself will be ruined, and every city or household divided against itself will not stand. If Satan drives out Satan, he is divided against himself. How then can his kingdom stand? And if I drive out demons by Beelzebul, by whom do your people drive them out? So then, they will be your judges. But if it is by the Spirit of God that I drive out demons, then the kingdom of God has come upon you. (Matt. 12:25–28)

Here is a more formal way to see what Jesus is saying:

1. If Satan were divided against himself, his kingdom would be ruined.
2. But it is not ruined (since demonic activity continues). To think otherwise is absurd.

---

52. Merold Westphal, "Onto-Theology, Metanarrative, Perspectivism, and the Gospel," in *Christianity and the Postmodern Turn: Six Views*, ed. Myron B. Penner (Grand Rapids: Brazos, 2005), 146–47.

53. For a more detailed rebuttal of the ontotheological objection, see Andrew I. Shepardson, *Who's Afraid of the Unmoved Mover?* (Eugene, OR: Pickwick, 2019), 100–115.

3. Therefore, (a) Satan does not drive out Satan.

4. Therefore, (b) Jesus cannot free people from Satan by satanic power.[54]

To claim that God is relational and not logical is a false dichotomy. God is both relational and logical.

Second, while natural theology does not result in showing us the God of the Bible, it does lend support to key aspects of God's nature as definitively revealed in the Bible. As you will see in this book, arguments for the existence of God show that there is a God who is a creator, and he is powerful, eternal, personal, and good. Ultimately, how we understand the ways in which we seek to know God must be governed by the Bible, but that should not prohibit us from seeking evidence for God in the world around us.[55] This leads to the third problem with the ontotheological objection, the notion that apologetics creates an idol out of reason or out of the god of the philosophers. For evangelicals, the goal of apologetics is not to worship the idea of a god that is the result of some philosophical argument. The goal is to provide intellectual support for my belief in God and to show others that there is a God who exists. In a way, it does matter who is doing natural theology. For evangelicals, our high view of Scripture will never threaten our investigations outside of Scripture, so the risk is not that we worship a false god, but that we fail to seek God in everything we do, including our reflections on the world around us. For those who are not part of the Christian faith, apologetics may help to open their hearts to the Holy Spirit, prompting them to ask, "If there is a God revealed in the natural world, could this God have revealed God's self in other ways?" Finally, if engaged with Christian convictions, apologetics does not attempt to use human intuition or secular reason to discover, control, or manipulate God. For Christians, we start the whole discussion with the doctrine of revelation. God has spoken and shown God's self in the Scriptures definitively and through

---

54. Douglas Groothuis, *On Jesus*, Wadsworth Philosophers Series (Belmont, CA: Wadsworth/Thomson Learning, 2003), 34–35.

55. Even Paul at Mars Hill did not immediately identify the "Lord of heaven and earth" with the God of Abraham, Isaac, and Jacob. And he used the concept of the unknown God to point to the God who raised the "man he has appointed" from the dead (Acts 17:24–31).

"what has been made" (Rom. 1:20). If the source material is God's own revelation, then God controls the discussion around who God is and what God has done. The apologist is firmly on the other side as the grateful listener. Indeed, apologetics moves us to worship the God of the Bible even more, through seeing the manifold ways in which the evidence of God's greatness and goodness are displayed throughout the world![56]

Indeed, God is the source of all of our knowledge of God, but God is also the source of salvation. And some Christians are wary of apologetics because of concerns that the apologist tries to take God's place in how someone comes to faith. Let's examine this final objection to apologetics.

5. APOLOGETICS TRIES TO USURP THE ROLE OF THE HOLY SPIRIT IN BRINGING SOMEONE TO FAITH

The most common objection to doing apologetics is "Arguments don't save people. The Holy Spirit saves people." The person who objects in this way is concerned that the apologist is trying to fill a role that only God can fill. After all, attempting to play God in bringing someone to faith would be prideful presumption. We could not agree more, but this is too quick of a dismissal of the ministry of apologetics. Think about how Jesus pointed to his works as evidence for his identity: "Do not believe me unless I do the works of my Father. But if I do them, even though you do not believe me, believe the works, that you may know and understand that the Father is in me, and I in the Father" (John 10:37–38). He was saying that his listeners, in this case his opponents, should believe in him based on the things they could see in the world around them. He did not say, "Believe in me as you hear the still, small voice." This does not challenge the work of the Holy Spirit, because Jesus was saying that God speaks through evidence. This does not challenge the importance of a still, small voice, either, because God, of course, speaks "at many times and in various ways" (Heb. 1:1). We can also consider how Paul, the person who converted after a vision of Christ, used arguments and evidence in his sharing of the gospel. In Ephesus, "Paul entered the

---

56. We think here of the lyrics to the hymn "How Great Thou Art."

synagogue and spoke boldly there for three months, arguing persuasively about the kingdom of God" (Acts 19:8).

Sometimes people who make this objection are thinking that what is needed is simply that we love people and provide simple presentations of the gospel. However, this is misleading as well, as apologist Greg Koukl explains: "You cannot love someone into the kingdom . . . many people who were treated with sacrificial love and kindness by Christians never surrendered to the Savior. Many who have heard a clear explanation of God's gift in Christ never put their trust in him."[57] Whether it is through arguments, acts of service, simple gospel presentations, or prayer, what is necessary is for God to move upon human souls. The great thing is that God chooses to work concurrently with human efforts: "So we are Christ's ambassadors; God is making his appeal through us. We speak for Christ when we plead, 'Come back to God!'" (2 Cor. 5:20 NLT). This is precisely the role apologists attempt to fill. They are bold in their representation of the King who sends them out to spread the word of His dominion. When people ask them to defend their King, they gladly accept the challenge, defending God's existence, nature, and work according to the rules of engagement (Christian virtues) set down by the King in his written guidelines (the Bible).

There is a final thing to think about when reflecting on the work of the Holy Spirit through apologetics. When someone comes to know God through faith in Christ, that person indeed receives knowledge from God that Christianity is true. However, knowing that Christianity is true is different from explaining to someone that Christianity is true. William Lane Craig makes this distinction. "Although arguments and evidence may be used to support the believer's faith, they are never properly the basis of that faith"; the Holy Spirit is the basis of the believer's knowledge that Christianity is true.[58] But for the unbeliever, "independent warrant [arguments and evidence] for Christian truth claims apart from the Spirit's witness could help predispose an unbeliever to respond to the drawing of the Holy Spirit when he hears

---

57. Greg Koukl, *Tactics: A Game Plan for Discussing Your Christian Convictions*, 10th Anniversary ed. (Grand Rapids: Zondervan, 2019), 44.

58. William Lane Craig, *Reasonable Faith: Christian Truth and Apologetics*, 3rd ed. (Wheaton, IL: Crossway, 2008), 46.

the gospel."[59] That is, the unbeliever may be shown that Christianity is true through arguments and evidence. This distinction does nothing to threaten the Spirit's power; in fact, apologetics works as a servant to the Holy Spirit. Consider what happens in your soul[60] when you hear an argument for the existence of God. You may form the thought *God exists*. That thought is perfectly at home in a soul where the Holy Spirit is testifying to you about Jesus forming a different thought: "I should believe in Jesus." In this case, the thought that is formed about God's existence serves the Spirit's testimony. Thinking about it this way highlights the fact that arguments and the Holy Spirit both interact with the same central aspect of human thought and personality: the soul. This means that the causal power of arguments and the Holy Spirit both act upon the same realm of reality: the soul.[61] Cooperation, with the Holy Spirit in the lead, is natural (or one might say "supernatural").

So the Holy Spirit's power is not threatened or denied by apologetics. Nor is apologetics contrary to authentic Christian faith. Nor do apologists worship reason. We have shown in this chapter that while there are many important theological objections to apologetics, they ought not to succeed in dissuading followers of Jesus in engaging in the ministry of apologetics. We have shown that the Holy Spirit takes the lead in bringing people to faith, but that arguments can play a role in confirming the truth of the Spirit's testimony. We have shown that while defending Christian truth claims may be offensive, the manner in which we defend the truth does not need to be offensive. The remainder of this book is dedicated to helping you to explain your faith, lovingly showing others all of the good reasons to believe the Christian message with boldness.

---

59. Craig, 48.

60. We have a couple of presuppositions here about the nature of human minds and thoughts: (1) Humans are a soul-body unity, meaning that there is a key aspect to human beings that is mental and nonphysical. It is by this aspect of human being that one can have thoughts. (2) Thoughts are abstract, nonphysical objects that inhere in minds. The thought *I should believe in Jesus* is nonphysical and is something that exists in the mind. For a defense of substance dualism, see J. P. Moreland, *The Soul: How We Know It's Real and Why It Matters* (Chicago: Moody, 2014). For more explanation on why some Christians are wrongly predisposed against substance dualism, see Andrew I. Shepardson, "An Outline of the Pentecostal Ethos: A Critical Engagement with James K. A. Smith," in *Quadrum* 3, no. 1 (July 2020): 24–25.

61. For a deeper look into the cooperation between apologetic arguments and the Holy Spirit, see Andrew I. Shepardson, "The Spirit of Truth and the Unmoved Mover: The Presence of the Holy Spirit in Natural Theology," in *Quadrum* 2, no. 1 (July 2019): 36–48.

STUDY QUESTIONS

1. Which of the theological objections to apologetics do you find compelling, if any? Why?
2. Discuss any objections to apologetics not mentioned in this chapter and respond to them logically and biblically.
3. If someone thinks apologetics is unbiblical, how might this affect their witness and spiritual life?

SUGGESTED READING

Bailey, Kenneth E. *Paul through Mediterranean Eyes: Cultural Studies in 1 Corinthians.* Downers Grove, IL: IVP Academic, 2011.

Barrett, Justin L. *Born Believers: The Science of Children's Religious Belief.* New York: Free Press, 2012.

Brunner, Emil, and Karl Barth. *Natural Theology Comprising "Nature and Grace" by Professor Dr. Emil Brunner and the Reply "No!" by Dr. Karl Barth.* Translated by Peter Fraenkel. London: Centenary, 1946.

Copan, Paul, and Kevin D. Litwak. *The Gospel in the Marketplace of Ideas: Paul's Mars Hill Experience for Our Pluralistic World.* Downers Grove, IL: IVP Academic, 2014.

Craig, William Lane. *Reasonable Faith: Christian Truth and Apologetics.* 3rd ed. Wheaton, IL: Crossway, 2008.

Edgar, William K., and K. Scott Oliphint, eds. *Christian Apologetics Past and Present: A Primary Source Reader.* Vol. 2, *From 1500.* Wheaton, IL: Crossway, 2011.

Griffiths, Paul J. *An Apology for Apologetics: A Study in the Logic of Interreligious Dialogue.* Maryknoll, NY: Orbis, 1991.

Groothuis, Douglas. *On Jesus.* Wadsworth Philosophers Series. Belmont, CA: Wadsworth/Thomson Learning, 2003.

_____. *Truth Decay: Defending Christianity against the Challenges of Postmodernism.* Downers Grove, IL: InterVarsity, 2000.

Guinness, Os. *Fool's Talk: Recovering the Art of Christian Persuasion.* Downers Grove, IL: InterVarsity, 2015.

Haddad, Jonah. *Insanity: God and the Theory of Knowledge.* Eugene, OR: Wipf and Stock, 2013.

Henry, Carl F. H. *God, Revelation and Authority, Volume II: God Who Speaks and Shows: Fifteen Theses, Part One.* Wheaton, IL: Crossway, 1999.

Koukl, Gregory. *Tactics: A Game Plan for Discussing Your Christian Convictions.* 10th Anniversary ed. Grand Rapids: Zondervan, 2019.

McDermott, Gerald R. *Can Evangelicals Learn from World Religions? Jesus, Revelation & Religious Traditions.* Downers Grove, IL: InterVarsity, 2000.

Moreland, J. P. *The Soul: How We Know It's Real and Why It Matters.* Chicago: Moody, 2014.

Moreland, J. P., and Garrett DeWeese. *Philosophy Made Slightly Less Difficult: A Beginner's Guide to Life's Big Questions.* 2nd ed. Downers Grove, IL: IVP Academic, 2021.

Nash, Ronald. *Worldviews in Conflict: Choosing Christianity in a World of Ideas.* Grand Rapids: Zondervan Academic, 1992.

Netland, Harold. *Christianity and Religious Diversity.* Grand Rapids: Baker Academic, 2015.

_____. *Encountering Religious Pluralism: The Challenge to Christian Faith and Mission.* Downers Grove, IL: IVP Academic, 2001.

Penner, Myron B. ed. *Christianity and the Postmodern Turn: Six Views.* Grand Rapids: Brazos, 2005.

Rowe, C. Kavin. *World Upside Down.* Oxford: Oxford University Press, 2010.

Shepardson, Andrew I. *Who's Afraid of the Unmoved Mover? Postmodernism and Natural Theology.* Eugene, OR: Pickwick, 2019.

Sire, James W. *The Universe Next Door: A Basic Worldview Catalog.* 6th ed. Downers Grove, IL: IVP Academic, 2020.

CHAPTER 3

PHILOSOPHICAL OBJECTIONS
TO APOLOGETICS

When I (Doug) was an undergraduate philosophy major and young Christian at the University of Oregon from 1976–79, my professors assumed that arguments for God's existence were passé at best and irrational at worst. In my history of philosophy courses, some place was given to Aristotle's argument for a prime mover or Aquinas's Five Ways or Leibniz's design argument, but these were considered to be more relics than live options in philosophy. I was taught that natural theology had been killed primarily by David Hume and Immanuel Kant a long time ago. None of my professors—even my one Christian professor—took any stock in any arguments for the existence of God.

This troubled me, but I thought that Christianity explained the world and human beings far better than any other worldview. My faith was nurtured in this by writers such as C. S. Lewis, Os Guinness, and Francis Schaeffer, and I was growing spiritually through Bible study and Christian fellowship. Later, for a time, I embraced an apologetic method (presuppositionalism) that avoided natural theology but still advanced a strong case for the rationality of the Christian worldview and was strong on negative apologetics, which is the discipline of finding logical, evidential, and existential weaknesses in non-Christian worldviews.[1]

---

1. The leading thinkers in this school in a previous generation were Cornelius Van Til, Gordon H. Clark, and Carl F. H. Henry. On presuppositionalism, see Douglas Groothuis,

When I returned to the University of Oregon in 1990 for doctoral studies in philosophy, much had changed concerning natural theology—even if none of my professors had softened their views on it. Since the late 1970s, William Lane Craig has been championing the kalam cosmological argument. The design argument—in cosmology and biology—was gaining new strength through the intelligent design movement and through work on the fine-tuning of the universe for the emergence of intelligent life. The ontological argument, although much debated even in the 1960s and 1970s, was being addressed at high levels as well. Major scholarly reference volumes such as *The Blackwell Guide to Natural Theology*,[2] *The Oxford Handbook of Natural Theology*,[3] and *Debating Christian Theism*[4] have advanced natural theology. It turned out that my doctoral dissertation featured a concluding chapter defending a version of the cosmological argument as well.[5]

Despite the rise in natural theology in philosophical circles in the last four decades or so, certain salient philosophical criticisms are still brought against it. Although subsequent chapters will marshal constructive arguments for God's existence and for other aspects of the Christian worldview, this chapter addresses several recurring objections to the project of apologetics generally and of natural theology in particular. We address here the following philosophical arguments against Christian apologetics:

1. The concept of God is contradictory.
2. Natural theology just as easily leads to belief in many gods as it does to belief in a creator God.
3. If God is invisible, then no one is justified in believing that God exists.

Christian Apologetics: A Comprehensive Case for Biblical Faith, 2nd ed. (Downers Grove, IL: IVP Academic, 2022), 57–63. For more on the distinction between negative and positive apologetics, see Ronald H. Nash, *Faith and Reason: Searching for a Rational Faith* (Grand Rapids: Zondervan, 1988), 14–16.

2. William Lane Craig and J. P. Moreland, *Blackwell Guide to Natural Theology* (Hoboken, NJ: Wiley-Blackwell, 2012).

3. Russell Re Manning, ed., *The Oxford Handbook of Natural Theology* (New York: Oxford University Press, 2013).

4. J. P. Moreland, et al., *Debating Christian Theism* (New York: Oxford University Press, 2013).

5. Douglas Groothuis, "To Prove or Not to Prove? Pascal on Natural Theology" (PhD diss., University of Oregon, 1993). Our chapter, "The Cosmological Argument," gives a version of my original argument.

4. If the universe needs a creator/designer, then God needs a creator/designer.
5. Natural theology says so little about God that God might as well be a flying spaghetti monster as the deity of any monotheistic religion.
6. God of the gaps: God is arbitrarily invoked by apologists to make up for the lack of a natural explanation for certain aspects of the natural world.
7. "God" is just a projection of our psychological desires and hang-ups.
8. The objective truth required for apologetics to be successful is impossible (the postmodern objection).

This chapter will outline and rebut these objections, showing how Christian apologetics is a philosophically sound enterprise that legitimately seeks to show the reality of God and God's interaction with the universe.

THE CONCEPT OF GOD

Some critics have claimed that the project of natural theology is bankrupt from the beginning because the very idea of God is contradictory. Since what is contradictory cannot possibly exist, there could be no argument for its existence. For example, a circle that is, at the same time, a square cannot possibly exist, so one could never give a good argument for the existence of a square circle. Now some concepts of God—that is, some understanding of divine attributes—may be contradictory, but is the classic monotheistic conception of God one of them?

The subject of the divine attributes can become complex, and philosophers have written entire books on it. Let us start with a succinct and serviceable definition of God from Descartes. A "supreme God" is "eternal, infinite, immutable, omniscient, omnipotent, and the creator of all things other than himself."[6] Although Descartes did not add "all-good"

---

6. René Descartes, *Discourse on Method and Meditations on First Philosophy* (Indianapolis: Hackett, 1999), 73, Kindle.

(or "omnibenevolent"), it is implied by the attributes he does list. This concept of God has well served Judaism, Christianity, and Islam (though with variations) for centuries. But some claim the divine attributes are an unstable compound. That is, (1) several of the attributes of God do not cohere or (2) some individual attribute of God in itself is contradictory.

Consider the divine attribute of omnipotence. The kalam cosmological argument (see ch. 4) concludes that a being has the power to bring everything out of nothing (in Latin, *ex nihilo*). It seems that only an omnipotent being could accomplish that unique task of creating everything out of nothing (or exnihilation).[7] Roughly put, an omnipotent being has the power to actualize any state of affairs that is not logically impossible. But the "paradox of the stone" challenges the very idea of omnipotence as a coherent concept. You may have heard this one growing up: "Can God create a stone so heavy that he cannot lift it?" If God cannot create such a stone, he is not omnipotent, since there is something that God cannot create (the stone). If God can create such a stone, then he is not omnipotent, since there is something he cannot accomplish (lifting the stone). Another way to put this is in another question: "What happens when the irresistible force meets the unmovable object?"

We can answer in two ways. First, if the paradox of the stone succeeds, it only shows that there cannot be an *omnipotent* God; it does not show that no divine being whatever exists. Perhaps a less than omnipotent God exists. But the first option need not worry us, since the paradox of the stone is a ruse and not a problem for the concept of God. The concept of omnipotence cannot include logical contradictions, since no being of any power can make a contradiction true. Contradictions—such as square circles and objects that are entirely blue and entirely red at the same time—are simply impossible states of affairs. The simultaneous claims that there is (1) an unliftable stone and (2) an all-powerful being do not logically cohere. Therefore, this is an impossible state of affairs.[8]

Acres of pages have been taken up with this question of the coherence

---

7. See Douglas Groothuis, "Metaphysical Implications of Cosmological Arguments," in *In Defense of Natural Theology*, ed. James Sennett and Douglas Groothuis (Downers Grove, IL: InterVarsity, 2005).

8. George Mavrodes, "Some Puzzles concerning Omnipotence," *Philosophical Review* 72, no. 2 (1963): 221–23.

and nature of divine attributes, but for our purposes we will proceed on the assumption that some coherent rendering of an orthodox concept of God is available for natural theology and apologetics. This is justifiable in light of the work done to defend the coherence of theism.[9]

TOO MANY GODS

An objection raised by the Scottish skeptic David Hume and many others after him is that even a successful piece of natural theology would underdetermine the God of the Bible. That is, even if we can conclude that the universe is created and designed by a force outside of itself, these arguments cannot tell us much about the Creator and Designer. Perhaps several beings—a transcendent committee of gods or godletts— are responsible for the cosmos. Here's what Hume said in his *Dialogues concerning Natural Religion*: "A great number of men join in building a house or a ship, in rearing a city, in framing a commonwealth: Why may not several Deities combine in contriving and framing a world?"[10] If this argument holds, then its polytheistic conclusion hardly serves as an argument for the one true God of Christianity (or of Judaism or Islam either).

Hume, despite his great influence, is overrated on this and on many other points, as many philosophers of religion have argued.[11] First, the appeal to simplicity in explanation rules out more than one Maker. If one ultimate Creator-Designer explains what needs to be explained, then to posit multiple makers is sheer whimsy. To put it more formally, we should not multiply explanatory factors or entities beyond what is

---

9. See Ronald Nash, *The Concept of God* (Grand Rapids: Zondervan Academic, 1983); and J. P. Moreland and William Lane Craig, "The Coherence of Theism I" and "The Coherence of Theism II," in *Philosophical Foundations for a Christian Worldview* (Downers Grove, IL: IVP Academic, 2017).

10. David Hume, "Dialogues concerning Natural Religion, Part V," in *Dialogues and Natural History of Religion*, ed. J. C. A Gaskin, Oxford World's Classics (Oxford: Oxford University Press, 1998), 69.

11. For a book-length critique of Hume on natural theology, see James Sennett and Douglas Groothuis, eds., *In Defense of Natural Theology* (Downers Grove, IL: InterVarsity, 2005). For a critique of his denial of miracles, see *In Defense of Miracles: A Comprehensive Case for God's Action in History*, ed. R. Douglas Geivett and Gary R. Habermas (Downers Grove, IL: IVP Academic, 1997).

necessary.[12] If a jury is investigating a murder, and the guilt of one man is a simpler explanation than the guilt of many, then we should prefer the simpler explanation, all things being equal.[13]

Second, a collection of gods means that each god is itself a finite and contingent being, unlike the God of monotheism. If so, given the principle of sufficient reason (which we later address in more detail), each of these entities would require an explanation for its existence, and so on *ad infinitum*. In that case, no ultimate explanation is offered, which is exactly what Hume is attempting to show with the many gods argument. On the other hand, a monotheistic God serves as the ultimate and sufficient explanation for the cosmos because that being is self-existent and eternal by definition. As Paul said, "And he is not served by human hands, as if he needed anything. Rather, he himself gives everyone life and breath and everything else" (Acts 17:25). The metaphysical[14] buck stops here.

WHERE IS GOD?

When I (Doug) was a teaching assistant in graduate school, the subject of God came up in a large lecture class. A student rather indignantly said, "I don't believe in God for the same reason that I don't believe there is a 747 in this room. I don't see God." Although I was not teaching the class, I responded by saying that the student believed in a lot of things that he could not directly see, such as moral principles and other people's minds. The professor did not acknowledge my point and dismissed my comment by saying that the class had to understand that I was a campus minister as well as a philosophy student. I was concerned about people's souls. The assumption was that my comment could be dismissed. Despite my Christian convictions to treat such mocking with patience and grace, I silently fumed.

---

12. This principle is known as Occam's razor.

13. See Richard Swinburne, "How We Explain Things," in *Is There a God?* (New York: Oxford University Press, 1996).

14. Metaphysics is the philosophical discipline that deals with the nature of existence and reality.

The professor's response committed at least two logical fallacies. First, my status as a campus minister was irrelevant to the point I was making. This is the fallacy of the *red herring*. Second, he *poisoned the well* by assuming that a campus minister couldn't make a good philosophical point on this matter because he was biased. But is it possible that I could be interested in people's souls and still make good philosophical arguments? Absolutely! Let me explain.

The objection made by the student is based on the invisibility of God. It assumes that for something to exist, it must be visible or potentially visible. As J. P. Moreland puts the objection, "For someone to be rational in believing that P exists, that person must be able to sense P with the five senses."[15] If God is invisible, he cannot exist, and there is no point in constructing arguments for an invisible being's existence any more than there is in constructing arguments for a square circle or a married bachelor. This claim is abundantly false, but I will limit my response to four points.

First, we find counterexamples to the claim. As I said to the student in that philosophy class, we believe in many things that are not in the category of the directly perceptible. Most people—even relativists when pressed—believe that there are moral principles that apply to all people, and that are not reducible to any physical state. Consider statements such as "Rape is always wrong" or "Murder is always wrong." These principles do not have a color, shape, weight, or smell. They are not physical things, but they are still objectively real. Moreover, when talking to you, I rightly believe that you are having thoughts pertaining to our conversation. Yet I cannot directly perceive your thoughts. I must infer their existence from your activities. It is true that you are having thoughts even though I cannot see them.

Nor can I perceive a subatomic particle, but I can infer its existence from the behavior of things that are perceptible. This is exactly what the Bible says about God, as Paul wrote, "For since the creation of the world God's invisible qualities—his eternal power and divine nature—have been clearly seen, being understood from what has been made, so that people are without excuse" (Rom. 1:20).

---

15. J. P. Moreland, *Scaling the Secular City: A Defense of Christianity* (Grand Rapids: Baker, 1987), 226. P is simply a placeholder for any proposition or idea.

Second, the claim that "in order for someone to be rational in believing that P exists, that person must be able to sense P with the five senses," is itself not the kind of thing that can be perceived by the five senses. Thus, the statement refutes itself, and is therefore false. It is a thought, and one can no more perceive a thought in oneself than in another person. We can infer thoughts in others through their behavior, and we can experience our own thoughts through pure subjectivity (or direct awareness) that does not require any sensory observation.

Third, to require that God be visible to exist is to commit the fallacy of a *category mistake*.[16] A category mistake attributes a property to something to which it cannot belong, such as looking for the *esprit de corps* as a physical property in an army platoon or identifying the color of a note in music. The Christian God is by definition an infinite and invisible Spirit, not an object in the physical and visible world. As Paul wrote, "Now to the King eternal, immortal, invisible, the only God, be honor and glory for ever and ever. Amen" (1 Tim. 1:17; see also 1 John 4:12).

But fourth, God *can* be apprehended through the senses in Jesus Christ. Paul wrote that the "Son is the image of the invisible God, the firstborn over all creation" (Col. 1:15). And Jesus said, "Anyone who has seen me has seen the Father" (John 14:9). Christianity is unique on this score, for Christians affirm that God is invisible, yet God is with us in the man Jesus Christ, so seeing the man Jesus is seeing God. We will cover this truth more in chapter 9, but for now, it is clear that there is nothing lacking in the concept of God due to the fact that God is not physically observed in the world around us right now. Thus, this objection fails.

WHO CREATED GOD?

A commonly heard objection to arguments for God's existence is that if the universe needs a creator-designer, then God himself would need a creator-designer. If so, then this god would not be God at all, since God's existence would be dependent on something outside himself.

---

16. Philosopher Gilbert Ryle coined this term.

This objection is often reduced to a question: "Then who created God?" In fact, it was with this objection that my (Ike's) PhD adviser summarily dismissed all cosmological arguments for the existence of God.

The short answer is, "No one created God." This is simply because the very idea of a monotheistic God is one of a self-existent and eternal being, who thus has no origin outside of himself. Consider Moses' words:

> Before the mountains were born
> or you brought forth the whole world,
> from everlasting to everlasting you are God.
> (Ps. 90:2; see also Acts 17:25)

No argument from natural theology we have ever seen—outside of errant student papers and false accusations by Bertrand Russell—claims that *everything that exists* requires a cause or reason outside itself. On the contrary, the claim is that anything that is contingent and finite requires an explanation outside of itself. God is necessary, not contingent. (Being necessary means that God depends on no other thing for his existence, and he exists in any possible world or version of reality. Contingent things may just so happen to exist, but are not necessary; they have a ground for existence outside themselves.) God is infinite, not finite. God is self-existent—meaning that he is the source or *cause* of his own existence.[17] God is also the *reason* for his own existence, as we will see in discussing the principle of sufficient reason cosmological argument.

Richard Dawkins has tried to be clever by saying that if a complex universe needs to be explained by design (that is, by God), then how much more so a God who must be more complex than the universe.[18] So, the quip goes, "Who designed the Designer?" If Dawkins is correct, then the God explanation for design fails, since God would be subject to the very idea that supposedly served as an argument for God's existence. If God needs to be designed, then he is not God at all.

---

17. *Cause* here does not mean linear causation. Nothing can cause itself in that sense, since it would have to precede itself in order to bring itself into being. That is impossible. I mean *cause* in the sense of a self-existent being requiring no cause outside of itself for its existence.

18. Richard Dawkins, "Why There Is Almost Certainly No God," in *The God Delusion* (Boston: Houghton Mifflin, 2007).

There are two basic responses. First, a long-standing theological tradition has argued that God is ultimately simple and not made up of parts. If God is not composed of parts, then God cannot be more complex than the universe, as Dawkins suggests, and would not require the sort of explanation he demands. In this case, the objection fails. Second, even if God is not simple (and I am not committed to the idea), his discrete attributes are those of an eternal and self-existent being (Acts 17:25). As such, they are not contingent features of his being. That is, if he is noncontingent, he requires nothing outside of himself to explain himself, and his own identity is eternally solid and stable. Thus, God alone is the undesigned designer of all else. Therefore, God, even if complex, does not require an explanation outside himself.[19] Even more, if God himself needed to be designed by something else, we would be left with a vicious infinite regress that would explain nothing.

THE FLYING SPAGHETTI MONSTER OBJECTION

Some skeptics have tried to mock intelligent design natural theology by saying that the universe might have been created by a "flying spaghetti monster" (or FSM for short). A man named Bobby Henderson concocted this idea in a 2005 "satirical letter to the State Board of Education of Kansas to protest the use of textbook stickers promoting Intelligent Design."[20]

No one believes in this FSM (although those who claim to do so call themselves Pastafarians), but the charge is that natural theology says so little about the creator and designer of the universe that it might as well be a flying spaghetti monster as the deity of any monotheistic religion. This is an attempted *reductio ad absurdum* (reducing to the absurd) argument.

The argument fails, however, for two reasons. First, as we will see in chapter 7, a successful intelligent design argument observes that the

---

19. See Douglas Groothuis, "Who Designed the Designer? A Dialogue on Richard Dawkins's *The God Delusion*," *Think* 8, no. 21 (Spring 2009): 71–81.

20. William Lane Craig, "Question of the Week: God and the Flying Spaghetti Monster," Reasonable Faith with William Lane Craig, December 3, 2007, https://www.reasonablefaith.org/writings/question-answer/god-and-the-flying-spaghetti-monster. This article gives a thorough response to the FSM challenge.

universe (physics and cosmology) is fine-tuned, which requires that there is a transcendent mind outside of the universe with the necessary intelligence to set up all the myriad conditions needed for life. The concept of a flying spaghetti monster is something within the universe, which itself would have to be designed. This is an important clarification for apologetics. When we are defending and commending the faith, we must be able to clearly explain what we are talking about when we are talking about God. God is not something inside the universe that might just as well be an FSM. God is outside the universe, so the FSM objection misses the mark.

Second, the intelligent design argument pertaining to the origin and development of life (biology) indicates that some intelligent agent is required to explain the specified complexities of life. Given the vast amount of information invested in the living cell and the vast biosphere, the ability to design such life-forms is certainly beyond the ken of said FSM as well.

When you factor in successful cosmological, moral, and other arguments for God, the divine résumé fills out considerably. God is the creator and designer of the universe, the source of the moral law, the creator of human consciousness and cognition, and more. Moreover, we can add to this the arguments from history for the reliability of the Bible, the resurrection of Jesus, and more. The FSM is nowhere to be found. While a clever idea, the FSM crashes and burns as a supposed refutation of intelligent design arguments (or of any part of natural theology). The crucial difference between the FSM and God is that the FSM is postulated as an ad hoc and finite being—totally unlike the God of natural theology and so unable to explain the universe or even account for its own existence (since there is no evidence for it).

METHODOLOGICAL NATURALISM AND THE GOD OF THE GAPS

Inasmuch as our society grants intellectual authority to anything outside of personal experiences, it grants authority to "science." We often hear comments such as "The science says so-and-so," and this means it is verified as true. Or we hear, "That's unscientific," meaning something is unwarranted by the evidence and thus untrue. Appeals to "science" were constant during the COVID-19 pandemic, although the sources sometimes disagreed or were later discredited. Apologetics today can draw much strength from scientific discoveries, especially in biology and cosmology, as we will see in later chapters. There is ample evidence from these sciences that God was involved at the creation of the world (physics and cosmology) and since the creation of the world (biology).[21]

Despite this evidence, one materialistic account of science discounts any possible evidence for the existence of God taken from any of the sciences. This protocol is called *methodological naturalism* (MN), and its sworn enemy is *the God of the gaps*. Methodological naturalism affirms that every scientific explanation must be naturalistic. Thus, we must account for the origin of life on earth (abiogenesis) only on the basis of undirected, unplanned natural processes explicable on the basis of chemistry, biology, and physics. The fact that no such theory is even remotely forthcoming, as Stephen C. Meyer has argued, is irrelevant to this perspective.[22] According to this view, any naturalistic explanation (or lack thereof) is better than any explanation that traces a cause outside of the material world. Methodological naturalists claim that science can, in principle, never produce evidence for supernatural beings or causes. The position is summed up well by scientist Stephen Jay Gould, who argues that science and religion are "Non-Overlapping Magisteria . . . science covers the empirical realm: what the universe is made of (fact) and why does it work this way (theory). The magisterium of religion extends over questions of ultimate meaning and moral value. The two magisteria do not overlap."[23] Therefore, the method used by scientists will rule out, in principle, any investigation into supernatural causation. That is, the methodology used by good scientists is naturalistic, or so MN holds.

To try to further strengthen their case, those who hold to MN charge that an explanation from outside the natural world would commit the

---

21. For a defense of Christian advocacy and involvement in the sciences, see Andrew I. Shepardson, *Who's Afraid of the Unmoved Mover?* (Eugene, OR: Pickwick, 2019), 155–59.

22. Stephen C. Meyer, *The Signature in the Cell* (New York: HarperOne, 2009).

23. Stephen Jay Gould, *Rocks of Ages: Science and Religion in the Fullness of Life* (New York: Ballentine, 1999), 5–6.

God-of-the-gaps error, which is an epistemic disorder in which God is arbitrarily invoked to make up for the lack of a scientific (meaning naturalistic) explanation. As I (Doug) heard a physics teacher say, "Before gravity was discovered, religious people thought that angels pushed the planets around. How silly. Now we know better." The idea is that natural explanations will always trump any attribution of divine causation. Thus, if we have no good explanation for abiogenesis (the beginning of life), then give it time. We will. The alternative is unthinkable and off-limits. This mentality was aptly and honestly summed up by notable American evolutionary biologist Richard Lewontin in a now famous quote.

> We take the side of science in spite of the patent absurdity of some of its constructs, in spite of its failure to fulfill many of its extravagant promises of health and life, in spite of the tolerance of the scientific community for unsubstantiated just-so stories, because we have a prior commitment, a commitment to materialism. It is not that the methods and institutions of science somehow compel us to accept a material explanation of the phenomenal world, but, on the contrary, that we are forced by our a priori [meaning: prior to and independent of experience] adherence to material causes to create an apparatus of investigation and a set of concepts that produce material explanations, no matter how counterintuitive, no matter how mystifying to the uninitiated. Moreover, that materialism is an absolute, for we cannot allow a Divine Foot in the door.[24]

Notice that Lewontin equates science (an epistemic program) with materialism (a metaphysical commitment). He opts for counterintuitive and mystifying material explanations over any "Divine Foot in the door." Why is that? Lewontin and others assume that if a divine cause be posited to explain, say, the fine-tuning of the universe or the origin of life, then that cause, who is a personal being, could do anything and upset the whole applecart of scientific investigation. Methodological naturalism claims not to make any *metaphysical* commitments about the

---

24. Richard Lewontin, "Billions and Billions of Demons," *New York Review of Books,* January 9, 1997, 31.

existence of God since it is only a *method*. In fact, some theists adopt this philosophy of science. They are always theistic evolutionists who accept Darwinism but try to leave some room for God somewhere. This is not a promising proposal.[25]

A similar procedure is applied when historians demand that all explanations appeal only to natural causes. For example, when skeptic Bart Ehrman was debating William Lane Craig on the resurrection of Jesus, Ehrman claimed that there could be no historical case for anything supernatural.[26] Craig retorted that if that was how Ehrman wanted to view things, then he could grant that the resurrection could not be established on the basis of history so defined, but that the evidence still favored the resurrection.

The error of MN is epistemic gerrymandering. Gerrymandering is when a political party in power changes the boundaries of voting districts to ensure that they have the most power advantage moving forward. Proponents of MN attempt to arrange the conceptual landscape so that some realities are forbidden from showing up—even if they exist and are detectable through the proper method. Consider the old adage "What my net don't catch ain't fish." But perhaps there are bona fide fish that your net does not catch. The problem is with the net, not the fish. Methodological naturalism is the attempt to gag God from speaking in his creation through nature (Ps. 19:1–6; Rom. 1:18–21).

Further, the leading scientists in Europe during what was called the *scientific revolution* were Christians, or at least theists who did not hold to methodological naturalism.[27] Isaac Newton is often charged with invoking a miracle of God to correct one of the anomalies in his account of physics, which otherwise relied on uniform patterns. Stephen C. Meyer, however, has shown this to be untrue. Newton did no such thing, nor did he need to, given his system.[28]

---

25. For a thorough critique, see J. P. Moreland et al., *Theistic Evolution* (Wheaton, IL: Crossway, 2017).

26. Bart Ehrman and William Lane Craig, "Is There Historical Evidence for the Resurrection of Jesus?," debate, College of the Holy Cross, Worcester, Massachusetts, March 28, 2006, https://www.physics.smu.edu/~pseudo/ScienceReligion/Ehrman-v-Craig.html.

27. See Stephen C. Meyer, *Return of the God Hypothesis: Three Scientific Discoveries That Reveal the Mind behind the Universe* (New York: HarperOne, 2021).

28. Meyer, 427–29.

Methodological naturalism is afraid of a "God of the gaps" who doesn't exist. If we appeal to a designing intelligence for the fine-tuning of the universe, we appeal to a reliable and repeatable method for finding design outside of physics—one used every day, and in a variety of fields, as we will discuss in chapter 7. These arguments are not based on ignorance but, rather, on *the increase of knowledge* in physics and biology. In Darwin's day, little was known about the cell. We now know it is a highly sophisticated assemblance of molecular machines, which cry out, "I am designed." Similarly, in 1900 there was little evidence from physics to infer a big bang. As the decades went by, the evidence became conclusive, as we argue in chapter 4. In good cases of natural theology, God is not called forth as a *deus ex machina*, but is rather the best explanation for a rich range of data, whether from science or elsewhere.

Another fear of those who advocate MN is that if you allow God as the designer of nature, then that God might do anything and so destroy the regularities of nature that are needed for the practice of science. Consider Lewontin's statement above about not letting "a Divine Foot in the door." If God were an arbitrary being, this would be a worry.[29] However, the God of the Bible is not so. While God may intervene in history to demonstrate his character, his judgments, and his care for his people, the laws of nature are regular and predictable. In fact, it was scientists with Christian convictions and motivations who solidified and strengthened the notion that nature was law-governed, as Meyer has documented.[30] This notion was necessary for the advancement of science.

GOD AS A HUMAN PROJECTION

Some try to preempt any arguments for God's existence by claiming that the very idea of God is no more than a projection of the human mind. It is in the same category as fairies, unicorns, and leprechauns—although

---

29. Stanley Jaki argues that the Islamic conception of God as an arbitrary will was not conducive to the development of science, since it could not ground the idea of natural law. Stanley Jaki, *The Savior of Science* (Grand Rapids: Eerdmans, 2000), 207, quoted in Rodney Stark, *For the Glory of God: How Monotheism Led to Reformation, Science, Witch-Hunts, and the End of Slavery* (Princeton, NJ: Princeton University Press, 2003), 155–56.

30. Meyer, "Part 1: The Rise and Fall of Theistic Science."

far more people believe in God than in any creatures in that imaginary menagerie. This argument takes several forms, but we will limit our responses to two of the most common: the social argument and the psychological argument.

The social argument, advanced by philosopher Karl Marx and others, is that religion (he was thinking primarily of Christianity) offers an imagined compensation for the difficulties of labor, employment, and politics in general. Because people are disappointed in the social order—the backbreaking work, the poverty, the lack of influence in politics—they turn to religion as a means of comfort in a heartless world, to paraphrase Marx. Even if earth punishes, heaven awaits and rewards. Marx thought religion was a necessary stage in the advancement toward a better society, but he claimed that it was false, an "opiate for the masses."

To respond, first, even if some people hold religious beliefs in a way that comforts them, that does not imply that Christianity is false. My wife comforts me, after all, but that fact does nothing to lessen the possibility of my wife's existence! It might be that the God who is there gives comfort based on the realities of his character and promises. In this way, the projection objection begs the question of God's existence in favor of atheism. Yes, perhaps theism is comforting, but the question of God's actual existence (rather than the emotion of belief) must be addressed. If any of the arguments from natural theology are successful, then we have evidence independent of human wishes for the existence of God.

Second, Marxism claims that religion pacifies the masses to endure injustice. Thus, religious folk will not take up the charge for revolution as they ought. Christianity has a strong social ethic and has been at the heart of beneficial social developments throughout Western history.[31] Historically, campaigns against infanticide, intoxication, slavery, Jim Crow, and colonialism were led by Christians in the West. Universal suffrage was based on the idea that all human lives have equal value, a uniquely Judeo-Christian concept (Gen. 1:26–28). While Christians are called to endure hardship with patience, they are also called to be salt and

---

31. See Rodney Stark, *The Victory of Reason: How Christianity Led to Freedom, Capitalism, and Western Success* (New York: Random House, 2005); and Tom Holland, *Dominion: How the Christian Revolution Remade the World* (New York, Basic Books, 2019).

light in society (Matt. 5:14–16), to minister to "the least of these" (Matt. 25:31–46), and to seek the welfare of the city where God has placed them (Jer. 29:7; Acts 17:26). That is hardly a prescription for quietism.

The philosophical objection to God was given by Ludwig Feuerbach (1804–72), who claimed that the essence of theology was really anthropology. The concepts of God as omnipotent, omniscient, and omnipresent are merely objectified human attributes multiplied to infinity and then said to apply to a God who is not there. *"Man is the God of Christianity, Anthropology the mystery of Christian theology,"* he said.[32] If this fictional deity is exalted, human beings are debased. The more we worship a nonexistent God, the more alienated we become from ourselves. We should, therefore, leave deity behind and trust only in humanity.

Feuerbach assumed there is no God and attempted to explain why so many people believe in God anyway. Given the success of natural theology—a case we make in this book—there is no need for such a deconstruction of faith into illusion. Further, Feuerbach's critique remains theoretical concerning how false beliefs about the deity might be formulated. A strong historical apologetic for the deity of Jesus— another case we will make in this book—puts such speculation to rights. The philosopher was also wrong that the Christian concept of God degrades human beings since God is taken to be finite and they are finite. On the contrary, the Bible teaches that humans are made in the image and likeness of God and so possess unique value and dignity (Gen. 1:26–28). However, these image-bearers find their ultimate fulfillment in worshiping and serving God in humility.

The psychological objection came primarily from psychologist Sigmund Freud in his small but influential book, *The Future of an Illusion*. Freud noted that we seek the protection and the love of a father in this dangerous world. But human fathers often disappoint us or even betray us. Even the best father cannot deliver us from death, disease, and many human miseries. Because of this, heartsick mortals invented the notion of a heavenly Father who is free from all human ills and who is all-good and all-powerful.

---

32. Ludwig Feuerbach, *The Essence of Christianity*, trans. George Eliot (New York: Harper & Row, 1957), 336, italics in original.

Freud's psychoanalytical account breaks on the rocks of any successful natural theology that is not based on human desires or subjective experience, just as Marx's account fails in light of any natural theology not tied to political desires by oppressed people. But Freud's claim can be turned on its head. If there is a personal God, he could have well designed us to be brought up in families with fathers—some better than others—who serve as a rough analogy of his character. Humans, unlike many animals, come into the world helpless and totally dependent on their parents. This, too, is an analogy of our dependence on God for all things. If there is a heavenly Father, then all earthly fathers are derivative of his ultimate fatherhood, and that fact does nothing to call belief in God into question.[33]

Despite our rejection of the social and psychological critique of theism, these kinds of critiques alert us to the dangers of idolatry, of making a god in our own image. The Bible constantly warns against this error, which is a form of false religion. The apostle John, for example, concluded his first letter by writing, "Dear children, keep yourselves from idols" (1 John 5:21). If our ideas of God are based solely on our social circumstances or psychological propensities and not derived from biblical revelation (God's self-disclosure), our theology will be impoverished at best and blasphemous at worst. Nevertheless, there is a God to whom we are responsible (Heb. 4:13).

THE POSTMODERN OBJECTION

Christians who have adopted a postmodern approach to philosophy reject natural theology (and classical apologetics in general) because they deny that objective truth is knowable through the operations of a universally valid reasoning process. Instead of taking truth to mean a correspondence to reality, these thinkers claim that truth is constructed and shaped by cultures. Reason itself is deemed a cultural product and cannot claim any perennial or cross-cultural authority. The classic laws

---

33. Freud, like sociologist Emil Durkheim, also advanced a fanciful genealogical account of religion that has no basis in history. See Winfried Corduan, *In the Beginning God: A Fresh Look at the Case for Original Monotheism* (Nashville: B&H Academic, 2013), 286–97.

of logic, as formulated by Aristotle, for example, are not more than culturally constructed patterns of thought. Apologetics, if done at all, is more about telling a meaningful story than it is providing compelling evidence that should convince a fair-minded thinker. Worse yet, the apologist who tries to use rigorous logic for Christianity is being coercive and even violent in this approach, so this must not be done.

Postmodernism rightly draws attention to the cultural and affective aspects of belief and belief-systems. We are more than logic chopping machines, but that is not news. Although we do not have room to thoroughly critique postmodernism, a few points suffice.[34]

First, any dissolving of Christian doctrine into relative and constructed forms of thought eliminates entirely the category of divine revelation and knowable reality. Christianity makes hard, strong, and sure truth claims that oppose any worldview that denies them. God exists. Christ died. Christ is risen. Christ will come again. These claims may be said in any language and presented in various rhetorical ways, but truth claims about objective reality they remain—and they confront all who receive them.

Second, the essential laws of logic are necessary for all thought and communication; they are not socially constructed or relative. The mother of all logic is the law of noncontradiction, formulated (but not invented) by Aristotle. As he put it in *Metaphysics*, "It is impossible for the same thing to belong and not to belong at the same time to the same thing and in the same respect."[35] God cannot exist and not exist. Christ cannot be God incarnate and not God incarnate. The Bible cannot be without error and also have errors. In addition, the basic argument forms of deduction, induction, and inference to the best explanation (abduction) are valid forms of reasoning. Each deductive, inductive, or abductive argument must be tested for soundness, but none of these argument forms is culturally relative. This book argues for the truth of Christianity through arguments. These arguments should be culturally sensitive, but the logic we employ and the facts we cite are not.

Some detractors have gone so far as to say that the use of reason in

---

34. For a thorough critique of postmodern rejections of apologetics, see Shepardson, *Who's Afraid of the Unmoved Mover?*

35. Aristotle, *Metaphysics*, bk. 4, pt. 3.

the manner just described entails the deification of reason or even the worship of reason, which is idolatry and unfitting for any apologist.[36] This is flatly absurd. Reason is a God-given tool that makes up part of what it means to be made in God's image and likeness. God himself is the source of all reason as the *Logos*, which is Greek for "Word" in John 1:1–2.[37] Since God is the *Logos* and gives us our reasoning abilities, the use of reason in natural theology and apologetics in general is hardly a practice of idolatry.

Third, is the quest for convincing argumentation a kind of violence against unbelievers? This is a strong charge, since, if it is true, nearly the whole history of apologetics would be nullified as unethical. To respond, we need only to make a simple distinction. Apologetics may be done in a heavy-handed and threatening manner, with plenty of finger-pointing and with raised voices. That is wrong since Peter tells us to defend the faith "with gentleness and respect" (1 Peter 3:15). However, giving a strong argument based on facts and logic is not coercive, let alone violent, if given in a reasonable and gentle manner. Whether an unbeliever accepts, say, a cosmological argument for God's existence is between the unbeliever and God. The apologist can make no demands but should simply speak the truth in love and give rational support for their claims.

Other philosophical objections to natural theology might be addressed, but this chapter covered what we take to be the most significant arguments that have been marshaled to stop natural theology in its tracks. To our reckoning, no such stoppage has occurred, so we press on into an open field to consider specific arguments for the existence of God.

---

36. See the section "Apologetics Turns Reason into an Idol and Produces a 'God' Who Is Nothing Like the God of Abraham, Isaac, and Jacob" in the previous chapter. For advocates of this position, see Carl A. Raschke, *The Next Reformation: Why Evangelicals Must Embrace Postmodernity* (Grand Rapids: Baker Academic, 2004), 81–82; Myron Bradley Penner, *The End of Apologetics: Christian Witness in a Postmodern Context* (Grand Rapids: Baker Academic, 2013), 62; and Merold Westphal, "Onto-Theology, Metanarrative, Perspectivism, and the Gospel," in *Christianity and the Postmodern Turn: Six Views*, ed. Myron B. Penner (Grand Rapids: Brazos, 2005), 146–47.

37. On the *Logos*, see Gordon Clark, *The Johannine Logos*, 2nd ed. (Unicoi, TN: Trinity Foundation, 1989); and Carl F. H. Henry, *God, Revelation, and Authority*, 6 vols. (Waco: TX, 1976–83), vol. 3, thesis 9, "The Mediating Logos."

STUDY QUESTIONS

1. Explain the difference between a philosophical objection to apologetics and a theological objection to apologetics.
2. Do you find any of the objections cogent? If so, why?
3. Might there be other philosophical objections to apologetics that are worth considering?

SUGGESTED READING

Clark, Gordon. *The Johannine Logos.* 2nd ed. Unicoi, TN: Trinity Foundation, 1989.

Corduan, Winfried. *In the Beginning God: A Fresh Look at the Case for Original Monotheism.* Nashville: B&H Academic, 2013.

Dawkins, Richard. *The God Delusion.* New York: Mariner, 2006.

Gould, Stephen Jay. *Rocks of Ages: Science and Religion in the Fullness of Life.* New York: Ballentine, 1999.

Groothuis, Douglas. "To Prove or Not to Prove? Pascal on Natural Theology." PhD diss., University of Oregon, 1993.

Henry, Carl F. H. *God, Revelation, and Authority.* 6 vols. Wheaton, IL, Crossway, 1976–83. Vol. 3, thesis 9, "The Mediating Logos."

Holland, Tom. *Dominion: How the Christian Revolution Remade the World.* New York: Basic Books, 2019.

Hume, David. *Dialogues and Natural History of Religion.* Edited by J. C. A. Gaskin. Oxford World's Classics. Oxford: Oxford University Press, 1998.

Jaki, Stanley. *The Savior of Science.* Grand Rapids: Eerdmans, 2000.

Lewontin, Richard. "Billions and Billions of Demons." *New York Review of Books,* January 9, 1997.

Manning, Russell Re, ed. *The Oxford Handbook of Natural Theology.* Oxford: Oxford University Press, 2013.

Mavrodes, George. "Some Puzzles concerning Omnipotence." *Philosophical Review* 72, no. 2 (1963): 221–23.

Meyer, Stephen C. *Return of the God Hypothesis: Three Scientific Discoveries That Reveal the Mind behind the Universe.* New York: HarperOne, 2021.

———. *The Signature in the Cell.* New York: HarperOne, 2009.

Moreland, J. P. *Scaling the Secular City: A Defense of Christianity.* Grand Rapids: Baker, 1987.

Moreland, J. P., and William Lane Craig. *Philosophical Foundations for a Christian Worldview.* 2nd ed. Downers Grove, IL: IVP Academic, 2017.

Moreland, J. P., et al. *Theistic Evolution: A Scientific, Philosophical, and Theological Critique*. Wheaton, IL: Crossway, 2017.

Nash, Ronald H. *The Concept of God*. Grand Rapids: Zondervan Academic, 1983.

_____. *Faith and Reason: Searching for a Rational Faith*. Grand Rapids: Zondervan, 1988.

Sennett, James, and Douglas Groothuis, eds. *In Defense of Natural Theology*. Downers Grove, IL: InterVarsity, 2005.

Shepardson, Andrew I. *Who's Afraid of the Unmoved Mover? Postmodernism and Natural Theology*. Eugene, OR: Pickwick, 2019.

Stark, Rodney. *The Victory of Reason: How Christianity Led to Freedom, Capitalism, and Western Success*. New York: Random House, 2005.

Swinburne, Richard. *Is There a God?* New York: Oxford University Press, 1996.

PART 2

GOD

EXISTS

CHAPTER 4

THE COSMOLOGICAL ARGUMENT

A theists claim that the cosmos is all that there is. There is no supernatural realm of God or spirits. All is natural—what can be explained by the material processes found in chemistry, biology, and physics. For them, the universe explains itself thoroughly and without gaps. This is what Francis Schaeffer called "the uniformity of cause and effect in a closed system."[1] Naturalists today may call it "the causal closure principle." The cosmos is closed in on itself, and there are no supernatural causes to violate its self-enclosed integrity.[2]

Theists demur. Using natural theology, Christian apologists argue that the cosmos has a Creator who has left a record of his creation in the cosmos. There is a First Cause of the cosmos that is transcendent to the cosmos. According to this worldview, as Schaeffer said, we live in "the uniformity of natural causes in an open system."[3] If it is an open system, then God and people can meaningfully act in nature. Miracles and revelation are possible, as is the supernatural salvation of the new birth in Christ (John 3). We then move to history to find what God may

---

1. Francis A. Schaeffer, *How Should We Then Live? The Rise and Decline of Western Thought and Culture*, L'Abri 50th Anniversary ed. (Wheaton, IL: Crossway, 2009), loc. 1743, Kindle.
2. See also C. S. Lewis, "The Naturalist and the Supernaturalist," in *Miracles: A Preliminary Study* (New York: HarperOne, 1994).
3. Schaeffer, *How Should We Then Live?*, locs. 1716–17.

have done. If the cosmos is a closed system, then we are on our own, and there is no salvation. Tremendous consequences flow from how we answer this—existentially, politically, culturally, and religiously.[4]

From theism's view of the cosmos come two basic types of natural theology: cosmological arguments and design arguments, each of which receive a chapter in this volume. Cosmological arguments search for a cause of the universe and try to account for its very existence. Design arguments consider particular features of the cosmos (in part or the whole) that indicate a designing intelligence behind it that accounts for these features.

There is no one cosmological argument, just as there is no one ontological argument, moral argument, or design argument. Rather, there is a family of cosmological arguments. All of them trade on the need for the cosmos to have been created by a cause outside itself; but each of them considers a different element of the cosmos's need for an external explanation. That is, in one way or another, all cosmological arguments take some element of the cosmos to be *contingent* on something outside of itself, although contingency is rendered in different ways in the different arguments. For apologetic strategy, if *any* of these cosmological arguments are successful, then there is a cause behind the cosmos, and atheism is defeated. However, different arguments secure different attributes of God. For example, the principle of sufficient reason (PSR) argument does not conclude that God created the cosmos out of nothing, although it is logically compatible with that claim. On the other hand, the kalam cosmological argument and the original causation argument do conclude that God is the creator of the universe out of nothing (*ex nihilo*). That is, God brought about a new order of being outside of himself that had a first moment in time.

Before starting our cosmological quest, we should note that these arguments have no force for those who deny the existence of the physical universe, since *cosmo*-logical arguments take as a given that a *physical cosmos* exists—that it is not an illusion or a collection of ideas. Other arguments might jostle immaterialists and idealists out of their

---

4. See Francis Schaeffer, "The Abolition of Truth and Morality," in *A Christian Manifesto* (Wheaton, IL: Crossway, 1981), and *How Should We Then Live?*

framework, but that is beyond our scope.[5] Our argument assumes that a material universe composed of finite entities exists objectively. Because of its wide acceptance, this premise will not be argued for, although it has been criticized in the history of philosophy and in some religious traditions, especially those from the mystic East.

This chapter takes up the PSR, the kalam argument, and the original causation argument. It will not address the venerable Thomistic cosmological argument, which has notable contemporary defenders.[6] This argument, if successful, shows that the universe depends on God for its existence, but it does not argue for creation out of nothing. Thomas Aquinas (1225–74) thought that we are reliant on biblical revelation for that doctrine and that it cannot be established philosophically. He explicitly, but briefly, rejected the kalam cosmological argument.[7] Let us first examine the PSR.

THE PRINCIPLE OF SUFFICIENT REASON COSMOLOGICAL ARGUMENT

Suppose you experience a bizarre and unexpected event. As you sit in a classroom listening to a lecture on metaphysics, all of a sudden and out of nowhere, a miniature, purple hippo appears floating in midair between the teacher and the students. It then begins spinning around quickly, puffing smoke from its mouth, while saying, "Jazz is not dead." Then it disappears as quickly as it appeared.

How might you respond? Since we interpret the bizarre in light of the normal, you might think, *Did I just hallucinate something?* But you

---

5. René Descartes argued from the idea of God in the mind to the existence of God outside the mind in *The Meditations*. He gave this argument before he argued for the existence of the physical world. For a treatment of this argument, see Douglas Groothuis, *Philosophy in Seven Sentences: A Small Introduction to a Vast Topic* (Downers Grove, IL: IVP Academic, 2016), 90–97.

6. See Brian Davies, *Thinking about God* (Eugene, OR: Wipf and Stock, 2010), ch. 1; Robert Koons, "A New Look at the Cosmological Argument," in *American Philosophical Quarterly* 34 (1997): 193–211; Glenn Siniscalchi, "Contemporary Trends in Atheistic Criticism of Thomistic Natural Theology," in *Heythrop Journal* 59 (2018): 689–706.

7. For an excellent treatment of Thomas, see Norman Geisler, *Thomas Aquinas: An Evangelical Appraisal* (Eugene, OR: Wipf and Stock, 2003).

find that the other students saw the same event. Now explanations are harder to find. *Could this be a hologram?* But you find no evidence of any devices in the room to produce a hologram. You may get more desperate: *Maybe aliens beamed this down to us for some reason,* or *maybe some evil scientist is trying this out.* We'll stop there. The point is that no matter how phantasmagoric, surreal, anomalous, or spectacular the event, we naturally seek out *some explanation for it.* No one in the room would think, *This event has no explanation at all. It's not just that* we *cannot explain it, but that there is no sufficient reason for it at all. Now let's get back to the lecture.*

This thought experiment sparks our intuition and common reasoning that things have explanations. The point is not that we know the proper explanation. Many things are beyond our ken, either temporarily or permanently. Before Newton discovered gravity, the uniform behavior of objects was something of a mystery. After Newtonian mechanics, much more was explained. Other items may be beyond any human knowing, such as the timing of the second coming of Jesus (Acts 1:7).

Things have explanations. To state this principle differently, for any state of affairs, there is some sufficient reason why it is what it is. This has been called the *principle of sufficient reason* and was first formulated by the German philosopher Gottfried Wilhelm Leibniz (1646–1716). He put it this way: "Nothing happens without a sufficient reason; that is to say, that nothing happens without it being possible for him who should sufficiently understand things, to give a reason sufficient to determine why it is so and not otherwise."[8] Notice that Leibniz said that it is "possible" to give an explanation for one "who sufficiently understands things." This shows that the principle is one of *metaphysics* (the way things are), not of *epistemology* (how we know things). The PSR fuels our epistemology (we seek explanations), but it is a claim about the order and intelligibility of the cosmos. We seek explanations because we know at least some of them can be found. Where we despair of finding an explanation, we still grant that one exists even if it is unattainable to mere mortals. This was the purpose of our mini purple hippo example.

---

8. G. W. F. von Leibniz, "Principles of Nature and Grace" (1714), in *Leibniz Selections*, ed. Philip P. Wiener (New York: Scribner, 1951), 527.

We now face two questions: (1) What is the logical status of the PSR, and (2) how does it relate to a cosmological argument?

To the first question: The basic laws of logic cannot be denied without absurdity. The law of noncontradiction, for example, is required for any rational thought or communication. Few thoughtful people dispute that. In other words, the principle of noncontradiction is a *necessary truth* with the same standing as definitional truths such as "a triangle has three sides" and "bachelors are unmarried males." Some claims are true but are not necessarily true, such as "Alaska is the forty-ninth state of the United States." This claim corresponds to reality, but it was *possible* that Alaska never became a state or that it became the fiftieth state because Hawaii preceded it in statehood. So the statement "Alaska is the forty-ninth state of the United States" is a *contingent truth*; it is true but not necessarily so. But what of the PSR?

Let us say that the PSR is false and consider where that takes us. To do that, we will reverse Leibniz's formulation: "Some things happen without a sufficient reason; that is to say, that something can happen without its being possible for anyone to give a reason sufficient to determine why it is so and not otherwise."

We will call this the principle of insufficient reason (PIR). This principle doesn't mean that nothing happens for a reason or that nothing can be explained, but, rather, that some things can or might happen in that way. So, according to PIR, that mini purple hippo could pop in and out of existence without any explanation for its appearance or disappearance. According to PIR, stuff happens—supposedly.

I take the PSR to be a necessary truth, but all we need for this cosmological argument to work is that the PSR is more likely true than false. If so, how does it work for a theistic argument?

Given the PSR, for any particular item, we can ask, "Why did it happen?" We seek explanations for the outcome of political elections, character flaws, weather patterns, and everything else. There is no reason not to apply the PSR to the cosmos as a whole, as opposed to applying it only for specific things that are systems within it. If we are seeking an explanation for the entire cosmos, we cannot appeal to anything within the cosmos to provide that explanation. But some think the cosmos itself explains itself adequately. To affirm this, the cosmos must itself be a necessary being, otherwise its contingency needs to be explained by something outside itself. That is a bad move philosophically, as Richard Taylor noted. "For we find nothing whatever about the world, any more than in its parts, to suggest that it exists by its own nature. Concerning anything in the world, we have not the slightest difficulty in supposing that it should perish, or even that it should never have existed in the first place. We have almost as little difficulty in supposing this of the world itself."[9]

Pascal explained the idea of contingency regarding himself and the implication he derived from it. "I feel that it is possible that I might never have existed, for myself consists in my thought; therefore I who think would never have been if my mother had been killed before I had come to life; therefore I am not a necessary being. I am not eternal or infinite either, but I can see that there is in nature a being who is necessary, eternal, and infinite."[10]

Since the world is a terrible candidate for being the explanation for itself, some will simply deny that the PSR applies to the cosmos as a whole. As Bertrand Russell said in a debate with Frederick Copleston, "The universe is just there."[11] It is a brute fact with no reason for its existence. However, this is hard for most of us to live with as meaning-seeking beings, because the implication is that the cosmos and life itself is meaningless. This is a matter of axiology, or the study of value. If the cosmos is "just there," then it is without design, purpose, or objective value.

That was the view of atheistic existentialist, Jean-Paul Sartre (1905–80). Having denied that God gives the world any essential meaning, we are left to define that meaning individually and for ourselves without any transcendent reference point. He said, "What do we mean here by 'existence precedes essence'? We mean that man first exists: he materializes in the world, encounters himself, and only afterward defines himself."[12]

---

9. Richard Taylor, *Metaphysics*, 4th ed. (New York: Pentice-Hall, 1992). See also William Lane Craig, *Reasonable Faith: Christian Truth and Apologetics*, 3rd ed. (Wheaton, IL: Crossway, 2008), 108–9.

10. Blaise Pascal, *Pensées* (New York: Penguin, 2017), 37, Kindle.

11. Bertrand Russell, "A Debate on the Existence of God," in *The Existence of God*, ed. John Hick (New York: Macmillan, 1964), 175.

12. Jean-Paul Sartre, *Existentialism Is a Humanism* (New Haven, CT: Yale University Press), 22, Kindle.

Since there is no explanation or reason for humanity, "there is no human nature since there is no God to conceive of it."[13] Despite all his heroic assertion of autonomous value in a valueless and ethics-free world, Sartre must confess that "Man is a useless passion."[14] This is not the place for a thorough critique of existentialism,[15] but this philosophy (which is on the rise) is one attempt to live with the results of denying that the PSR applies to the cosmos, of taking the cosmos to be all that exists.

Since we ought to accept the universal application of the PSR (for metaphysical and axiological reasons), and because the cosmos cannot explain itself, we are brought to something outside the cosmos that explains it. That being would need to be either personal or impersonal. But an impersonal being is insufficient as an explanation for a world populated by personal and rational beings who legitimately seek explanations for phenomena. Unless this being is also subject to being explained by something outside itself, we deem it a necessary being. The reason for this being is intrinsic, not extrinsic. It is self-explanatory. As a personal, rational, and necessary being distinct from the cosmos, this being lines up with the God of monotheism, although history and experience will have much more to say about him in the project of apologetics.

THE KALAM COSMOLOGICAL ARGUMENT

The kalam cosmological argument (hereafter "kalam") has received much attention in the last forty years, largely through the efforts of William Lane Craig, who helped revive it from obscurity through his academic and popular writing as well as through numerous lectures and debates with atheists. Rather than canvassing all the aspects of this argument and the case made against it, we will instead outline its structure, the major evidence for it, and some of the rebuttals made

---

13. Sartre, 22.

14. Jean-Paul Sartre, *Existentialism and Human Emotions* (New York: Philosophical Library, 1957), 90.

15. See James W. Sire, "Existentialism," in *The Universe Next Door: A Basic Worldview Catalog*, 6th ed. (Downers Grove, IL: InterVarsity, 2020); and Douglas Groothuis, "Jean-Paul Sartre and the Resurgence of Existentialism," *Christian Research Journal* 40, no. 4 (2017), https://www.equip.org/article/jean-paul-sartre-and-the-resurgence-of-existentialism.

against it. Even in brief compass, it should be clear that this argument packs a powerful punch in favor of theism.

The kalam was invented and developed by Arabic philosophers under the Muslim Abbasid caliphs al-Ma'mun (reigned 813–33 CE) and al-Mu'tasim (reigned 833–42 CE)[16] before it was used by Christian apologists.[17] Since Muslims and Christians agree that God created the universe out of nothing, both may benefit from a successful prosecution of the argument. The Christian apologist will continue to argue that God is a Trinity, that Jesus is God incarnate, that salvation is through faith in Jesus, and so on. The Muslim will appeal to the Qur'an for particular doctrines about God (Allah) and so deny the Trinity, incarnation, and salvation through faith in Jesus.

The kalam is simple and elegant.

1. Whatever begins to exist has a cause.
2. The universe began to exist.
3. Therefore, the universe had a cause.

The argument form is deductive, which means that if the premises are true, the conclusion must be true. (This is unlike an inductive argument, the conclusion of which is only probable if the premises are true.) Thus, to defeat the argument, either one of the premises must be refuted. The question of how much the conclusion tells us about the cause of the universe—whether it can be considered God—must be explored as well. We will consider each premise first.

Premise 1: Whatever Begins to Exist Has a Cause

First, premise 1 does not affirm that "anything that exists has a cause." That principle generates a vicious infinite causal regress that would ill serve any cosmological argument.[18]

---

16. For the Muslim perspective, see Mohammed Hijab, *Kalam Cosmological Arguments* (S.A.L.A.M Publications, 2019). See also Ya'qub ibn Ishaq al-Kindi, *Al-Kindi's Metaphysics: A Translation of Ya'qub ibn Ishaq al-Kindi's Treatise "On First Philosophy"* (fi al-Falsafah al-Ula), trans. Alfred L. Ivry (Albany, NY: State University of New York Press, 1974).

17. For the history of the kalam and a presentation of the argument, see William Lane Craig, *The Kalām Cosmological Argument* (Eugene, OR: Wipf and Stock, 2000).

18. This was discussed in chapter 3, "Philosophical Objections to Apologetics."

Premise 1 is a principle that appeals to rational intuition. It is not a matter of empirical observation or inductive inference. The statement is universal: *whatever* begins to exist has a cause. To put it negatively: *nothing* begins to exist without a cause. Another way of conceiving this principle is that things do not pop into existence out of nothing. An old Latin phrase sums it up: *ex nihilo, nihil fit*: out of nothing, nothing comes. Or as Maria sings while wondering over being loved by Captain von Trapp in *The Sound of Music*, "Nothing comes from nothing."[19]

As with the PSR, some deny that this principle is true. That is, things could begin to exist without any antecedent causation. Put another way, acausal events do or could occur. Some appeal to quantum physics to make the point, saying that some particles appear out of nothing. There are two defects to this response. First, this is but one interpretation of quantum physics, not the only one or necessarily the best one. Second, the idea of acausal events is so wildly counterintuitive that to cite evidence of their occurrence seems to run against reason itself.

Whether premise 1 is a necessary truth (like the PSR) or is more likely true than false does not affect its rationality. I take it to be a necessary truth. We are on safer ground to hold premise 1 to be true than to deny it. If so, we can move to premise 2.

Premise 2: The Universe Began to Exist

There are two routes to justifying this claim: empirical and philosophical. First, the empirical, through the avenue of science.

Cosmology is the study of the nature of the cosmos as a whole and in its particular operations. Contemporary cosmology—which involves physics and astronomy—speaks to whether the cosmos had a beginning in time. While it is a matter of some debate, the consensus view is what came to be called the *big bang*. On this view, the entire universe came into existence about fourteen billion years ago from an initial singularity. The view, also called the *standard model*, developed over several decades, beginning with Einstein's general theory of relativity (1917), which, when corrected, predicted an expanding universe.

---

19. Richard Rodgers, "Something Good," *The Sound of Music* (soundtrack), SME and RCA/ Legacy, 1965.

The theory was then corroborated by various kinds of evidence, such as the "red shift," which further indicated that the universe was expanding. At the end of World War II, three scientists calculated that if the cosmos began through a tremendous explosion, this event would have produced intense radiation that would still exist to some extent in the contemporary universe. In 1965 Arno Penzias and Robert Wilson detected evidence of just such radiation, thus confirming that the expansion of the universe had a definite beginning. More evidence could be cited.[20] Physicist Alexander Vilenkin, director of the Institute of Cosmology at Tufts University, says, "With the proof now in place, cosmologists can no longer hide behind the possibility of a past-eternal universe. There is no escape: they have to face the problem of a cosmic beginning."[21]

If the big bang is well established by cosmology (*that* it occurred), we need to ask *how* it could have occurred. In this, we move beyond science proper into philosophy, which is entirely appropriate, since we cannot expect science to answer every question or have the final word on all matters. Science tells us that there was an absolute beginning. Since the cosmos cannot create itself (nothing can), it either popped into existence out of nothing or was caused by something outside of itself. Given premise 1, the universe could not have come into being out of nothing. Thus, the cosmos requires a cause outside of itself. We will explore the nature of this cause later in this chapter.

The second route to the beginning of the cosmos concerns two concepts of infinity in relation to time. A *potential infinite* series is one that is always finite but increases without end, such as the age of a person who begins to exist but never ceases to exist. The endless bisection of a finite line is another example of a potential infinite. An *actual infinite* "is a set considered as a completed totality with an actual infinite number of members."[22] No new members can be added to it, unlike a potential infinite.

20. For a superb account of how science has confirmed the beginning of the universe, see Steven C. Meyer, *Return of the God Hypothesis: Three Scientific Discoveries That Reveal the Mind behind the Universe* (New York: HarperOne, 2021), chs. 4–6.

21. Alexander Vilenkin, *Many Worlds in One World: The Search for Other Universes* (New York: Hill and Wang, 2006), 176. Vilenkin, however, does not accept a creator.

22. J. P. Moreland, *Scaling the Secular City: A Defense of Christianity* (Grand Rapids: Baker, 1987), 20–21.

But what does this have to do with the cosmological argument or the beginning of the cosmos? Consider two scenarios:

1. If the cosmos is infinitely old—that is, if it had no beginning— then it would have to have existed for an actually infinite amount of time.
2. If the cosmos began to exist a finite time ago, then it would exist in a potentially infinite series—limited, but ever increasing. The cosmos would age every day but never reach an absolute age.

Option 1 is beset with difficulties. First, the very idea of an actual infinite is troublesome. Consider a library with an actually infinite number of books. Half of the books are blue, and the other half are red. If a library had one million books, there would be no problem. Five hundred thousand would be red and five hundred thousand would be blue. But if the holdings of the library were actually infinite, the number of blue books would be actually infinite and the number of red books would be actually infinite. That means that each half of the holdings of the library ends up being equal to its entire holdings, which is impossible, since a whole is greater than the sum of its parts.

Second, even if the idea of an actual infinite is not illogical, problems arise when we consider its playing out (or being instantiated) in the space-time world.

1. If the past is made up of an actually infinite series of moments (or events), then we would never reach the present moment.
2. But we have reached the present moment.
3. Therefore, the past cannot be made up of an actually infinite series of events.

Consider premise 1. An actual infinite cannot be traversed in time because progress could never be made. If dinner is served at 6:00 p.m. and it is now 12:00 p.m., there are six hours until dinner. You can last if you are patient. But if you are told dinner will be served an actually infinite number of hours from 12:00, you will starve to death because that moment never arrives. To give another example, we can neither count from one to infinity nor count down from infinity to one. With an infinite distance to travel, we never arrive. As the great philosopher of mathematics Bertrand Russell put it, "classes which are infinite are given all at once by the defining property of their members, so that there is no question of 'completion' or of 'successive synthesis.'"[23] Technically, this is called "the impossibility of traversing (or crossing) the actual infinite by successive addition."

Both the empirical-scientific and the philosophical arguments lead to a beginning to the universe in time. If either one of these arguments works, then the universe had a birth date. It came from somewhere by a cause, since it cannot materialize out of nothing (premise 1).

Conclusion: The Universe Had a Cause.

We can infer that this cause, since it is outside the cosmos, transcends space, time, and matter, since those are all part of the cosmos itself. This cause would have the immense power required for the creation of everything from nothing. We can further infer that this cause is personal, not impersonal, since creation at a particular point in time requires a decision and decisions require persons to make them. We can also lean on the design argument to know that this cause is personal, since its design requires a designing *mind*. This is starting to look a lot like the creator God of the Bible—a spaceless, timeless, immaterial, tremendously powerful personal being who transcends the cosmos. But the skeptic may not be convinced.

First, if the actual infinite cannot exist or if the actual infinite cannot be traversed by successive addition, then that implies that God himself cannot exist since he exists in an actual infinity of moments or events. So, the principles of the kalam return as a boomerang to cut off its head. Defenders of the kalam have responded to this charge in several ways. First, the conclusion of the kalam is that God is outside of time (at least as we know it), so he does not exist in an actual infinity of moments or events. God must be somehow related to the temporal universe in order

---

23. Bertrand Russell, *Our Knowledge of the External World as a Field for Scientific Method in Philosophy* (London: Allen and Unwin, 2011), 141, Kindle.

to antecedently cause it, but that does not imply that he occupies time in the same manner as the cosmos.

Second, the skeptic says that monotheism claims that God himself is infinite in his being. But if the kalam argument disallows the infinite, that would disallow God himself from existing as infinite. Thus, the kalam destroys itself. However, this objection is based on confusion over the idea of the infinite. God is infinite with respect to his perfections, metaphysically and morally. That is, God is infinitely or maximally powerful and good. This description, however, is not quantitative but qualitative. No series of numbers, moments, or events is involved. Therefore, the argument does not backfire on God himself.

The kalam has generated a vast literature in the last forty years. It can be addressed in a much more sophisticated way than what has been done here. Still, the basic features of the argument are straightforward and, to our minds, quite compelling.[24] William Lane Craig often presents the basic argument in his debates with atheists before audiences of nonacademics.[25] We commend this argument as an invaluable tool in your belt as you defend the Christian faith.

THE TEMPORAL FIRST CAUSE ARGUMENT

This cosmological argument depends on the notion of contingency, so it is critical to state clearly what contingency is supposed to involve.[26] First, contingency means that for any finite object, it is possible for that object not to have been caused to exist or for the object to have existed in a different form or context than it does exist. Even if a determinist tells us that things must be the way they are because of inescapable

---

24. For a detailed and technical treatment of the kalam, see William Lane Craig and James D. Sinclair, "The Kalam Cosmological Argument," in *The Blackwell Companion to Natural Theology*, ed. William Lane Craig and J. P. Moreland (Malden, MA: Wiley-Blackwell, 2009). For a less technical but still rigorous version, see Craig, *Reasonable Faith*, 111–56.

25. See Craig's Reasonable Faith with William Lane Craig web page for video and transcripts of these debates: www.reasonablefaith.org.

26. What follows is an abbreviated and simplified version of Douglas Groothuis, "Defending Cosmological Theism," in "To Prove or Not to Prove? Pascal on Natural Theology" (PhD diss., University of Oregon, 1993).

causal conditions, we can still imagine another very different, equally inescapable set of causal conditions. As Ludwig Wittgenstein put it,

> The insidious thing about the causal point of view is that it leads us to say: "Of course, it had to happen like that." Whereas we ought to think: it may have happened like that—and also in many other ways.
>
> We can also conceive that no set of causal conditions exists at all, because there might have been nothing instead of something. So we may wonder why something is as it is or wonder why it is at all.[27]

To put it another way, there must be some causal explanation for the existence of a mountain that is not intrinsic to the mountain itself: it was made through volcanic upheaval centuries ago. Contingent truths may have failed to occur, and contingent things cannot explain themselves. They require an extrinsic cause for their existence that explains their existence, which may itself be another contingent thing.

If the concept of contingency is clear, we can proceed to question its role in deriving a noncontingent being from the existence of the universe. This argument claims that the universe is made up of finite objects and events whose existence is contingent on causal factors that provide a causal explanation for their existence. This is reflected in our question concerning any object or event: how did it come to be? That is, what causal factors produced this effect—whether it is a mountain, a bicycle, or a mouse?

The argument against an infinite causal regress does not depend on the principle of sufficient reason; it depends on a principle of linear causation. J. L. Mackie, an atheist critic of all theistic arguments, claimed that the straightforward sense of linear causation needed for "the common sense [cosmological] argument" is more plausible than the principle of sufficient reason because "the notion that an effect depends on a temporally earlier cause is part of our ordinary understanding of causation; we all have some grasp of this asymmetry between cause and effect."[28] To reach

---

27. Ludwig Wittgenstein, *Culture and Value* (Chicago: University of Chicago Press, 1980), 37e.
28. J. L. Mackie, *The Miracle of Theism* (Oxford: Clarendon, 1980), 92.

this causal understanding, we must first deal with a few examples of dependency relationships that intimate the principle to which we will appeal to ground the temporal First Cause cosmological argument.

ON INFINITE CAUSAL CHAINS

The argument for a First (chronological) Cause has been rejected by many philosophers simply because the notion of an infinite causal series seems possible and not intrinsically absurd or problematic. Some philosophers are sanguine about the plausibility of an infinite and contingent causal series. William Rowe, for instance, endorsed the idea in one sentence by saying that "there seems to be no good reason for making [the] assumption" that "every causal series must stop with a first member somewhere in the distant past."[29] The claim, made by Hume and others, is that every contingent being is caused by some other contingent and antecedent being. This amounts to saying that for any and every contingent being in the causal series, that being is explained on the basis of another preceding contingent being that serves as its cause. Yet this common response contains hidden difficulties regarding the nature of contingency when contingency is understood as part of an *infinite* causal series. This difficulty can be illustrated by two examples that isolate a common principle employed for cosmological ends.

Analogies for Original Causation[30]

Consider a linear series of causally related events where each event depends on a previous event such that event B depends on C and C depends on D, and so on. Suppose I desire to borrow one hundred dollars from B, but B must first borrow the money from C, who must first borrow the money from D, and so on *ad infinitum*. I will never receive the hundred dollars if no one in the linear, dependent causal series ever originally possesses the money required for there to be any borrowing.

---

29. William Rowe, *Philosophy of Religion* (Belmont, CA: Wadsworth, 1978), 22.
30. These examples are given in Richard Purtill, *Reason to Believe: Why Faith Makes Sense* (Grand Rapids: Eerdmans, 1974), 83–84. I have adapted them for my purposes.

The notion of an original lender is intelligible and required for the subsequent and dependent causal chain, while the notion of a borrower logically presupposes a lender who originally possesses the needed funds.

Similarly, if I seek permission from a governmental official to build an addition to my home and he grants it, the permission is explained by virtue of the official's authority. But if official 1 must ask for permission from official 2 who must ask permission from official 3, *ad infinitum*, I will never receive permission to build the addition to my home, because in this scenario there is no original authority from which to secure permission. Again, the notion of endless contingency is problematic when the state of affairs in question—permission in this case—is not traceable to a noncontingent first term.

The examples cited, despite their differences with respect to the stipulated dependency conditions, assume a more general and formal proposition. J. L. Mackie noted that this general principle is used by temporal First Cause arguments: "When items are ordered in a relation of dependence, the regress must end somewhere; it cannot be either infinite or circular."[31]

To refer to our examples, real borrowing requires an original giver that makes the borrowing possible, not endless requests; actual permissions require an original permitter who makes the permissions possible, not endless permissions. The unifying and underlying concept is that some noncontingent, originating, and antecedent state must account for or explain the subsequent contingent states. And without this noncontingent originating state, the subsequent dependent states would not occur. We can make this principle of antecedent dependency more specific with respect to the linear causation of physical states—which is what we need for this cosmological argument—in this way:

> *The principle of linear causation*: For any contingent physical state of affairs in a linear series, there must be some antecedent and original state of affairs that serves as the causal explanation of the resulting physical state of affairs that is itself not contingent on any antecedent state of affairs.

---

31. Mackie, *The Miracle of Theism*, 90.

Therefore, there cannot be an antecedent infinite series of similarly contingent states because this precludes the "antecedent and original state of affairs that serves as the causal explanation of the resulting series." We may now take this principle and apply it to the case of the physical existence of a cosmos consisting of contingent beings and events.

The Principle Applied to the Cosmological Argument

If there is an infinite causal series of contingent beings, then no contingent being can now exist because these antecedent beings would lack a necessary causal explanation—just as the home builder would lack permission to build and the receiving of money without a giver would never occur. Since we live in a world of contingent things, this infinite and contingent causal regress cannot be the case. There must be a beginning and an Originator of the entire series.

To put the case positively, if any contingent being exists, it must receive its existence from a noncontingent being—however distant that noncontingent being might be on the finite causal chain. Otherwise, the series of contingent beings would be endlessly contingent without an original cause and could therefore not exist. The only escape from the problem of endless contingency is found by granting the existence of a noncontingent or ontologically independent (noncontingent) First Cause. If we grant that this Being brought the universe into existence, then we are freed from the conundrums attendant upon an infinite contingent causal series. This being, as the noncontingent First Cause, would be different in kind from any physical and contingent state of affairs and would be self-existent. This description fits the God of the Bible. As Paul said in Athens, God "is not served by human hands, as if he needed anything. Rather, he himself gives everyone life and breath and everything else" (Acts 17:25). This being would be the Creator, who is distinct from the contingent universe.

The critic may object in several ways. First, he may say that the analogies invoked are significantly disanalogous to the case of an infinite and contingent causal series, and if this is so, the concept of such a series has not been rendered problematic. Second, he may argue that the infinite causal series itself is not contingent but necessary in some way. I respond to each in turn.

Questioning the Cosmological Analogies

What about the examples employed against an infinite causal series? The skeptic may retort by making the general claim that for any and every contingent physical state of affairs that state of affairs is caused by an antecedent state of affairs that serves as its immediate explanation *ad infinitum*. Therefore, no contingent state of affairs is ever really left begging for a causal explanation, as is the case in the cosmological examples.

We dispute that this causal understanding can explain the existence of the set of all causal relations such that we can grant an infinite causal series that is not dependent on a First Cause. The true statement "X exists because caused by antecedent causal state Y" invokes the following true statement: "Y exists because of the antecedent causal state W," *ad infinitum*. We do not object to the verity of the first two statements, but to the *ad infinitum* qualifier that is meant to refer to an entire infinite causal chain. This is because without an originating cause, he claims, the chain itself hangs in midair. Put another way, we cannot jump out of a bottomless pit; yet we may climb out of the pit if the ladder is resting on rock bottom.

Just as the cases of borrowing and permission require a first term, so it is with the more general case of physical existence itself. Its existence must be traced to an original cause that is itself noncontingent. This understanding is admittedly more general than tracing the pathways that led to a borrowing or to a permission, but it appeals to the same logical insight that undergirds the examples. If the case of receiving physical existence or being is relevantly different from the cases cited above, it needs to be shown how they are relevantly different. But another example helps illustrate our point.

Consider a chandelier suspended from a ceiling. The chandelier is contingent on something fixed, and each link in the chain must refer back to the first supported link in the chain in order to explain how the chandelier can hang there at all. We cannot imagine a chain hanging in midair without a supported link. Even if we supply the chain with an infinite number of unsupported links, this will not yield a fixed point to insure a supported chain.

This example differs from those examples mentioned earlier that refer to antecedent causal states, because the fixed point *simultaneously* causes the chain to be supported (rather than preceding it in time), but it still illustrates the contention that contingency multiplied by infinity still lacks the required cause for any contingent causal state of affairs to exist.

The skeptic might try to legitimize the idea of an infinite causal chain by claiming that just as we can imagine an infinite set of numbers, we can likewise imagine an infinite series. Causes and effects are simply two types of punctiliar designators for an infinity of points comprising an infinite temporal series. This move tries to show that the idea of an infinitely extended series is not the problem that this cosmological argument contends it is.

However, this rejoinder confuses the difference between infinite sets of numbers and infinite sets of physical causes and effects. It is one thing to conceive of an infinite set of numbers (which have no physical existence); it is quite another thing to make sense of an infinite and contingent causal series comprised of physical objects. The latter involves concrete causal relations between contingent entities; the former requires nothing of the sort. They are two very different sorts of things, so the objection fails.

ENTER COSMOLOGICAL THEISM

The collection of cosmological arguments is larger than what we have surveyed here. For example, we have not explored the Thomistic cosmological argument, whose origin and pedigree are impressive. The whole family of cosmological arguments depend on the claim that there is some property or properties about the cosmos that require that its very existence be explained by a noncontingent or self-existent being outside of itself. Here is what we have concluded about God from the three cosmological arguments addressed.

1. God is the sufficient reason for the cosmos, which depends on God for its existence. If the cosmos exists, then God exists (principle of sufficient reason argument and temporal First Cause argument).
2. God is the First Cause or creator of the universe. Since the cosmos came into being at one point, God is the cause of its beginning to exist (kalam cosmological argument).

3. From 1 and 2, we infer that:

4. God is self-existent, since God explains the existence and origin of the universe.

5. What is self-existent is eternal, since nothing could bring about or threaten its existence.

6. As the creator of the cosmos, God decided to create the cosmos, which makes God a personal being as opposed to an impersonal set of conditions.

7. Since God created the cosmos, he is outside of time and space, since they had their origin at creation.

8. God is immensely powerful, given the act of *creation ex nihilo*. Creating a good argument, a good syllabus, or a good omelet is hard enough. Imagine creating an entire cosmos. In fact, we cannot imagine an act more powerful than creation *ex nihilo*, which means that God is omnipotent.[32]

Statements 1 through 8 establish a vigorous metaphysical basis for theism, even apart from other specimens of natural theology, such as design, ontological, and moral arguments. While no cosmological argument concludes that God is a Trinity or that God became incarnate for our salvation in Jesus Christ, it does set the stage of history for such a revelation, as we will find in chapters 8–10. We must be patient to follow all the arguments through to their conclusions and implications.

STUDY QUESTIONS

1. What is the basic idea of a cosmological argument that unites all the various versions of this argument?

2. Which version of the cosmological argument trades on scientific theories, and how does it do so?

3. How does the principle of sufficient reason cosmological argument differ from the kalam cosmological argument?

---

32. See Douglas Groothuis, "Metaphysical Implications of Cosmological Arguments," in *In Defense of Natural Theology*, ed. James Sennett and Douglas Groothuis (Downers Grove, IL: InterVarsity, 2005).

SUGGESTED READING

Craig, William Lane. *The Kalām Cosmological Argument.* Eugene, OR: Wipf and Stock, 2000.

Craig, William Lane, and James D. Sinclair. "The Kalam Cosmological Argument." In *The Blackwell Companion to Natural Theology,* edited by William Lane Craig and J. P. Moreland. Malden, MA: Wiley-Blackwell, 2009.

Davies, Brian. *Thinking about God.* Eugene, OR: Wipf and Stock, 2010.

"A Debate on the Existence of God." In Bertrand Russell, *Bertrand Russell on God and Religion,* edited by Al Seckel. New York: Prometheus, 1986.

Geisler, Norman. *Thomas Aquinas: An Evangelical Appraisal.* Eugene, OR: Wipf and Stock, 2003.

Groothuis, Douglas. *Christian Apologetics: A Comprehensive Case for Biblical Faith.* 2nd ed. Downers Grove, IL: IVP Academic, 2022.

_____. "Jean-Paul Sartre and the Resurgence of Existentialism." *Christian Research Journal* 40, no. 4 (2017). https://www.equip.org/article/jean-paul -sartre-and-the-resurgence-of-existentialism.

_____. "Metaphysical Implications of Cosmological Arguments." In *In Defense of Natural Theology,* edited by James Sennett and Douglas Groothuis. Downers Grove, IL: InterVarsity, 2005.

_____. *Philosophy in Seven Sentences: A Small Introduction to a Vast Topic.* Downers Grove, IL: IVP Academic, 2016.

_____. "To Prove or Not to Prove? Pascal on Natural Theology." PhD diss., University of Oregon, 1993.

Hijab, Mohammed. *Kalam Cosmological Arguments.* S.A.L.A.M. Publications, 2019.

Koons, Robert. "A New Look at the Cosmological Argument." *American Philosophical Quarterly* 34 (1997).

Mackie, J. L. *The Miracle of Theism.* Oxford: Clarendon, 1982.

Meyer, Stephen C. *Return of the God Hypothesis: Three Scientific Discoveries That Reveal the Mind behind the Universe.* New York: HarperOne, 2021.

Moreland, J. P. *Scaling the Secular City: A Defense of Christianity.* Grand Rapids: Baker, 1987.

Pascal, Blaise. *Pensées.* New York: Penguin, 2017. Kindle edition.

Schaeffer, Francis A. *A Christian Manifesto.* Wheaton, IL: Crossway, 1981.

_____. *How Should We Then Live? The Rise and Decline of Western Thought and Culture.* L'Abri 50th Anniversary ed. Wheaton, IL: Crossway, 2009. Kindle edition.

Siniscalchi, Glenn B. "Contemporary Trends in Atheistic Criticism of Thomistic Natural Theology," *Heythrop Journal* 59 (2018): 689–706.

Sire, James W. "Existentialism." In *The Universe Next Door: A Basic Worldview Catalog* by James W. Sire. 6th ed. Downers Grove, IL: InterVarsity, 2020.

Vilenkin, Alexander. *Many Worlds in One World: The Search for Other Universes.* New York: Hill and Wang, 2006.

CHAPTER 5

THE ONTOLOGICAL ARGUMENT

My brother and I (Ike) are very close. We share a deep love for family, the Lord, Mexican food, and baseball. But when we were younger, we were not always the best of friends. He's eight years older than me, and when I was in elementary school, he tried to settle a few disputes we had by flipping a coin. The only problem with his approach was that right before he flipped the coin, he would quickly say, "Heads I win, tails you lose." Now the first couple of times he did this, I didn't understand what he was saying and went along with it. However, I quickly realized that I was the victim of a verbal trick. These kinds of jokes usually leave the victim upset and the perpetrator laughing. Given his former duplicity, it is perhaps more accurate to say that with the passage of time, my brother and I *have become* very close.

Some people claim that our next argument for the existence of God is a verbal trick. To its detractors, it is "cute" at best or manipulative at worst. However, having detractors does not ruin a good argument, and as we investigate the ontological argument, we will show that it is a fine piece of reasoning that points to the existence of God. The ontological argument claims that proper reasoning about the notion of a perfect being entails the conclusion that God exists. The argument is a bit different from other arguments, so we will take some time to explain it and some objections to it, and then we will carefully explore two versions of the argument: the first from the medieval philosopher-theologian Anselm of Canterbury (1033–1109) and the second from contemporary philosopher Alvin Plantinga (1932–), to whom much modern investigation into the argument is indebted.

A PRIORI AND *A POSTERIORI* ARGUMENTS

The first thing to get straight about the ontological argument is that it falls within a class of arguments known as *a priori* arguments. *A priori* is a Latin phrase that means that this argument uses reasoning gained from internal rational reflection. Its opposite, *a posteriori*, refers to something that one can reflect on only after observing or experiencing something in the external world. Here is a simple enough *a priori* statement: "All bachelors are unmarried men." Without any investigation into the external world, one is able to form knowledge that all bachelors are unmarried men. That is, the concept itself of "bachelorness" entails manhood and the status of being unmarried. Now something does not have to be a logical argument for it to be *a priori* or *a posteriori*. For example, you have a belief, "I exist," that you likely gained simply by internal reflection. Few of us ever set out to logically demonstrate or argue that our own selves exist. Your own existence is something that you know intuitively or *a priori*. The same is true with your belief that there are other minds (persons). You probably haven't developed an argument for this, but your *a posteriori* experience in the world has led you to the belief that there are other minds.

The thing about *a posteriori* thinking is that it is easy to use to argue for a particular phenomenon or item of experience to which others may be able to relate. Imagine you're in Cocoa Beach, Florida, and you keep happening to see red cars. You form a belief that there are more red cars than cars of any other color in Cocoa Beach. Then you turn to your friend and exclaim, "Have you ever seen more red cars in your life?!" Perhaps then your friend protests, "Are you kidding? I've never seen more black cars in my life." So you both start counting cars in the beach parking lot to get a sample. Now, assuming you have a big enough beach parking lot, you may be able to solve your disagreement. This is what *a posteriori* investigation can do. In fact, *a posteriori* argumentation is exactly what we did in the previous chapter on cosmological arguments. Consider the kalam cosmological argument again. This argument states that everything that begins to exist has a cause. Now why do we know that? The answer is that we can catalog all kinds of phenomena which have both come into existence and have a cause. Then you set out to examine the universe. There are empirical features of the universe that seem to indicate that it had a beginning (red shift, cosmic radiation, etc.). However, something different begins to come into play when one starts to think about the concept of an actual infinity. When one examines what an actual infinity entails, this is where one starts to use *a priori* reasoning (for example, the library of infinite numbers of red and blue books). So the kalam argument uses primarily *a posteriori* reasoning but has a role for *a priori* investigation into the concept of an actual infinity.

This distinction is easy enough, but there are some cultural challenges to using *a priori* argumentation. We discussed how North American culture grants a great deal of authority to a particular conception of science. Science is primarily an *a posteriori* discipline in its investigations into the natural world. This does not mean that our culture denies personal experiences; however, personal experiences are relativized when they are made to serve as templates for larger truths. For example, you may have had a religious experience that led you to the belief that Jesus is the Lord and true king of the universe. That is a personal experience that has universal ramifications. Our culture would augment the personal side of that experience and deny its universal implications by applauding you for "speaking your truth." That is, our culture has a lot of respect for your personal experiences and thoughts as long as you do not attempt to apply those experiences or thoughts to others. However, the findings of mainstream science are in a different position with respect to accept-ability.[1] J. P. Moreland illustrates science's cultural authority in a story rehearsing a conversation with his nurse at the hospital, who asked about

---

1. This is not the case in North American evangelicalism, where many Christians have an attitude of suspicion toward science and scientists. For the negative impact of this attitude, see David Kinnaman with Aly Hawkins, *You Lost Me: Why Young Christians Are Leaving Church . . . and Rethinking Faith* (Grand Rapids: Baker, 2011), ch. 7.

his academic background. He explained that he had a bachelor's degree in physical chemistry, a ThM in theology, an MA in philosophy, and a PhD in philosophy.

> She mused out loud that I had taken two very unrelated, divergent paths. Before she could explain, I asked if this was what she meant: I started off in science, which deals with reality—hard facts—and conclusions that were proved to be true. But theology and philosophy were, well, fields in which there were only private opinions or personal feelings, where no one was right or wrong, or if they were, no one could know who was right. Science was cognitive, and theology and philosophy were personal and emotional. . . . She acknowledged that my understanding was exactly what she had in mind.[2]

This bias is called *scientism*, the notion that knowledge is gained only through the sciences, and it negatively affects how people consider *a priori* argumentation. Of course, scientism is self-refuting and false. Consider the claim "Knowledge is gained only through the sciences." This claim itself is not scientific; it is philosophical and is thereby crushed under its own weight. Moreover, science requires a number of philosophical presuppositions to simply get off the ground: the reliability of our cognitive faculties, the existence of objective truth, the orderliness of the external world, and an account for the truths of mathematics. And there is plenty of knowledge that is nonscientific, including moral knowledge, knowledge of history, and logic.[3] As people who love science ourselves, we reject scientism, and we must affirm the authority of *a priori* knowledge. Just think about how much more basic your knowledge is that 2 + 2 = 4 compared to an experiment where you add two quarts of water to two quarts of milk to see what will result. The first item of knowledge is *a priori* and foundational for any *a posteriori* application.

---

2. J. P. Moreland, *Scientism and Secularism: Learning to Respond to a Dangerous Ideology* (Wheaton, IL: Crossway, 2018), 25–26.

3. Moreland provides a devastating critique of scientism in *Scientism and Secularism*. For the purposes of this discussion, see esp. chs. 4–7.

THE ONTOLOGICAL ARGUMENT IN BRIEF

So with this confidence in *a priori* argumentation, we return to our consideration of the ontological argument for the existence of God by providing brief presentations of two versions of the arguments, from Anselm and Plantinga. Then we shall consider some objections to ontological arguments in general. Later we will go deeper on Anselm's argument and specific objections to it and on Plantinga's version and specific objections to it. We will see that the ontological argument is sound, and it can be helpful when used in conjunction with other arguments to support the truth and rationality of the Christian worldview.

First, let's start with Anselm's argument. He defined God as "something than which nothing greater can be thought." Even the "Fool" who has said in his heart, "There is no God" (Ps. 14:1), understands the concept of God in his mind even though he does not agree that God exists in reality. However,

> surely that-than-which-nothing-greater-can-be-thought cannot exist
> in the mind alone. For if it exists solely in the mind, it can be
> thought to exist in reality also, which is greater. If then that-than-
> which-nothing-greater-can-be-thought exists in the mind alone, this
> same that-than-which-nothing-greater-can-be-thought is that-than-
> which-a-greater-*can*-be-thought. But this is obviously impossible.
> Therefore, there is absolutely no doubt that something-than-which-
> a-greater-cannot-be-thought exists both in the mind and in reality.[4]

If your head is twisting in knots a bit, that is okay. Anselm may have been overselling it when he wrote the word "obviously." His meaning is actually not that obscure, however. He was saying that the concept of God (that-than-which-nothing-greater-can-be-thought; a simpler way to say this would be "the greatest possible being") exists in the mind, even in the mind of someone who denies God's existence. But the person who

---

4. Anselm of Canterbury, "Proslogion," in *The Major Works: Including Monologion, Proslogion, and Why God Became Man*, Oxford World's Classics, ed. Brian Davies and G. R. Evans (Oxford: Oxford University Press, 1998), 87–88.

denies God's existence thinks that the concept of God can merely be in the mind without God actually existing in reality. Here the atheist has it wrong, because if one is thinking of the greatest possible being, that being would necessarily exist in reality. Greatness of this kind—you might call it "maximal greatness"—is only maximally great if it is real. So the thought the atheist has of God, a maximally great being, is not really a thought about a maximally great being, because it would be possible to conceive of something even greater. That greater thing would be to conceive of a maximally great being who actually exists. Since the atheist's concept of God is impossible (a being which does not exist but is, somehow, still the greatest being we can think of), it leaves us with the conclusion that a maximally great being must actually exist. We will evaluate this argument below, but one can see that the argument trades on the notion of conceivability. That is, God's existence is something that can be thought of in one's mind.

Second, let's take a look at Alvin Plantinga's version of the argument. One of the greatest philosophers of religion in the last hundred years, Alvin Plantinga dedicates space to the ontological argument in a number of his books, but the most straightforward formalization of the argument comes to us from *God, Freedom, and Evil*, where he talks about the idea of a maximally great being existing in "a possible world," a concept used by philosophers to consider a complete set of states of affairs that could all exist in a coherent reality. The reality that we live in is one possible world, but there are other possibilities for how reality could have been (for example, a reality where *only* God exists or one where H_2O is poisonous).[5] William Lane Craig helps us understand what Plantinga means by the idea that God exists in at least one possible world. "To say that God exists in some possible world is just to say that there is a possible description of reality which includes the statement 'God exists' as part of that reality."[6]

---

5. Don't get tripped up by the word "world." Plantinga is not talking about other planets or parallel universes. A "world" in philosophy is just a complete set of states of affairs. It's a way of talking about every true statement about a possible reality.

6. William Lane Craig, "Richard Dawkins on Arguments for God," in *God Is Great, God Is Good: Why Believing in God Is Responsible and Reasonable*, ed. William Lane Craig and Chad Meister (Downers Grove, IL: InterVarsity, 2009), 28.

Now for Plantinga's argument:

1. There is a possible world in which maximal greatness is instantiated.
2. Necessarily, a being is maximally great only if it has maximal excellence in every world.
3. Necessarily, a being has maximal excellence in every world only if it has omniscience, omnipotence, and moral perfection in every world.[7]

Plantinga concludes, "There actually exists a being that is omnipotent, omniscient, and morally good."[8] Here is a summary: If God exists, then God is an "instantiation" or an actual instance of a maximally great being. Now, it is possible that God exists. That means that there is at least one possible world in which God exists. Step back for a second, though. If a being were to be maximally great, then that being would not just exist in one possible world; that being would exist in *every* possible world. After all, if a being existed in just one possible world, it would not be maximally great, because it could have existed in others as well, making it even greater. So God exists in every possible world, including *the actual world*, since our reality is one of the possible worlds.

Now what does "maximal excellence" mean in this case? Plantinga answers this question by stating that the being would be omnipotent, omniscient, and morally good. If a being were to be maximally great, this greatness would apply to every possible world, but excellence has to do with a being's properties in the actual world. He is saying that excellence in the actual world logically follows from greatness in all possible worlds. Premise 3 just makes it clear what excellence entails. So (1) sets out an easily acceptable premise. Is it possible that God exists? Yes. Premise (2) makes it clear that if a being with maximal greatness (God) exists, then this greatness (which includes existing in all possible worlds) logically entails that the being has excellence in the

---

7. Alvin Plantinga, *God, Freedom, and Evil* (New York: Harper Torchbooks, 1974), 111. We have edited the numbers used by Plantinga for clarity.

8. Plantinga, 112.

actual world ("in every world"). And (3) just teases out what is meant by maximal excellence.

From a logical perspective, so far so good. But Plantinga here expresses a hesitation. He thinks that the argument is logically sound, meaning that its premises relate to one another in the proper logical form to generate a valid argument, but he claims that the argument does not prove that God exists. He concedes, "Not everyone who understands and reflects on its central premise—that the existence of a maximally great being is *possible*—will accept it."[9] The argument's failure, then, is that it is not convincing to everyone. But is this a reason to reject it? We don't think so, and to be fair to Plantinga, he does not think so either. But he claims that the argument only establishes the rational acceptability of believing in God; it fails to demonstrate in a convincing way that God exists.

We will take up Plantinga's hesitation below, but let us consider the significance of Anselm's and Plantinga's arguments. If successful, these arguments show that God exists without doing any investigation into the empirical world. These ontological arguments instead show *a priori* that God exists. In this way alone, they are important to other kinds of natural theology. Consider how an *a priori* mathematical equation supports reflection on the actual world. Since we are not mathematicians, look at $2 + 2 = 4$. This is something that one can rationally accept without doing any investigation into adding two items to two other items in the actual world. If we understand the concepts of the number two, the number four, and of addition, we cannot fail to see its truth. However, consider how the *a priori* truth of $2 + 2 = 4$ supports every *a posteriori* investigation into adding two things to two other things. The person doing the *a posteriori* investigation has an *a priori* truth ringing in her mind as she does her investigations, and each subsequent *a posteriori* confirmation of the *a priori* truth builds her confidence again and again of the truth that, in this simplistic case, $2 + 2 = 4$. Likewise, *a priori* support of God's existence can only bolster one's *a posteriori* investigation into God's existence.

---

9. Plantinga, 112.

GENERAL OBJECTIONS TO ONTOLOGICAL ARGUMENTS

Of course, as Plantinga concedes, not everyone will accept this kind of reasoning about God. We will go deeper on critiques of Anselm's and Plantinga's individual arguments below, but let's consider some objections to ontological arguments in general. The evolutionary biologist Richard Dawkins calls the argument "infantile" and "logomachist trickery" (a logomachist is someone who enjoys arguing about words), for he holds "a deep suspicion of any line of reasoning that reached such a significant conclusion without feeding in a single piece of data from the real world."[10] Please note the bias against *a priori* thinking and what seems to be an implicit precommitment to methodological naturalism.[11] But is the argument actually a trick? Dawkins's way of affirming this charge is to state parodies of arguments for the existence of God that he finds humorous. For example, here is the argument that God does not exist, credited to Douglas Gasking:

1. The creation of the world is the most marvelous achievement imaginable.
2. The merit of an achievement is the product of (a) its intrinsic quality, and (b) the ability of its creator.
3. The greater the disability (or handicap) of the creator, the more impressive the achievement.
4. The most formidable handicap of a creator would be non-existence.
5. Therefore, if we suppose that the universe is the product of an existent creator we can conceive a greater being—namely, one who created everything while not existing.
6. An existing God therefore would not be a being greater than which a greater being cannot be conceived because an even more formidable and incredible creator would be a God which did not exist.

---

10. Richard Dawkins, *The God Delusion* (New York: Houghton Mifflin, 2006), 82.

11. Of course, Dawkins is a metaphysical naturalist; however, the only kind of inquiry he will accept is that which uses data from the "real" (read: "natural") world. On methodological naturalism, see our chapter, "Philosophical Objections to Apologetics."

Ergo:

    7. God does not exist.[12]

Dawkins presents this and other parodies of natural theology as jokes, supposedly trying to show how absurd theistic arguments like the ontological argument are. If you found this odd set of statements difficult to follow, it is because it *is* a verbal trick, unlike the ontological argument that it parodies. Consider premise 4: "The most formidable handicap of a creator would be non-existence." He is saying in premise 3 that a creator gets more credit for a creation if the creator has some challenge to overcome. This makes sense. A five-year-old deserves more credit for coloring in the lines than does a fifteen-year-old, and this is because the five-year-old lacks some properties, such as that of having the fine-motor control that the fifteen-year-old possesses. But how does one lack the property of existing? A thing that lacks the property of existence is no-thing, a nonexisting thing. This is a category mistake. Dawkins (and Gasking) are conflating having and lacking creative-enabling properties with having or lacking the property of existence. This is just a verbal joke, of course, but the fact that it is silly does not mean that it is insightful. William Lane Craig concludes, "A being who creates everything while not existing is a logical incoherence and is therefore impossible."[13]

A more common retort to the ontological argument is that it lacks existential punch, meaning that it is difficult to connect the argument's affirmation with one's basic orientation toward life and meaning. Contrast it with the moral argument (see chapter 6), which argues from the existence of objective moral laws to an objective moral lawgiver. The moral argument immediately connects with something that people care about: the moral universe. You care if someone hurts you and those you love. You care (or should care) about large-scale injustices, and so the argument packs an existential punch in its ability to draw someone's eyes from their moral convictions to the Source of moral conviction, goodness, and justice. While we concede that the argument may lack

---

12. Dawkins, *God Delusion*, 83.
13. Craig, "Richard Dawkins on Arguments for God," 29–30.

this kind of punch for many, this is not necessarily the case. Anselm's initial formulation of the argument was in the form of a prayer, after all. He prefaced the argument like this: "Well then, Lord, You who give understanding to faith, grant me that I may understand . . . that we believe You to exist, and that You are what we believe You to be."[14] Anselm's spirituality was deeply tied to this philosophical reflection, and we should not impugn the argument simply because we may lack the same reaction. To do so would be to be guilty of recency bias. Consider someone who hears Plantinga's possible worlds ontological argument and concludes that God exists and is then hastened to discover if God was disclosed in other ways. Would it be right to disparage that person's conviction and questioning just because the argument is obscure and does not necessarily carry an emotional punch? We do not think so, and our contention is that this argument may indeed serve such a function as part of a larger cumulative case for the truth of Christianity. But before we get too much more involved in the argument's place in an apologetic strategy, let's go a bit deeper on its versions, first Anselm's and then Plantinga's.

ANSELM'S ARGUMENT IN DEPTH

Anselm's argument has captured legions of advocates and detractors. In this section, we will carefully explain and defend Anselm's argument, and we will show where its detractors have gone wrong. The reader will recall that Anselm made his argument based on the idea of God that exists even in the mind of the "Fool."[15] But the idea of God cannot exist merely in the mind, given Anselm's definition of God: "That-than-which-nothing-greater-can-be-thought." If one were to conceive

14. Anselm of Canterbury, "Proslogion," 87.

15. The passage in which the "Fool" appears is Psalm 14:1–2, "The fool says in his heart, 'There is no God.' They are corrupt, their deeds are vile; there is no one who does good. The LORD looks down from heaven on all mankind to see if there are any who understand, any who seek God." We affirm God's right to judge humanity, and our ability to call sin "sin," but do not take it as permission to make ourselves the judges of others. We will continue to refer to the "Fool" in this explanation of Anselm without putting ourselves in the judgment seat of any atheists who say that there is no God.

of God in the mind, then one could conceive of God in reality, and critically, existing in reality is greater than existing in the mind. But it is absurd to think that there could be something greater than the greatest possible being or "That-than-which-nothing-greater-can-be-thought." So Anselm concluded, "Therefore, there is absolutely no doubt that something-than-which-a-greater-cannot-be-thought exists both in the mind and in reality."[16] Here's a formalized version of the argument as laid out by Anselm:

1. Definition of God:
   That-than-which-nothing-greater-can-be-thought.
2. Fool's premise: God exists in the understanding but not in reality.
3. Existence in reality is greater than existence in the understanding alone.
4. A being having all of God's properties plus existence in reality can be conceived in the mind.
5. A being having all of God's properties plus existence in reality is greater than God (based on premises 2 and 3).
6. A being greater than God can be conceived in the mind (based on premises 4 and 5).
7. But it is false that a being greater than God can be conceived in the mind (based on premise 1).
8. Therefore, it is false that the concept of God exists in the mind only but that God does not actually exist in reality by *reductio ad absurdum.*
9. Therefore, God exists in reality.[17]

We came across the phrase *reductio ad absurdum* when, in chapter 2, we talked about Jesus' use of logical argumentation in claiming that it was absurd to believe that he was driving out demons by the power of Satan. This kind of argument teases out, or "reduces," an idea to its logically absurd conclusion. Anselm was saying that it is absurd to think

16. Anselm of Canterbury, "Proslogion," 87–88.

17. This formalization is deeply indebted to Alvin Plantinga in *God and Other Minds: A Study of the Rational Justification of Belief in God* (Ithaca, NY: Cornell University Press, 1967), 29.

that the concept of God could exist only in the mind. In this case, it is absurd to think that one could conceive of God as existing only in the mind when it is possible to conceive of something greater than God. After all, God is That-than-which-nothing-greater-can-be-thought!

So is there something wrong here? Is this just a verbal trick? We do not think so. Let us examine Anselm's detractors. The earliest challenge to this argument came from the monk Gaunillo, who did not reject the conclusion that God exists but rejected Anselm's way of arriving at the conclusion. Consider the thought of an island that "is more excellent than all other countries, which are inhabited by mankind, in the abundance with which it is stored."[18] This is the greatest of all possible islands, the Island-than-which-no-island-greater-can-be-conceived. This is something that one could conceive of in one's mind. Gaunillo states that, of course it is better to exist in reality than just in the mind. By Anselm's reasoning, this island actually exists since it is better to exist in reality than in the mind only, or so Gaunillo charges. If this was all Gaunillo was getting at, it's not actually that significant. So there's a greatest of all possible islands? So what? Well, it seems that Gaunillo was mocking Anselm, saying that Anselm's reasoning could be used to conceive of the greatest of all possible candy bars or the greatest of all possible cars. What really seems to be at stake here is the definition of God. If an island is good because it has pineapples, you could keep adding pineapples to it. If God is good, what if God was just a little *more* good? The implication here is that Anselm's conception of God is unintelligible, just like that of the greatest of all islands.

But this is a category mistake. God is completely unlike islands. For example, islands have properties that do not necessarily get better when one adds to them. How many pineapples make up the greatest of all islands? How many trees are there, and how blue is the surrounding water? There is not a clear way to conceive of the maximal amount of pineapples, trees, and blueness that would necessarily make one island greater than all others. However, conceiving of maximal goodness and power does seem possible. The properties that we attribute to God are not like the properties that we attribute to islands. For example, God

---

18. Gaunillo, "On Behalf of the Fool," quoted in Plantinga, *God, Freedom, and Evil*, 89.

is omniscient, and it is impossible to conceive of a being that has more knowledge than that. In the same way, one cannot add just a bit more goodness to an all-good God. So this is just a bad analogy.

The next rejection of this argument comes from the great German philosopher Immanuel Kant (1724–1804). Kant claimed that Anselm is guilty of some conceptual trickery by arguing that the concept of God is greater when one adds the idea of existence to it. Kant was accusing Anselm of saying this:

GOD IS. > GOD

Kant was charging Anselm with saying that if one adds "existence" or "being" (represented in the word "is") to the concept of God, then one has something greater in mind than just the concept of God by itself. But Kant's reply was that one adds nothing to the concept of God by adding "is." When one describes God by saying things like "God is omnipotent," one uses the word "is" to say something about God, in this case omnipotence. But Kant claimed that the word "is" by itself does nothing except show the relation of what is said to the one about whom it is said. (In grammar "what is said" is the predicate, and "the one about whom it is said" is the subject.) So when one says, "God is omnipotent," one uses the word "is" to merely connect the idea of omnipotence (predicate) with the idea of God (subject). So far so good. However, Kant claimed that when one adds the word "is" by itself to the concept of God (for example, "God is"), one has done nothing noteworthy. This is because the concept of "being" or "existence" cannot be predicated of any subject. He was saying that there is no difference between the idea "God" and the idea "There is a God." From Kant himself: "*'Being'* is obviously not a real predicate; that is, it is not a concept of something which could be added to the concept of a thing. . . . If now, we take the subject (God) with all its predicates (among which is omnipotence), and say 'God is,' or 'There is a God,' we attach no new predicate to the concept of God."[19] To understand Kant's objection, we need to think

---

19. Immanuel Kant, *The Critique of Pure Reason*, trans. Norman Kemp Smith (London: Macmillan, 1929), 504; in Alvin Plantinga, *The Ontological Argument: From St. Anselm to Contemporary Philosophers* (New York: Anchor Books, 1965), 61.

about what the ontological argument is doing. The argument begins by suggesting that the "Fool" could have the concept of God in his mind while still thinking that God does not exist. But if one adds "existence" to God, one has not really done anything.

If this is what Anselm was doing, then we might rightly reply that existence is indeed a meaningful predicate sometimes. Consider the child who reads a story that has a lion and a unicorn in it and asks her mother, "Are the animals real or just in the story?" Adding the predicate of existence to the lion but not to the unicorn is perfectly logical.[20] However, this is not actually what Anselm was doing in the argument anyway. Anselm was saying that the Fool has a concept of a God in his mind while denying God's existence. The problem for the Fool is that if one is thinking of God *without* thinking about a God who exists, then one is not actually thinking about God. The argument's power is in showing that if one is thinking of a God that does not exist, one is not actually thinking about God, since the greatest possible being has the property of existence.

Here's how Plantinga defends Anselm: "If he started with some concept . . . and then annexed *existence* to it—then indeed his argument would be subject to Kant's criticism. But he didn't, and it isn't."[21] Anselm was saying that if one concedes that it is possible to conceive of God (which seems obvious), then one is conceiving of a being who exists necessarily. ("Necessarily" here means something that could not have been otherwise. The opposite of necessary is contingent. For example, it is a necessary fact that $2 + 2 = 4$, but it is a contingent fact that Evangeline and Matilda Shepardson are blondes.) If one is thinking about God, then one is thinking about a being who in fact exists and could not possibly fail to exist. So, for the ontological argument to fail, one would have to claim that it is impossible to conceive of God, which is absurd as well.[22]

---

20. Douglas Groothuis, *Christian Apologetics: A Comprehensive Case for Biblical Faith*, 2nd ed. (Downers Grove, IL: IVP Academic, 2022), 192.

21. Plantinga, *God and Other Minds*, 37.

22. Now here someone might claim that we are simply begging the question in favor of our own concept of God, a being than whom nothing is greater, and adding the concept of existence to it. We answer with Anselm that maximal greatness entails existence, and the burden of proof falls on the one who would deny that this is the case. For how could something be maximally great and not exist?

The final objection to Anselm's argument is fairly simple. Anselm seemed to be saying that it is better for God to exist than not exist. That is, one of the properties that is entailed by greatness is existence. So it would seem that to exist is better than not to exist. However, this is obviously not true. Think about COVID-19. It is clearly better for that virus to lack the property of existence. This means that it would be better if COVID-19 were merely an idea rather than a reality.[23] So was Anselm saying that existence is necessarily better than nonexistence? It seems that Anselm did not really address this question, but it is clear that he was making an argument about God, not by comparing God to other kinds of concepts, but by considering what the concept of God, as a unique kind of thing, entails. That is the key to responding to this objection. Anselm was talking about God as a unique kind of being, indeed a perfect being. A perfect being is in its own class in terms of which properties add to its greatness. A person cannot simply compare the idea of God to other kinds of ideas when thinking about which properties are entailed by greatness. Since Anselm was not making an argument by analogy anyway, this objection fails with the others. Anselm's argument, though much maligned, stands on solid ground for the person who seeks to show that God exists. Even so, it is fortunate for the apologist that another form of the ontological argument exists: Plantinga's ontological argument.[24]

PLANTINGA'S ARGUMENT

We only briefly outlined this argument above, so here we will dedicate more space to Plantinga's ontological argument. You will recall that Plantinga's argument trades on the idea of possible worlds. Possible worlds are conceptual devices used by philosophers to help us consider which kinds of propositions are true, which are false, which are possible,

---

23. Groothuis, *Christian Apologetics*, 193.
24. There are other formulations of the ontological argument as well. In particular, Descartes' ontological arguments are strong. For a solid introduction to Descartes's arguments, see Yujin Nagasawa, *The Existence of God: A Philosophical Introduction* (London: Routledge, 2011), pt. 1, sec. 3.

and which are impossible. A possible world, then, is really just a list of propositions. Think about the following list as a list of possible worlds (PW) with the ellipses (. . .) representing all of the other propositions about that world:

PW1: $2 + 2 = 4$, H_2O is poisonous, there are many persons . . .
PW2: $2 + 2 = 4$, H_2O is nourishing, there are many persons . . .
PW3: $2 + 2 = 4$, H_2O is nourishing, there is only one person . . .

Of course all of these worlds are possible; however, it is the case that only PW2 represents something like our actual world. Another way to think about possible worlds is to think about which propositions are necessarily true and which are only contingently true. A necessary truth is something like $2 + 2 = 4$. That is, it is not possible for $2 + 2$ to equal anything but 4. So in all possible worlds (including the actual world) $2 + 2 = 4$. This is because $2 + 2 = 4$ is necessarily true. It could not be otherwise. However, the fact that H_2O is nourishing is a contingent truth. It just so happens that H_2O is nourishing, and it is logically possible that H_2O is poisonous. There is some possible world in which H_2O is poisonous.

Now back to the ontological argument that states that God exists necessarily. Now, if God exists necessarily, then this means that God exists in all possible worlds (including the actual world). However, this is exactly what is in dispute between theists and nontheists. So Alvin Plantinga gives an argument for this line of thinking. Here is his formalized argument:

1. There is a possible world in which maximal greatness is instantiated.
2. Necessarily, a being is maximally great only if it has maximal excellence in every world.
3. Necessarily, a being has maximal excellence in every world only if it has omniscience, omnipotence, and moral perfection in every world.[25]

---

25. Plantinga, *God, Freedom, and Evil*, 111.

He argues from the idea that it is possible that a maximally great being exists in some possible world.[26] From there, he simply shows the logical necessity of God's existence given God's possible existence. If a being who has the property of being maximally great exists in one possible world, then that being exists in all possible worlds. That is, the property of maximal greatness entails existence in all possible worlds. Maximal greatness is not maximal if it is only contingently instantiated, say in one possible world. Maximal greatness entails necessity. In addition, Plantinga's argument teases out what is meant by maximal greatness in that maximal greatness implies maximal excellence in the areas of omniscience, omnipotence, and moral perfection. What does it mean to be maximally great? Well, it means that one possesses various great-making properties to a maximal degree. Knowledge, power, and goodness are great-making properties that a maximally great being has. This is a clear upside for Plantinga's argument. As you'll see throughout this book, good natural theology is typically modest when ascribing various attributes to God. From a Christian perspective, this is appropriate as the Bible is the definitive authority on the nature of God. However, Plantinga's ontological argument gives philosophical confirmation to the fact of God's omniscience, omnipotence, and moral excellence as authoritatively revealed in the Bible (Pss. 106:1; 147:5; Jer. 32:27; Mark 10:18; Luke 1:37; 1 John 3:20; Rev. 19:6).

As we described above, Plantinga is modest about this argument, but in a different way. Plantinga suggests that the argument may be lacking. He claims that the argument is valid, which is how philosophers refer to an argument that is in the proper form, and he claims that the argument is sound, meaning that it has true premises, indicating that the argument shows something true about reality. However, Plantinga is concerned that the argument will not be convincing to everyone, and he thus rules it out as a "successful piece of natural theology." He says, "It must be conceded that not everyone who understands and reflects on its central premise—that the existence of a maximally great being

---

26. It is worth noting that the argument could fail at this point if the idea of a maximally great being is logically contradictory; however, there is no reason to believe that this is so. In fact, the argument's strength is that it begins with a highly plausible premise in the possibility of the existence of a maximally great being.

is *possible*—will accept it."[27] Plantinga makes a distinction between
the rational acceptability of theism and the truth of theism in arguing this way. The ontological argument shows that theism is rationally
acceptable, but it fails to establish the truth of theism due to the fact
that not everyone will accept the argument. In our experience doing
apologetics, we have often encountered people who will not accept
arguments for the existence of God. This is not surprising. People fail
to accept good arguments all the time. However, the fact that people
fail to accept good arguments should do nothing to change in our minds
the fact that good arguments are indeed good. Plantinga is correct in
saying that people do not always accept good arguments, but he is wrong
in his assessment of his own fine argument. Whether an argument is
true is a matter of fact. However, whether an argument is convincing
is relative to the individual considering the argument and is subject to
a million biases, presuppositions, and mental peculiarities. Plantinga's
argument shows us the existence of God and should be accepted for its
philosophical success. But if it is not always accepted, this should not
diminish our assessment of it.

Even so, there is something to be said for the argument's lack of
appeal. At this point, you have read a whole chapter on the ontological
argument, and if it is your first time encountering the argument, your
head may be spinning a bit. That's okay. The argument is complicated,
and a first glance at it may leave you with some questions. After all, the
argument is *a priori*, and in modern Western culture, we are not used to
forming arguments about big ideas this way. We usually think about evidence from an *a posteriori* perspective. Again, the fact that culture has
conditioned us thusly should not diminish the fact that the ontological
argument shows that God exists, but we should still be realistic about
its prospects. For many, the ontological argument provides an additional
logical confirmation of God's existence and nature. Viewed alongside
cosmological arguments, the moral argument, and design arguments,
the ontological argument further buttresses the truth of theism. When
presented with a larger case for the Christian worldview, we have further

---

27. Plantinga, *God, Freedom, and Evil*, 112.

support for a good, powerful, and wise God. All of these arguments together lead us to wonder at God's greatness and to worship him:

> Oh, the depth of the riches of the wisdom and knowledge
>> of God!
> How unsearchable his judgments,
> and his paths beyond tracing out!
> "Who has known the mind of the Lord?
> Or who has been his counselor?"
> "Who has ever given to God,
> that God should repay them?"
> For from him and through him and for him are all things.
> To him be the glory forever! Amen.
>> (Rom. 11:33–36)

STUDY QUESTIONS

1. How does the ontological argument differ from cosmological arguments?
2. Do you think the God of the ontological argument is too abstract to be identical to the God of the Bible?
3. Sometimes people claim the ontological argument is illicit because it simply posits an idea of God as existing without giving a real argument. Respond to this charge.

SUGGESTED READING

Anselm of Canterbury. *The Major Works: Including Monologion, Proslogion, and Why God Became Man*. Oxford World's Classics. Edited by Brian Davies and G. R. Evans. Oxford: Oxford University Press, 1998.

Craig, William Lane. "Richard Dawkins on Arguments for God." In *God Is Great, God Is Good: Why Believing in God Is Responsible and Reasonable*, edited by William Lane Craig and Chad Meister. Downers Grove, IL: InterVarsity, 2009.

Dawkins, Richard. *The God Delusion*. New York: Houghton Mifflin, 2006.

Groothuis, Douglas. *Christian Apologetics*: *A Comprehensive Case for Biblical Faith*. 2nd ed. Downers Grove, IL: IVP Academic, 2022.

Kant, Immanuel. *The Critique of Pure Reason*. Translated by Norman Kemp Smith. London: Macmillan, 1929.

Kinnaman, David, with Aly Hawkins. *You Lost Me: Why Young Christians Are Leaving Church . . . and Rethinking Faith*. Grand Rapids: Baker, 2011.

Moreland, J. P. *Scientism and Secularism: Learning to Respond to a Dangerous Ideology*. Wheaton, IL: Crossway, 2018.

Nagasawa, Yujin, *The Existence of God: A Philosophical Introduction*. London: Routledge, 2011.

_____. *Maximal God: A New Defence of Perfect Being Theism*. New York: Oxford University Press, 2017.

Plantinga, Alvin. *God and Other Minds: A Study of the Rational Justification of Belief in God*. Ithaca, NY: Cornell University Press, 1967.

_____. *God, Freedom, and Evil*. New York: Harper Torchbooks, 1974.

_____, ed. *The Ontological Argument: From St. Anselm to Contemporary Philosophers*. New York: Anchor Books, 1965.

CHAPTER 6

THE MORAL ARGUMENT

The 2020 Olympics were a strange affair. For one, these Olympics did not take place in the year 2020. The COVID-19 pandemic delayed the games by a year, and the decision to still hold the games was highly contentious, even with all of the extra precautions planned by the International Olympic Committee. Only a limited number of media and sports professionals were even allowed to see the games live, and the 2020 Olympics were actually held in 2021 (with all of the Olympic paraphernalia still branded as Tokyo 2020). Then there was the "Russian Olympic Committee," who took third place in the total number of medals earned despite the fact that Russia, as a country, was banned from officially sending athletes as part of their "punishment" for a doping scheme that went on for years. So the Russian Olympic Committee sent athletes to the games as an unofficial group, albeit with standard outfits with the colors of the Russian flag artfully displayed.

But then there was the beautiful story of Gianmarco Tamberi of Italy and Mutaz Barshim of Qatar. These men competed in the high jump competition, and it was a fierce contest. They were neck and neck the entire time, each one working his way closer to the top until they were left as the last two competitors. This was fitting for them, as they had known each other for years and often trained together and competed against one another. Indeed, they had become great friends and held each other as men and as athletes in high esteem. However, neither was able to edge the other out. Despite successfully conquering the gradual increase in height of the bar, each failed three times to best one another by hitting the Olympic record height of seven feet, ten inches. In their exhaustion, Barshim made an offer to the official in the hearing of Tamberi: "Can we have two golds?" Tamberi nodded his head in stunned agreement, and the official said that this arrangement was within the rules. The two exploded in celebration, leaping and hugging one another in a display that seemed to celebrate the precise fraternal spirit behind the Olympic games. This exchange and the result became a seminal moment in the 2020 (2021?) games and is likely to be remembered for years to come.[1]

One marvels at such moral beauty. If nothing else, Tamberi and Barshim's story points us to a kind of transcendent beauty that can be realized in the messy immanence of athletic competition. But why is this story so beautiful? Why do we see such displays as full of beauty and hope? Conversely, why do we rightly disdain the hypocrisy in the enabling of the "Russian Olympic Committee" to send athletes while officially banning "Russia" from doing so? What is it about this inconsistency that irritates our moral sensibilities? After all, we live in a world where many cheat and get away with it, and many people do beautiful, morally courageous things and get no credit for them. More importantly for our project, what is it about our moral sensibilities that tells us something bigger about the way things are? Is there indeed something transcendent in acts of moral beauty? Is there some kind of objective standard that is violated when people cheat and lie? If so, is there a good explanation for these moral values?

This chapter will outline the moral argument for the existence of God, which points to a moral authority behind objective rights and wrongs. Moral arguments establish that there are such things as moral truths, exemplified in moral values like courage or compassion and in moral duties like the duty not to commit murder. From these moral truths, apologists show that God is the reason these values and duties exist. Take Moreland and Craig's version of the argument:

---

1. *Guardian* Staff and Agencies, "'Just Magical': Joy for Tamberi and Barshim as They Opt to Share Gold in Men's High Jump," *Guardian*, August 1, 2021, https://www.theguardian.com /sport/2021/aug/02/tamberi-barshim-share-olympic-gold-mens-high-jump-reaction.

1. If God did not exist, objective moral values and duties would not exist.
2. Objective moral values and duties do exist.
3. Therefore, God exists.[2]

Since this form is valid (it is a *modus tollens* argument, which means "in the method of denying"), the argument attempts to defend (1) why God's nonexistence would entail that there would be no such things as objective moral values and duties and (2) the existence of those objective moral values and duties. This chapter will start by challenging key cultural and philosophical rejections of the idea of objective morality: relativism, Darwinian pragmatism, and Eastern pantheism's illusion view of moral values. All of these deny statement 2. After showing that these alternative views are false, we will outline C. S. Lewis's famous moral argument and J. P. Moreland and William Lane Craig's version of the argument. Then we will consider some objections to the moral argument, with special attention paid to philosopher Erik Wielenberg's "Godless Normative Moral Realism," which affirms statement 2, but denies statement 1. Then the chapter will conclude with a brief look at the problem of evil, showing that the existence of evil, long held to be a major challenge to Christian belief, is actually evidence of a moral universe over which God is the divine Lawgiver.

THE FAILURE OF DENYING OBJECTIVE MORALITY

The most popular way in Western culture to invalidate the moral argument is to deny the existence of objective moral values and duties. However, the motivation of those who deny objective morality is not necessarily to deny God's existence. Instead, the cultural mood seems to be that morality is deeply personal, moral judgments are private, and what is right differs from person to person. But this is not the only way objective morality is denied. Some who reject God's existence also rule

---

2. J. P. Moreland and William Lane Craig, *Philosophical Foundations for a Christian Worldview*, 2nd ed. (Downers Grove, IL: IVP Academic, 2017), 505.

out objective moral values and duties as well. For these atheists, morality is indeed dependent on God, and God's nonexistence entails a denial of objective morality. There are also many others who live every day as if there is such a thing as morality but also believe that despite the fact that we have moral commitments, ultimate reality is really beyond the categories of good and evil. Typically influenced by Advaita Vedanta Hinduism or Mahayana Buddhism, these people believe there is no real objective morality. We will address all three of these objections in this section.

Before we do, it is best to start by making a distinction between subjective and objective values and duties. Subjective values are everywhere. Ike values electronic access to books and articles so that he can access resources wherever he happens to be working that day. Easy access makes Ike's dual vocation as technologist and professor possible. Doug values a large physical library so that he can hold resources in his hands while he reads and writes. The physicality of books reminds Doug of the importance of knowledge. Neither of us thinks the other is wrong as we both affirm the other's preference. These are subjective values. Subjective duties are common as well. Ike considers it a duty to call each member of his family on their birthday to make sure they hear a birthday greeting from him personally rather than through the less personal medium of a text message. Doug considers it a duty to write letters to friends and loved ones to encourage them and to let them know that he is thinking about them. These are subjective duties that we would never lay upon others' shoulders. Objective values and duties are different. Courage and compassion are good values regardless of anyone's particular preference or place in the world. Worshiping God alone and avoiding theft are duties that apply to all humankind regardless of preference or background. So when we talk about objective moral values and duties, we are talking about principles that exist regardless of one's personal eccentricities, proclivities, background, and biases. "To say that there are objective moral values is to say that something is good or bad independent of whatever people think about it. Similarly, to say that we have objective moral duties is to say that certain actions are right or wrong for us regardless of what we think about them."[3]

---

3. Moreland and Craig, 501.

A clear challenge to the objective/subjective distinction is the notion that what is good and bad and right and wrong is merely a matter of taste or background. This is moral relativism, and it comes in two varieties. First, there is moral subjectivism, the idea that what is moral differs from person to person. Second, there is cultural relativism, the idea that what is moral differs from culture to culture. If either of these relativistic positions is true, then the moral argument fails because it affirms the existence of objective moral values and duties. This is because, according to relativism, all moral values and duties are subjective, and no law-giving God is required to explain what is subjective.

Well, should we accept relativism? For the Christian, the answer is unequivocally no. This does not entail any lack of respect for different cultures and people with different perspectives, for relativism undermines a respect for cultures and persons. Consider the classic notion of tolerance, the idea that people should be able to believe what they believe without fear of coercion. Now imagine someone whose personal sense of right and wrong includes the idea that people should be coerced to agree on some moral principles. If we hold to the moral subjectivist version of relativism, we are required to legitimize one person's view that people should be coerced to agree on moral beliefs!

There are many other reasons to reject moral relativism. First, consider prejudices like anti-Semitism and practices like child marriage, foot binding, or female genital mutilation. These are often encouraged at the cultural level. A misguided version of tolerance, with cultural relativism in the background, would say that what is moral differs from culture to culture, so who are we to pass judgment on such things? Well, that is an absurd perspective. Anti-Semitism is wrong, and practices like child marriage, foot binding, and female genital mutilation are wrong, and those who practice these things deserve moral accountability. Yet relativism would prohibit any moral critique of another culture.

Second, think about moral reformers like Dr. Martin Luther King Jr. Dr. King critiqued and challenged the dominant white Southern culture in the United States for its racism and injustice. However, moral relativism would offer that racism was good *for* the white Southern culture (cultural relativism) or that racism was good *for* individuals like George Wallace (moral subjectivism), the segregationist governor of Alabama.

This entails that Dr. King was wrong to impose his egalitarian views on race onto other persons or cultures, and that is absurd.

Third, most of us think that people and societies can go through a kind of moral progress or advance. For example, George Wallace later became a born-again Christian and publicly repented of his earlier views. He appointed many black people to positions of power in the Alabama state government. On relativism, this is merely moral *change*, not growth or progress. Wallace believed racism was justified but later changed his mind. Yet that does not capture the whole story, right? He held views that were wrong, and he became a better person later in life. But this kind of moral progress is impossible on relativism.

Fourth, relativism leads to nihilism. Nihilism comes from the Latin *nihil*, meaning "nothing." You may have seen this word in the theological phrase creation *ex nihilo*. Nihilism is the idea that there are no such things as moral values, and our moral choices have no objective meaning. Relativism leads to nihilism in that if the good is only determined by the individual or group, then one person's or group's "good" is another person's or group's "evil." This means every moral action is both good and evil and neither good nor evil at the same time. This makes the moral actor completely alone, and their choices are without any ultimate meaning or purpose.[4]

Finally, relativism faces an empirical failure. Contrary to the progressive spirit of the times that would affirm otherwise, cultures have agreed on a number of common moral principles, including respecting elders, caring for children, honoring one's word, and being merciful to the weak.[5] Some might protest the fact that the Nazis or some other group has violated these laws; however, our moral revulsion at those who break these common moral principles underscores the fact that the moral standards are real, and groups who have betrayed these principles are morally wrong. So much for relativism. Those who claim that *what is believed to be moral* may differ from person to person or culture to culture are perhaps not altogether mistaken, but those who claim that

---

4. For more on how relativism entails nihilism, see James W. Sire, *The Universe Next Door: A Basic Worldview Catalog*, 6th ed. (Downers Grove, IL: IVP Academic, 2009), 107–13.

5. See C. S. Lewis, *The Abolition of Man (or Reflections on Education with Special Reference to the Teaching of English in the Upper Forms of Schools)* (New York, HarperOne, 1944), 83–101.

what is moral differs from person to person or culture to culture have many problems with which to contend.

However, relativism is not the only potential challenge to the moral argument. Indeed, some atheists simply reject the existence of objective moral values and duties, claiming that the nonexistence of God rules out the objective meaning of moral action in principle. What is ironic about this is that these atheists are essentially in agreement with theists in affirming premise 1 from above: If God did not exist, objective moral values and duties would not exist. However, God's nonexistence entails that there simply are no moral values and duties. Michael Ruse talks about it this way: "God is dead, so why should I be good? The answer is that there are no grounds whatsoever for being good. There is no celestial headmaster who is going to give you six (or six billion, billion, billion) of the best if you are bad. Morality is flimflam."[6] However, for Ruse, that is not the end of the story. Ruse offers a kind of Darwinian pragmatism in place of moral obligation. Humans thrive in our environment when we cooperate and act morally toward one another. "We succeed, each of us individually, because we are part of a greater whole and that whole is a lot better at surviving and reproducing than most other animals."[7] However, this invitation to self-centered prudence could easily meet its match in Ted Bundy. Bundy, the man who raped and murdered dozens of women and who recorded his conversations with many of them, agreed that the death of God (plus the Darwinian paradigm) entailed that there were no such things as objective morals. He reasoned,

> Why is it more wrong to kill a human animal than any other ani-
> mal, a pig or a sheep or a steer? Is your life worth more to you
> than a hog's life to a hog? Why should I be willing to sacrifice my
> pleasure more for the one than for the other? Surely, you would
> not, in this age of scientific enlightenment, declare that God or

6. Michael Ruse, "God Is Dead. Long Live Morality," *Guardian*, March 15, 2010, https://www.theguardian.com/commentisfree/belief/2010/mar/15/morality-evolution-philosophy. See also Ruse, *The Darwinian Paradigm: Essays on Its History, Philosophy, and Religious Implications* (London: Routledge, 1989). The phrase "six of the best" refers to corporal punishment in a British boys' school environment.

7. Ruse, "God Is Dead."

nature has marked some pleasures as "moral" or "good" and others as "immoral" or bad"?[8]

This is the embodiment of moral nihilism. Bundy rightly reasoned that Darwinism entails that each creature fight for its own pleasure, regardless of the consequences of one's actions on others. Yet Bundy also highlighted the fact that the denial of objective moral values and duties is simply unlivable. This means that Ruse (and of course, Bundy) may claim all day that the universe is godless and without objective moral significance, but this leads to the absurd conclusion that the Ted Bundys of the world deserve the same moral evaluation as the Mother Teresas of the world. Not only does this beg the question against the existence of God (which the first half of this book is carefully demonstrating), but it is unlivable.

One more worldview that denies objective moral values and duties deserves our attention: the Eastern pantheistic worldview embodied in religious expressions like Advaita Vedanta Hinduism and Mahayana Buddhism. These perspectives claim that morality is *maya*, an illusion, and part of enlightenment is to realize that objective reality is beyond the categories of good and evil. The Hindu theologian Śankara taught that ultimate reality is without qualities or attributes, so even though we speak about Brahman as good, we are really only interacting with a human projection about Brahman in our lower-level version of reality. When we look at reality as it really is, it is beyond good and evil. This is strange, however, because it requires believing that God both exists and that God is beyond description. But what is the statement "God exists" but a description about something that has the property of existence? This perspective is self-refuting because it uses descriptions about God to claim that God is beyond description.[9] Mahayana Buddhism similarly asserts that while virtues like charity are important at lower levels of the Eightfold Path, enlightenment reveals that "true knowledge *is* higher

---

8. Ted Bundy, quoted in *Moral Philosophy*, ed. Louis P. Pojman, 3rd ed. (Cambridge, MA: Hackett, 2008), 41. For more on this, see Douglas Groothuis, *Philosophy in Seven Sentences: A Small Introduction to a Vast Topic* (Downers Grove, IL: IVP Academic, 2016), 27–29.

9. Timothy C. Tennent, *Christianity at the Religious Roundtable: Evangelicalism in Conversation with Hinduism, Buddhism, and Islam* (Grand Rapids: Baker Academic, 2002), 46–55.

than ethical virtues."[10] This distinction effectively erases Buddhism's emphasis on the moral life and is subject to the critique that Mahayana Buddhism strangely affirms that ethics are both important and unimportant. When all is said and done, we know that our ethical intuitions about the reality of good and evil and the significance of the moral life are correct. Any attempt to deny the existence of the objective moral universe fails. With these things said, it is time to turn our attention to the moral argument itself.

C. S. LEWIS'S MORAL ARGUMENT

Oxford and Cambridge literature scholar Clive Staples Lewis (1898–1963) has awakened the moral and theological imaginations of countless children through The Chronicles of Narnia. Yet for many of us, he awakened us to the importance of the intellectual life for the Christian. It was through reading Lewis's *Mere Christianity* that I (Ike) discovered my calling to think well for Christ, and I was particularly emboldened by its appeal to reason in explaining the existence of God. Lewis's work on the moral argument actually first begins in his *The Abolition of Man*, a book seemingly written to counter some trends in the teaching of English literature in the British version of high schools. However, Lewis's goals were much greater, for he used a dispute about literature instruction to make a much larger point about the existence of objective moral value. Lewis began by pointing out that there are many who think that when someone makes an evaluation (and he particularly has in mind a *moral* evaluation), what they say tells you more about them than about whatever they are evaluating. For example, if you saw an older man say something like, "Children just don't have any respect," you might reasonably conclude that the older man himself lacks respect for children and perhaps is unable to understand the children. This point of view, however, is dangerous in that it reduces moral judgments to being statements that are merely "about the emotional state of the speaker."[11]

---

10. Tennent, 135. Emphasis in original.
11. Lewis, *Abolition of Man*, 4.

This anti-objectivism makes it impossible to evaluate any moral action or attitude. This perspective, to Lewis, was antihuman, for part of the moral life is giving our best judgments back to the world in our moral evaluations. This means dramatically struggling against evil and courageously contending for the good. But if there are no moral values and instead only emotive statements, we are all just "Men without Chests."[12] It is as if one loses one's soul. Lewis argued that the key to understanding the moral universe is a justified belief in the *Tao*, a word that Lewis used to stand for the idea of objective moral value. When one rejects the *Tao*, one is actually rejecting what it means to be human. Ironically, rejecting the *Tao* is like trying to control the moral universe by claiming that the individual has mastery over the universe, yet one is conquered by nature instead. If there are no duties or laws, then all that is left is one's subhuman instincts and baseless sentimentality, and this is what Lewis called "the abolition of man."[13] Lewis ended the book with an empirical argument for the *Tao* (again, the doctrine of objective moral value). He argued that moral principles such as duties like caring for children, honoring the elderly, and keeping one's promises are enshrined in moral teaching across the world's cultures. Consider the principle of honest financial gain:

"I have not stolen." (ancient Egyptian)
"Thou shalt not steal." (ancient Jewish; Ex. 20:15)
"Choose loss rather than shameful gains." (Greek)[14]

These three moral statements, albeit from different sources, cultures, and times, all speak of a similar principle of only pursuing honest financial gain. Lewis's argument is appealing to empirical evidence to claim that while there may be some cultural differences with respect to many moral positions, there is significant convergence on a number of key moral issues. It is false that what is believed to be moral differs from culture to culture. Indeed, many cultures have always agreed on some common moral principles. So there are such things as objective moral values.

---

12. Lewis, 25.
13. Lewis, 64.
14. Lewis, 93. Lewis is quoting the ancient Greek wise man Chilon.

Lewis picked up the argument in *Mere Christianity* but pushed further toward its logical conclusion.

> Men have differed as regards what people you ought to be unselfish to—whether it was only your own family, or your fellow countrymen, or every one. But they have always agreed that you ought not to put yourself first. Selfishness has never been admired. Men have differed as to whether you should have one wife or four. But they have always agreed that you must not simply have any woman you liked.[15]

Lewis called this evidence for "the law of nature." It is unimportant that people often do not abide by the law; instead, we know the law exists because we cannot shake its judgments in our psyches. We understand the law and rightly feel convicted when we break it. According to Lewis, there are only two explanations for the law's existence. The first is a materialist picture of the universe that claims that human beings along with everything else are the way they are by chance and material forces. But chance and matter cannot account for the law of nature. But there is a second explanation, the religious view. On the religious view, the law is revealed by Someone from beyond the universe to human hearts in the universe, urging us to do good and to avoid breaking the law. This law is delivered from an external source via an internal witness to human beings, a kind of "Director" or "Guide."[16] Here is a logical formulation of what Lewis was arguing:

1. If there is a universal moral law, there is a moral lawgiver.
2. If there is a moral lawgiver, it must be something beyond the universe.
3. There is a universal moral law.
4. Therefore, there is a moral lawgiver.
5. Therefore, the moral lawgiver is beyond the universe.[17]

---

15. C. S. Lewis, *Mere Christianity* (San Francisco, HarperSanFrancisco, 1952), 6.
16. Lewis, *Mere Christianity*, 23–25.
17. For a more detailed explanation of the development of Lewis's argument, see Andrew I. Shepardson, *Who's Afraid of the Unmoved Mover?* (Eugene, OR: Pickwick, 2019), 27–32.

Statement 1 is true because materialism does not have an account of why there are moral laws. Statement 2 is necessary because the only way for laws to be universal would be for them to have a source that transcends our cultures and contexts. Moreover, the source of moral law would have to be able to put its stamp internally onto all hearts, and we know of nothing inside this universe that could have that power. Statement 3 is from the arguments made in *The Abolition of Man* on the *Tao*. Statement 4 follows from statements 3 and 1. Statement 5 follows from statements 2 and 4. This argument is in a proper logical form, and Lewis has given a highly plausible defense for the premises. Therefore, we are justified in believing it to show that God exists. What this argument has going for it is its ability to connect with the human experience and our desire for an imaginative account for why we are the way we are. Lewis's scholarly ability to explain the existence of common moral principles and his artful demonstration of the "Director" or "Guide" within our hearts connects on a deeply personal level. For this reason, the argument has had staying power among apologists, capturing our minds along with our hearts in a way that defends the truth of God's existence to people who can already sense the internal witness of God's moral law inside their own consciences. As Christians, we rightly understand the nature of the source of the moral law: "Indeed, when Gentiles, who do not have the law, do by nature things required by the law, they are a law for themselves, even though they do not have the law. They show that the requirements of the law are written on their hearts, their consciences also bearing witness, and their thoughts sometimes accusing them and at other times even defending them" (Rom. 2:14–15). However, this is not the only form of the argument. Next we will consider J. P. Moreland and William Lane Craig's simpler version of the moral argument.

MORELAND AND CRAIG'S VERSION

To those of us who care about defending and commending the faith with evangelistic passion and intellectual care, J. P. Moreland and William Lane Craig have set incredible examples for us to follow. Their contribution to the moral argument is helpful for its precision and simplicity.

Precision and simplicity are values that all apologists should care about. If you, the reader of this book, have a discussion with someone you care about who does not yet know the Lord, you may want to share one of the arguments from this book to show your partner in dialogue that God exists. But after you have had a discussion, wouldn't it be that much better if your partner in dialogue could remember the wisdom you shared? Wouldn't it be helpful for your philosophical argument to be not just logically sound but also memorable? Moreland and Craig's argument is exemplary in this regard. Take a look:

1. If God did not exist, objective moral values and duties would not exist.
2. Objective moral values and duties do exist.
3. Therefore, God exists.[18]

This is a *modus tollens* argument, which means "in the method of denying," because premise 2 denies the consequent of premise 1.[19] Since it is false that there are no objective moral values and duties (that is, moral values and duties do indeed exist), then that entails that God exists. If 1 and 2 are correct, or at least more plausible than their denials, then 3 follows necessarily. This kind of logical argument is known as a demonstration, for it shows, or demonstrates, that the conclusion is true (and not just likely to be true).

The appeal of this argument is that many atheists, especially those vehemently opposed to Christianity, agree with statement 1. Remember Michael Ruse saying, "God is dead, so why should I be good? The answer is that there are no grounds whatsoever for being good"?[20] Without divine authority, there is no reason for any person to claim that certain moral judgments like "compassion is good" or "murder is evil" are about anything other than an individual's likes and dislikes. While there may be evolutionary accounts for why humans behave certain ways, these accounts cannot tell us how the world ought to be. To have the kind of

---

18. Moreland and Craig, *Philosophical Foundations*, 505.
19. The first premise has an antecedent "If God did not exist," and a consequent "objective moral values and duties would not exist." A *modus tollens* argument denies the consequent.
20. Ruse, "God Is Dead." See also Ruse, *Darwinian Paradigm*.

universal moral authority that is required to claim that compassion is good, there must be a universal moral lawgiver. If there is none, then there are no moral values. Premise 1 has a high degree of plausibility. Premise 2 simply relies on the near universal human desire for and affirmation of the existence of objective moral values and duties. It is self-evident to most people that good and evil exist. If you wish to claim that both torturing someone and nursing someone back to health are morally neutral, you will have many detractors. Even in a relativistic cultural context like North America where "To each his or her own" seems to be the rule of the day, most people would add the caveat "To each his or her own, as long as you're not hurting someone else." When one modifies the phrase this way, one may still be a relativist about many things, but one is effectively a moral absolutist about at least one big thing. This means that even this type of relativist agrees that there is at least one objective moral duty, and that is all that is needed for the argument to be successful. Regardless, when pressed, most people would still admit that it is always wrong to torture an innocent person, rape is never justifiable, courage and kindness are always good, and extreme greed is always bad.

The conclusion, then, obtains necessarily. There is a God who is the source of objective moral values and duties. This conclusion corroborates certain doctrines about the existence of a holy, good, and just God, whose will and nature are the source of the various goods that form the moral universe. The psalmist said, "The LORD is upright; he is my Rock, and there is no wickedness in him" (Ps. 92:15). Consider the words of God through the prophet Micah, "He has shown you, O mortal, what is good. And what does the LORD require of you? To act justly and to love mercy and to walk humbly with your God" (Mic. 6:8). Jesus said, "Why do you call me good? . . . No one is good—except God alone" (Mark 10:18). God is both the source of goodness itself and of our knowledge of the good.

OBJECTIONS TO MORELAND AND CRAIG'S ARGUMENT

Of course, the existence of God remains a contentious issue, and there are many who do not agree with the conclusion of the moral argument.

The argument's form is a simple *modus tollens*, and there is no issue with the form. Therefore, the argument's detractors take issue with the premises. We already discussed those who object to all moral arguments by rejecting Moreland and Craig's premise (2) by claiming that there are no objective moral values and duties. We have shown that the one who rejects (2) does so at the great risk of affirming a way of life that is unlivable. To live without belief in objective moral values or duties is absurd, and it leads to nihilism. In that world, indeed, living holds no greater value than dying, and most (rightly) will not concede this. However, there are some who reject premise (1) of Moreland and Craig's argument, claiming that there are objective moral values and duties, but we do not need God as a source or explanatory entity behind these values and duties. The two main types of atheistic moral absolutism are these:

1. reductive naturalistic moral realism and
2. godless normative moral realism.

We will explain these positions and terms and show that these two pathways, made famous by leading atheist scholars, are bankrupt in explaining how moral values and duties are objective.

Reductive Naturalistic Moral Realism

Paul Kurtz and Sam Harris are proponents of the first way in which some atheists reject premise 1: If God did not exist, objective moral values and duties would not exist. Their position can be summed up under the heading reductive naturalistic moral realism. Moral realism is a way of saying that there are objective moral values and duties. This is, of course, the position of traditional theism and of Christian theism in particular. However, Kurtz and Harris believe in a moral realism that is reductively naturalistic. This phrase means that naturalistic and *only* naturalistic explanations are necessary to describe and justify moral realism. In addition, the kinds of causes that impel human behaviors can only be explained on naturalistic grounds. In particular, human choices are caused by their biochemistry and material environment. Naturalism rejects the existence of God (indeed the existence of any gods or supernatural beings), and so Kurtz and Harris think that we can understand objective moral values and duties without any reference to God. Kurtz prefers to refer to objective moral principles such as the duty to be kind or to care for one's family. These emerge through human evolution and take shape as cultures and societies emerge. Therefore, "the commitment to moral principles becomes so significant in human civilization that they begin to take on a special kind of objective reality and are an integral part of the bio- and socio-cultural spheres. They have natural and objective foundations."[21] Kurtz uses the phrase "common moral decencies" to refer to these principles, and they are formed by evolutionary processes: "Be kind and considerate to the members of your tribe; be honest and truthful; do not maim, injure or harm needlessly; be sincere and keep your promises, etc."[22] Human awareness of these principles and adherence to them emerges over time through the development of more advanced societies and civilizations. However, these moral principles are indeed common to humanity despite the fact that cultures are different. "Given the fact that individuals have common biological needs and face similar problems of survival common norms have developed."[23]

Harris's view is similar, though also being influenced by neuroscience. For Harris, God is not necessary to explain any of our human concerns about the moral life. Instead, "meaning values, morality, and the good life must relate to facts about the well-being of conscious creatures."[24] We discover what the well-being of conscious creatures is by using a rational, neuroscientific approach to discovering the truth. Harris himself calls this a kind of "moral realism," a commitment to objective existence of moral facts, albeit ones derived from common experiences among conscious creatures who suffer and thrive in various ways.[25] Indeed, the things that cause suffering and thriving can be discovered by neuroscience, and they form a moral landscape with peaks of well-being and valleys of suffering. The baseline evil for Harris is whatever would cause "the worst possible misery for everyone."[26]

---

21. Paul Kurtz, *Forbidden Fruit: The Ethics of Humanism* (New York: Prometheus, 1988), 65.
22. Kurtz, 67–68.
23. Kurtz, 67.
24. Sam Harris, *The Moral Landscape: How Science Can Determine Human Values* (New York: Free Press, 2010), 6.
25. Harris, 62.
26. Harris, 201.

That starting point is the lowest valley and the evil that humans are duty-bound to avoid.

The problem with these views, which we have called reductive naturalistic moral realism, is that they both trade on objective moral values existing without an objective moral evaluator. Of course, it is obvious that societies thrive when we avoid needless injury or harm, and people suffer less when we seek to avoid "the worst possible misery for everyone"; however, there is a big difference between making the claim that some creatures suffer and the claim that suffering is bad. Of course, we agree that suffering is bad, but our thinking that it is bad cannot make it bad. This is because badness is a value that is different from suffering. Suffering is a descriptive concept, and badness is a value concept in the same way that "paints" is descriptive and "paints skillfully" is evaluative.

To have a conversation, then, about objective moral values requires that we have something more than neuroscientists who describe things. Instead, objective moral values require an objective moral evaluator. This is what some scholars call the "is versus ought fallacy." Science uses descriptions of the world to convey its findings, such as, "Upon an act of generosity, this neuron fired in such and such a fashion." However, ethics makes injunctions such as, "One ought to be generous." The former describes the world while the latter asserts the existence of, in this case, a moral duty. Values such as the goodness of generosity fall within the domain of ethics and not science as well.

Philosopher T. Edward Damer explains that scientific facts are not morals: "It is not logically appropriate to move in an argument from a factual claim, a so-called 'is,' to a moral claim, a so-called 'ought.' To do so is to commit the 'is-ought fallacy.' The only legitimate logical moves in argumentation are from factual claims to factual claims, a feature of most arguments, or from moral claims to moral claims, the unique feature of moral arguments."[27] Science is beyond its domain of authority to make moral claims since it is only a descriptive enterprise. This fact does not deny science's importance. In fact, one might say it underscores

---

27. T. Edward Damer, *Attacking Faulty Reasoning: A Practical Guide to Fallacy-Free Arguments*, 7th ed. (Boston, Cengage Learning, 2012), 25.

science's value as a vehicle of descriptive enterprise while keeping it in its appropriate domain.

Another problem with Kurtz and Harris's view is known as the "ought implies can problem." Reductive naturalism requires that human beings are solely the result of evolutionary processes that are governed by their biology and chemistry, chance and necessity, and external causes and effects over which they have no control. Reductive naturalism entails that "we are just puppets or electro-chemical machines. And puppets do not have moral responsibilities. Machines are not moral agents."[28] Mechanistic views of evolution require that humans are solely the result of external causal constraints, yet our basic intuitions regarding moral responsibility, praise, and blame require that a moral actor could have acted otherwise.[29] Indeed, in our culture, we make the proper distinction between someone who is guilty and someone who is guilty for reasons of insanity. That is because the person who falls into the latter category had less control over their moral actions than did someone who acted with malice aforethought. If an insane person did not have control of their actions, we may incarcerate them, but we would not as easily make the moral claim that they are evil, all things being equal. Thus, we conclude that Kurtz and Harris are unable to provide a rebuttal of premise 1, "If God did not exist, objective moral values and duties would not exist," that withstands scrutiny.

Godless Normative Realism

However, Kurtz and Harris are not the only atheists who deny premise 1. In recent years, an incredibly important challenge to premise 1 has arisen in the work of DePauw University professor of philosophy Erik Wielenberg. He calls his view "godless normative realism," which is a way of saying that there are real and objective moral values and duties that do not require a divine foundation. However, instead of locating those values and duties in human nature or experience as discovered by

---

28. William Lane Craig, "First Rebuttal," in *Sam Harris v William Lane Craig Debate "Is the Foundation of Morality Natural or Supernatural?"* University of Notre Dame, April 7, 2011. Transcript available at http://www.mandm.org.nz/2011/05/transcript-sam-harris-v-william-lan e-craig-debate-"is-good-from-god".html.

29. Even a Christian compatibilist would say that moral responsibility follows someone having the ability to approve or disapprove of their own good or evil desires.

science, Wielenberg claims that moral values and duties simply exist and do not require an explanation for their existence. They are brute facts that are not reducible to material states or properties like other aspects of the world around us. In fact, Wielenberg claims that there are no good arguments to explain or justify the existence of these moral values and duties, but—and this is key for his perspective—theism does not have a better explanation for their existence. Here, we will examine godless normative realism and provide a brief critique.

Godless normative realism is the notion that moral values and duties are real things. They form part of the fabric of reality. Wielenberg says, "Consider, for instance, the state of affairs in which it is morally wrong to torture the innocent just for fun and the state of affairs in which pain is intrinsically bad (that is, bad in its own nature, or in and of itself). These states of affairs obtain not just in the actual world but in all metaphysically possible worlds."[30] He is not simply saying that people have moral motivations and behaviors, which of course, they do. Instead, he is saying that things like the wrongness of murder and the goodness of charity are abstract objects that exist. In philosophy an abstract object is distinct from a concrete object in this way: Think of any sets of things that you could form into groups of three, like three pieces of pizza or three baseballs. These are all examples of concrete objects. Now think of the concept of "three." "Three" or "threeness" can exist in many different sets of concrete objects, and the reason for this is that the abstract object "three" is a real thing. The fact that you can recognize "three" as a commonality between the sets of baseballs and pieces of pizza is evidence for the existence of "three." Now, for Christians who believe in abstract objects, "three" exists in the mind of God and is a precondition for all concrete sets of three.[31]

The Greek philosopher Plato thought that "three" existed as a

---

30. Erik J. Wielenberg, "In Defense of Non-Natural, Non-Theistic Moral Realism," in *Faith and Philosophy* 26, no. 1 (January 2009), 26.

31. The existence of abstract objects has received a great deal of attention in recent years. For an introduction to this debate, see the symposium in *Philosophia Christi*: William Lane Craig, "God and Abstract Objects," *Philosophia Christi* 17, no. 2 (2015): 269–76; J. Thomas Bridges, "A Moderate-Realist Perspective on God and Abstract Objects," *Philosophia Christi* 17, no. 2 (2015): 277–83; and Peter Van Inwagen, "Did God Create Shapes?," *Philosophia Christi* 17, no. 2 (2015): 285–90.

nonphysical but real entity in the world of the forms and was ultimately dependent for its existence on the highest form, the form of the Good. For Wielenberg, moral values and duties are similar to "three," yet he does not attempt to explain how they exist or what kinds of things they are. He claims that an explanation is not required. It simply is the case that these moral values and duties exist. They are "basic ethical facts." These facts are exemplified in concrete moral situations through something that Wielenberg calls "supervenience." When there is a concrete situation, say, of someone causing pain just for the fun of it, the moral value of "wrongness" is necessarily attached to that situation. That is, the abstract moral property of wrongness is necessarily exemplified in the concrete situation of causing pain for fun. This means that a physical situation has a nonphysical moral value attached to it. Given Wielenberg's atheism, this relationship of physical and nonphysical might seem strange, but Wielenberg claims that the supervenience relationship between the moral value and the concrete situation is simply another "brute fact" that requires no explanation.

Now, one could respond to Wielenberg by asking, "Well, do you have an account for these facts? How did they come to be? What is their foundation?" His reply?

> To ask of such facts, "where do they come from?" or "on what foundation do they rest?" is misguided in much the way that, according to many theists, it is misguided to ask of God, "where does He come from?" or "on what foundation does He rest"? The answer is the same in both cases: They come from nowhere, and nothing external to themselves grounds their existence; rather, they are fundamental features of the universe that ground other truths.[32]

Wielenberg claims that ethical facts have the same status for him as God does for theists. Ethical facts do not require an explanation for his version of atheism in the same way that God does not require an explanation for theism. This could give the impression that atheism and theism have equal standing; however, all is not equal according to

---

32. Wielenberg, "In Defense of Non-Natural, Non-Theistic Moral Realism," 26.

Wielenberg. Godless normative realism lends atheism an advantage that theism does not have: simplicity. On theism, you have God who has no foundation for God's own existence but who serves as the foundation for moral values and duties. But on godless normative realism, you have only objective moral values and duties that do not require an explanation or foundation. Think about it this way:

Traditional Theism

Foundational: God → (is the foundation of) → Objective Morality

Wielenberg's Atheism

Foundational: Objective Morality

The whole system is simpler, and this is a philosophical virtue known as Occam's razor, in which, all things being equal, one should prefer simpler explanations over more complicated ones.

Now, the question for the Christian apologist should be, "Are all things equal here?" Is Wielenberg's godless normative realism to be preferred over theistic ethics for its relative simplicity? We think not, for Wielenberg's version of objective morality is lacking in some key ways. First, Wielenberg admits that he has no rationally compelling arguments for the existence of objective moral values and duties.[33] In this way, Christianity has a key advantage; objective moral values and duties are grounded in the character of the divine Lawgiver. Human moral intuitions are not accidental or arbitrary but result from the one who inscribed the moral law on human hearts (Rom. 2:14–15). Second, even if one might concede that Wielenberg has an account of moral values (that is, they simply exist), moral duties are different things altogether. Duties imply the existence of one to whom a moral actor is duty-bound. If moral properties simply exist, it is strange to think that someone might be morally bound to abide by a duty to a property. In this way, Wielenberg falls prey to the same "is versus ought" fallacy to which Harris and Kurtz fall prey. Perhaps we grant

---

33. Erik J. Wielenberg, *Robust Ethics: The Metaphysics and Epistemology of Godless Normative Realism* (Oxford: Oxford University Press, 2014), 4, 36–38.

that moral values exist; that does not entail that we have any obligations (duties) to do anything.[34] The Christian picture is that any objective obligations have an objective source in God. That is, Wielenberg's solution may be simple, but it does not actually account for moral duties. So it does not benefit from an appeal to Occam's razor. Third, the idea of supervenience is exceedingly strange. As Craig argues, "How is it that these abstract objects like *goodness* or *badness* come to be attached to physical situations? . . . How can a physical object somehow reach out and causally connect to a transcendent, causally isolated, abstract object?"[35] Christianity requires no strange causal connections between nonphysical and physical things.

Finally, Wielenberg's naturalism undermines his account of moral knowledge. If human beings are simply the result of evolutionary processes, it is hard to see how human beings could have knowledge of anything at all. This is part of the evolutionary argument against naturalism.[36] Wielenberg, like many naturalists, claims that humans are descended from lower forms of animal life. Now think about the reliability of the cognitive capacities of lower animals. They may be well adapted to their environments in some ways, but that does not entail that their thoughts aim at truth. Evolution selects for survival, and evolutionary processes are not aimed at truth. This entails that humans, though seemingly well adapted for survival, have no evolutionary advantage over lower animals with respect to the truth of their thoughts, and this means that if naturalism is true, then we should be deeply skeptical about all of our theories. So, if naturalism is true, we should also be deeply skeptical of Wielenberg's account of moral knowledge.[37] The moral argument, then, stands vindicated, due to the failure of these alternative accounts of objective morality.

---

34. Wielenberg grounds moral duties in having decisive reasons to act. However, this is incompatible with so-called supererogatory acts, such as sacrificing one's life to save another. In this case, one may have a duty to give up one's life that is in conflict with reasons related to preserving one's own life. See William Lane Craig, "Opening Speech," in *A Debate on God and Morality: What Is the Best Account of Objective Moral Values and Duties?*, ed. Adam Lloyd Johnson (New York: Routledge, 2021), 35.

35. Craig, "Opening Speech," 34.

36. See Alvin Plantinga, *Where the Conflict Really Lies: Science, Religion, and Naturalism* (Oxford: Oxford University Press, 2011), ch. 10.

37. Craig makes a similar argument in "Opening Speech," 36–38.

THE PROBLEM OF EVIL

There is more to say on the matter, however, because even if theism gives the best account for objective moral values and duties, there is a key challenge that Christian apologetics must consider to its view of God and the good. The problem of evil is the idea that there is a deep conflict between the idea of an all-powerful and all-good God and the human experience with suffering and evil. We have found this to be the most important objection to Christian faith for many around us. Human misery and suffering are found everywhere. This section will briefly address the existential, logical, and evidentiary problems of evil, and it will show that the existence of evil, long held to be a major challenge to Christian belief, is actually evidence of a moral universe over which God is the divine Lawgiver. A brief distinction is relevant here. When we speak of "the problem of evil," there are various ways in which the challenge to Christian faith could be construed. Some might say that the existence of any amount of evil is incompatible with the existence of God. This is the *logical problem of evil*. Others would say that it is not that evil *per se* is incompatible with a theistic worldview; rather, it is the amount and the intensity of evils in this world that are at odds with the existence of God. This is the *evidentiary problem of evil*. Yet likely for many that you will meet in your life, the problem is more personal, emotional, and existential. That is, many people feel as if the idea of God has let them down in the face of their personal experiences with evil. This is the *existential problem of evil*.

The Existential Problem of Evil

For many people, their experiences of their own suffering or their knowledge of how others have suffered evil makes the idea of God seem strange, offensive, or even obsolete. When Ike's wife, Kelsey, had a miscarriage early in their marriage, they felt alienated from God and numb toward his presence in their lives. When Doug's first wife, Becky, suffered a long illness that led to her death, there were times when Doug hated God and told him so.[38] This problem is unlike philosophical

---

38. See Douglas Groothuis, *Walking through Twilight: A Wife's Illness—A Philosopher's Lament* (Downers Grove, IL: InterVarsity, 2017).

objections to Christianity in that it does not tend to make claims that require analysis and rebuttal. Sure, in the middle of one's suffering, one may accuse God or make negative claims about Christianity, but the problem is much deeper. As apologists, we must see when someone's suffering or awareness of evil runs in the direction of the existential problem of evil, and provide a gentler and tenderer response. For both of us, our dogs were a key part of how we received God's grace in the middle of our suffering. For many people, considering Christ's rejection by his friends and his suffering on the cross helps them to receive God's touch in their lives. For those of us who care about our suffering friends, our silent and physical presence, charged by the Holy Spirit's indwelling presence, is often the proper response to someone's existential struggle with evil. Prayers of praise, thanksgiving, and lament are often important, and our humble acknowledgment of the sovereignty of God, the goodness of God's plans, and our inability to "explain it all" are helpful as well.

The Logical Problem of Evil

Yet many claim that God's existence is incompatible with the existence of evil. After all, classical theism, and Christianity in particular, claims that God is all-good, or "omnibenevolent." If God created a world in which evil exists, then either God is not all-good (which would undermine religious devotion and the point of the moral argument) or God does not actually exist at all. David Hume said it this way: "Is he willing to prevent evil, but not able? then he is impotent. Is he able, but not willing? then he is malevolent. Is he both able and willing? whence then is evil?"[39] First, it is important to note that Christian philosophers and theologians have typically been careful in how they articulate God's responsibility for evil. For example, Augustine claimed that evil is real, but that God did not create it. That is, evil is real, but it is not a thing that God made. Instead, evil is the result of some of the goodness of God's creation being removed, altered, or corrupted. Think about how eating is good but overeating is gluttony. Sex is good, but sex without

---

39. David Hume, "Dialogues concerning Natural Religion," in *Dialogues and Natural History of Religion*, ed. J. C. A. Gaskin (Oxford: Oxford University Press, 1993), 100. Hume's problem of evil was initially a skeptical detraction from the design argument; however, with the conspicuousness of evil in modernity, the problem of evil has come to be expressed as either a way of logically disproving the existence of God or of existentially asserting God's irrelevance.

commitment in marriage is harmful. Evil happens when the original goodness of things gets twisted or corrupted by humanity. But the real question is: Is God's existence logically incompatible with the existence of evil? It does not seem so. For all that God would need to have to justify the existence of evil are reasons that are good enough for allowing the existence of evil. What might these kinds of reasons be? Well, if God wanted humanity to have free will either to choose to love him or reject him, that would be a good reason. After all, love is not really possible without authentic choice, so God could have known that a world with authentic love and some evil would have been much better than a world without the freedom to love. In addition, God could have known that some struggle and opposition help to make people be more virtuous.

The careful reader may notice that we are not, at this point, claiming that these are reasons that God would have for allowing evil. We are simply saying that it is logically possible that God has reasons like these for allowing evil. If it is possible that God has reasons like these, then the logical problem of evil *necessarily* fails. Remember, the logical problem of evil claims that God's existence and the existence of evil are logically incompatible. A response to this problem needs only to provide a logical account for why God might allow the existence of evil. That said, many atheists have given up the logical problem of evil in favor of the evidentiary problem of evil.

The Evidentiary Problem of Evil

Among many atheists, one may hear a kind of astonishment and offense at the idea of God in light of egregious evils like the Holocaust. This seems to be at the heart of what some atheists say when they charge that a good God could not possibly exist given the amount and intensity of evil in the world. The British atheist Stephen Fry was asked what he would say to God if he was confronted by God. He said, "I'd say, Bone cancer in children? What's that about? How dare you? How dare you create a world in which there is such misery that is not our fault? It's not right, it's utterly, utterly evil."[40] The anger that one may perceive in Fry's remarks does not seem to be actually directed at God, for Fry is an atheist.

---

40. Jack Linshi, "Here's What Stephen Fry Would Say to God," *Time*, February 1, 2015, https://time.com/3691225/stephen-fry-god.

Instead, the anger seems to be directed at the very idea of God and perhaps those who believe in God. How could someone believe in God in a world where children seem to suffer needlessly, where nuclear bombs have been detonated, and where racism, rape, and torture are common? Indeed, it is one thing to say that God may have allowed some evils to exist for the attainment of greater goods, but it is much harder to see why God has allowed so much evil to exist. In response, we must address the notion of greater goods, the free will defense, the possibility for knowing God's reasons, and the cross and the resurrection of Jesus Christ.

First, we know that there are some good consequences that only result in a world in which evil exists. Consider the virtues of people like Major Richard D. Winters of the US 101st Airborne who served in the European theater in World War II.[41] Winters bravely led and inspired the men under his command with moral virtue and skill that saved many lives and contributed greatly to the war effort. The story of his leadership inspires many today, long after the events of World War II. Had the war not happened, it is unlikely that Winters's leadership would be known or appreciated, and the world would likely lack a key exemplar of courage, virtue, and self-sacrifice. That is, great goods have resulted from Winters fighting in the war. Now, no one would rightly claim that the good resulting from Winters's life and leadership would justify the whole war and all the lives lost. Winters himself surely would have wished to remain obscure and unknown if, by so doing, he could have saved the life of even one of his men. However, it is possible to see how great good can come out of tremendous evil. More broadly, this is the case with the virtues of courage, temperance, peacemaking, self-sacrifice, and patience. These virtues only obtain in a world where evil is a reality. It seems possible that God wants humanity to develop important virtues, and to that end, God may allow the existence of evil for a time.

Second, as we alluded to above, our choices figure greatly in the existence of evil. It would be wrong to say that God causes the evils that plague the human experience. As James said, "When tempted, no one should say, 'God is tempting me.' For God cannot be tempted by evil,

---

41. His story is told in various places but made most famous by Stephen A. Ambrose, *Band of Brothers: E Company, 501st Regiment, 101st Airborne from Normandy to Hitler's Eagle's Nest* (New York: Simon & Schuster, 2001) and in the HBO miniseries *Band of Brothers*.

nor does he tempt anyone; but each person is tempted when they are dragged away by their own evil desire and enticed. Then, after desire has conceived, it gives birth to sin; and sin, when it is full-grown, gives birth to death" (James 1:13–15). The free-will defense claims that the existence of free will may be one of God's reasons for allowing the existence of evil. If God's goals in making a universe are tied to the personal responses of some of God's creatures, then it seems that God may have desired to allow for the possibility of evil for a time. Consider the nature of love. Love requires a lover and a beloved, and the best kinds of love involve reciprocity between lover and beloved. However, reciprocal love could not exist without both the lover being able to choose to love the beloved and vice versa. There is no such thing as forced love. Yet had God created humanity without the powers involved in the exercise of free will, including the power to possibly reject love in favor of selfishness and all of the evil tied to selfishness, genuine love would not be possible. Perhaps God could still be the Lover and humanity the beloved, but the love would not be reciprocal. In fact, this power to choose (the power of free will) is key to the existence of genuine moral goodness in the world. Humans are at their best when they choose love in spite of themselves and regardless of the consequences, and it is easy to see why God might allow evil to make room for the possibility of the free will exercising itself in love.

One might still object that, though one can see why God would have allowed some evil for greater goods and for the sake of free will (and the goods that accompany it), it is hard to see why God would allow as much evil as God has, in fact, allowed. Again the evidentiary problem of evil trades on the amount and intensity of evil in our actual world. This is where we should ask if we are justified in thinking that we could have access to all of God's reasons for allowing the amount of evil God has allowed. Daniel Howard-Snyder thinks not. He considers a case where a person opens the refrigerator and rummages around, looking for the milk carton. After a few moments of failing to see a milk carton, the person is justified in saying, "We're out of milk."[42] In another case, a person is standing at the kitchen window, peering out at the garden one hundred

---

42. This thought experiment comes from William Rowe, "The Evidential Argument from Evil: A Second Look," in *The Evidential Argument from Evil*, ed. Daniel Howard-Snyder (Bloomington, IN: Indiana University Press, 1996).

feet away to see if he can spot any garden slugs. In that case, the person is not justified in saying, "There aren't any slugs." According to Howard-Snyder, human cognitive access to God's reasons is probably much more like the latter case than the former. In fact, given human cognitive limits compared to an all-knowing and infinite God, we have good reasons "to doubt whether it is highly likely that we would see a reason that would justify God in permitting so much evil if there were a reason."[43] This is not to cop out and cry "mystery," but it does situate the discussion of human knowledge about God's mind and suggest that we may not know comprehensively why God would allow so much suffering.

Does this exhaust how to address the problem of evil? Of course not, for Christian faith has a vital contribution to the discussion of the amount and intensity of evil that addresses the heart of the issue. In the person and work of Jesus Christ, we see God's plan to defeat and eliminate evil. Jesus committed no evil acts and yet lived as an oppressed minority under the Romans, endured religious persecution by his own people, and suffered and died to forgive the evil of all who would receive him. Through his death, he defeated the powers of evil; he "disarmed the powers and authorities, he made a public spectacle of them, triumphing over them by the cross" (Col. 2:15). And he rose from the dead to show us that evil does not have the last word in the human story. His resurrection is proof that the redemption of humanity and the elimination of evil is possible. Since he claimed that we would know that he is God through his rising from the dead (see Matt. 16:13–28), we can know that his further claim that he will eliminate evil will come to pass. As it is written in the book of Revelation:

> And I heard a loud voice from the throne saying, "Look! God's dwelling place is now among the people, and he will dwell with them. They will be his people, and God himself will be with them and be their God. 'He will wipe every tear from their eyes. There will be no more death' or mourning or crying or pain, for the old order of things has passed away."

---

43. Daniel Howard-Snyder, "God, Evil, and Suffering," in *Reason for the Hope Within*, ed. Michael J. Murray (Grand Rapids: Eerdmans, 1996), 138.

He who was seated on the throne said, "I am making everything new!" (Rev. 21:3–5)

Viewed from this perspective, there will be an eternity to come without
evil, and this means that the evils that we experience in this present
age, though egregious and lamentable, will be properly contextualized
in God's ultimate victory in the age to come. None of this is to belittle
people's experience of evil, but it does situate our experiences in the
eternity of bliss to come.

The Argument for the Existence of
God from the Problem of Evil

In closing this chapter, it is worth noting that an important issue
arises for Christian apologetics when addressing the problem of evil.
Anyone who raises any of the problems addressed above must concede
the reality of evil. Evil is not to be denied or dismissed. In all of these
objections, evil reveals itself as an objective moral value that requires
an objective moral evaluator. If such an evaluator does not exist, then
evil is merely an illusion or the result of the norms and customs of a
given culture. This gets serious very quickly. Consider our revulsion to
the practice of female genital mutilation. This revulsion is not simply
due to our culture or religion; it is at least partly due to the fact that a
true moral abuse has taken place when a woman is assaulted thusly. In
this way, we say that female genital mutilation is objectively evil, and
even though there are those who may try to defend the practice, we
correctly say that they are wrong to do so. That is, it is factually incorrect
to say that female genital mutilation may be permissible under certain
circumstances. The practice is evil. Here is how this forms a new kind
of moral argument.

1. For an action to always be evil, there must be an absolute moral
   lawgiver: God. (If there is not an absolute moral lawgiver, then
   female genital mutilation may be permissible.)
2. Some actions are always evil. (Female genital mutilation is
   always evil.)
3. Therefore, there is an absolute moral lawgiver: God.

Just as importantly, we have identified at least one objective moral value (female genital mutilation is wrong) and at least one objective moral duty (one ought not to practice female genital mutilation). Here is how this fits into Moreland and Craig's moral argument:

1. If God did not exist, objective moral values and duties would not exist.
2. Objective moral values and duties do exist.
   (1) Female genital mutilation is wrong.
   (2) One ought not to practice female genital mutilation.
3. Therefore, God exists.

So you see, far from evil being a defeater for the idea of God's existence; it is actually evidence of the Lawgiver, the good God who condemns evil and calls us to reach out for the righteous Judge. "Amen. Come, Lord Jesus" (Rev. 22:20).

STUDY QUESTIONS

1. What is the basic two-stage approach to the moral argument?
2. What are the best arguments against relativism, and why must relativism be defeated for the moral argument to work?
3. How do you respond to the question "But what makes God good"?

SUGGESTED READING

Ambrose, Stephen A. *Band of Brothers: E Company, 501st Regiment, 101st Airborne from Normandy to Hitler's Eagle's Nest.* New York: Simon & Schuster, 2001.

Bridges, J. Thomas. "A Moderate-Realist Perspective on God and Abstract Objects," in *Philosophia Christi* 17, no. 2 (2015): 277–83.

Craig, William Lane. "God and Abstract Objects." *Philosophia Christi* 17, no. 2 (2015): 269–76.

Craig, William Lane, and Sam Harris. *Sam Harris v William Lane Craig Debate "Is the Foundation of Morality Natural or Supernatural?"* University of Notre Dame, April 7, 2011. Transcript available at http://www.mandm.org

.nz/2011/05/transcript-sam-harris-v-william-lane-craig-debate-"is-good-from
-god".html.

Craig, William Lane, and Erik Wielenberg. *A Debate on God and Morality: What Is the Best Account of Objective Moral Values and Duties?* Edited by Adam Lloyd Johnson. New York: Routledge, 2021.

Damer, T. Edward. *Attacking Faulty Reasoning: A Practical Guide to Fallacy-Free Arguments.* 7th ed. Boston: Cengage Learning, 2012.

Groothuis, Douglas. *Philosophy in Seven Sentences: A Small Introduction to a Vast Topic.* Downers Grove, IL: IVP Academic, 2016.

_____. *Walking through Twilight: A Wife's Illness—A Philosopher's Lament.* Downers Grove, IL: InterVarsity, 2017.

Harris, Sam. *The Moral Landscape: How Science Can Determine Human Values.* New York: Free Press, 2010.

Howard-Snyder, Daniel. "God, Evil, and Suffering." In *Reason for the Hope Within*, edited by Michael J. Murray. Grand Rapids: Eerdmans, 1996.

Hume, David. "Dialogues concerning Natural Religion." In *Dialogues and Natural History of Religion*, edited by J. C. A. Gaskin. Oxford: Oxford University Press, 1993.

Kurtz, Paul. *Forbidden Fruit: The Ethics of Humanism.* New York: Prometheus, 1988.

Lewis, C. S. *The Abolition of Man (or Reflections on Education with Special Reference to the Teaching of English in the Upper Forms of Schools).* New York: HarperOne, 1944.

_____. *Mere Christianity.* San Francisco: HarperSanFrancisco, 1952.

Linshi, Jack. "Here's What Stephen Fry Would Say to God." *Time*, February 1, 2015. https://time.com/3691225/stephen-fry-god.

Moreland, J. P., and William Lane Craig. *Philosophical Foundations for a Christian Worldview.* 2nd ed. Downers Grove, IL: IVP Academic, 2017.

Plantinga, Alvin. *Where the Conflict Really Lies: Science, Religion, and Naturalism.* Oxford: Oxford University Press, 2011.

Pojman, Louis P., ed. *Moral Philosophy.* 3rd ed. Cambridge, MA: Hackett, 2008.

Rowe, William. "The Evidential Argument from Evil: A Second Look." In *The Evidential Argument from Evil*, edited by Daniel Howard-Snyder. Bloomington: Indiana University Press, 1996.

Ruse, Michael. *The Darwinian Paradigm: Essays on Its History, Philosophy, and Religious Implications.* London: Routledge, 1989.

Shepardson, Andrew I. *Who's Afraid of the Unmoved Mover?* Eugene, OR: Pickwick, 2019.

Sire, James W. *The Universe Next Door: A Basic Worldview Catalog.* 6th ed. Downers Grove, IL: IVP Academic, 2020.

Tennent, Timothy C. *Christianity at the Religious Roundtable: Evangelicalism in Conversation with Hinduism, Buddhism, and Islam.* Grand Rapids: Baker Academic, 2002.

Van Inwagen, Peter. "Did God Create Shapes?" *Philosophia Christi* 17, no. 2 (2015): 285–90.

Wielenberg, Erik J. "In Defense of Non-Natural, Non-Theistic Moral Realism." *Faith and Philosophy* 26, no. 1 (January 2009).

_____. *Robust Ethics: The Metaphysics and Epistemology of Godless Normative Realism.* Oxford: Oxford University Press, 2014.

CHAPTER 7

THE ARGUMENT
FROM DESIGN

Christianity teaches that God created and designed the universe for his purposes. The argument from design claims that God's designing fingerprints are all over creation. The arrangement of the parts of the universe—what eighteenth-century English Christian apologist and philosopher William Paley called "contrivances"—reveals a mind that designed these parts to work together to achieve certain ends. King David said,

> For you created my inmost being;
>> you knit me together in my mother's womb.
> I praise you because I am fearfully and wonderfully made;
>> your works are wonderful,
>> I know that full well. (Ps. 139:13–14)

On the contrary, atheist biologist Richard Dawkins asserts, "The universe that we observe has precisely the properties we should expect if there is, at bottom, no design, no purpose, no evil, no good, nothing but pitiless indifference."[1]

This chapter will explore several aspects of design and respond to

---

1. Richard Dawkins, *River Out of Eden* (New York: Basic Books, 1994), 133.

the charge that there is too much evil and ugliness in the world for anyone to conclude that it was designed by a Mind outside the cosmos.[2] Although we need to address the ugliness and seeming indifference of nature to suffering, as Dawkins states it above, we begin with the design argument from beauty. This argument may touch people more directly and viscerally than other design arguments.

THE ARGUMENT FROM BEAUTY

Nature often astounds us with its radiant beauty. We may see a majestic cloud at sunset or sunrise, one that we know no human being shaped, and still be entranced by its beauty—so much so that we feel gratitude or awe regarding it. A fellow graduate student and I (Doug) were beholding such a sight in the early 1990s in Eugene, Oregon. He remarked, "When I see this, I feel so grateful." I asked him to identify the object of his gratitude. He was slow to respond and was not sure what to say, but we later had several significant discussions about God. One can also feel humbled and in awe of the beauty humans create, whether it be a painting, a poem, or a piece of music. For example, many—myself included—have a sense of the transcendent when listening to *A Love Supreme* by jazz saxophonist John Coltrane (1964).[3] However, we will attend only to natural beauty.

The range of beautiful objects and systems in nature is vast and variegated. We need not agree on the nature of beauty or whether a particular thing is beautiful to realize that some aspects of nature evoke a sense of wonder, awe, and thanksgiving, given their beauty. This beauty is found, not made. This beauty is beheld, not used.

One can ponder the beauty of flowers, animal bodies and sounds, sunsets, sunrises, cloud formations, nebulae, and endless other earthly and heavenly treasures. As Roger Scruton wrote, this contemplation of natural beauty

---

2. The objection that any divine designer would require another designer to explain its existence was discussed in "Philosophical Objections to Apologetics."

3. See Douglas Groothuis, "John Coltrane and the Meaning of Life." All about Jazz, January 22, 2015: https://www.allaboutjazz.com/john-coltrane-and-the-meaning-of-life-john-coltrane -by-douglas-groothuis.

fills us with wonder, and prompts us to search for meaning and value in the cosmos, so as with Blake

> To see a world in a grain of sand
> And a Heaven in a wild flower. . . .

From the earliest drawings in the Lascaux caves to the landscapes of Cézanne, the poems of Guido Gezelle and the music of Messiaen, art has searched for meaning in the natural world.[4]

The wonder of nature leads us to ponder that reality in the arts, which themselves may become items of beauty, thus doubling the beautification. Read this short section by writer and nature mystic Annie Dillard.

> I salt my breakfast eggs. All day long I feel created. I can see the blown dust on the skin on the back of my hand, the tiny trapezoids of chipped clay, moistened and breathed alive. There are some created sheep in the pasture below me, sheep set down here precisely, just touching their blue shadows hoof to hoof on the grass. Created gulls pock the air, rip great curved seams in the settled air: I greet my created meal, amazed.[5]

This argument requires that beauty be something real and objective that needs to be explained. Aesthetic relativists or subjectivists will not be impressed, but I won't assault them here.[6] Beauty is more than the firing of brain neurons. Nor can it be reduced to Darwinian mechanisms, which do not require and would not be expected to produce the kind of beauty we often find in the natural world. And Darwinism in principle has nothing to say about the beauty world outside of biology, such as geology and astronomy. The atheist has nothing but time, space, chance,

---

4. Roger Scruton, *Beauty: A Very Short Introduction*, Very Short Introductions (New York: Oxford University Press), 65, Kindle.

5. Annie Dillard, *Holy the Firm* (New York: HarperCollins e-books), 25, Kindle.

6. On the objective beauty in Douglas Groothuis, see "True Beauty," in *Truth Decay: Defending Christianity from the Challenges of Postmodernism* (Downers Grove, IL: InterVarsity, 2000). See also Scruton, *Beauty*.

and brute natural law as the ingredients of that beauty, and no one put them all together.

If we call on the principle of sufficient reason (PSR), which we defended in chapter 4, we find that beauty needs an explanation.

1. Beauty exists in nature and in some aspects of art.
2. Beauty needs a sufficient explanation, given the PSR.
3. Materialism provides no explanation for the existence of beauty. (This is because beauty is more than brain chemistry or the arrangement of material parts in the external world.)
4. Theism proposes God as the author of nature (human and nonhuman). This explains beauty as the result of a purposive and artistic agent.
5. Therefore, God exists.

We can rule out pantheism as the conclusion, since its god is impersonal and thus not an artist. We can rule out polytheism as well, since we appeal to the simplest explanation unless compelled otherwise. We cannot always decipher the meaning of the Artist's work, and his world has been corrupted by human mismanagement and worse, yet his oeuvre is on display.

DESIGN AS INTELLIGIBILITY

Some scientists prize themselves on being strictly empirical and for eschewing philosophy, which is mere armchair reasoning. Stephen Hawking, one of the greatest physicists of all time, was blunt in saying that science has replaced philosophy in answering the greatest questions, such as these:

> How can we understand the world in which we find ourselves? How does the universe behave? What is the nature of reality? Where did all this come from? Did the universe need a creator? . . .
>
> Traditionally these are questions for philosophy, but philosophy is dead. Philosophy has not kept up with modern developments in

science, particularly physics. Scientists have become the bearers of the torch of discovery in our quest for knowledge.[7]

By claiming that physics is the royal road—or only road—to knowledge, Hawking contradicted himself by giving a philosophical statement in order to refute philosophy. This is a form of scientism, an epistemological claim that science alone conveys knowledge.[8] But that claim itself is not a matter of scientific discovery, so it refutes itself as well. Further, as noted in this book, there is strong scientific evidence combined with philosophical reasoning for the reality of a Creator-Designer. So we are thrown back to philosophy (but not without science!), especially concerning Hawking's first question, "How can we understand the world in which we find ourselves?"

That question can be answered with respect to the proper scientific methodology and instrumentality (microscopes, telescopes, seismographs), or it can be addressed philosophically. Albert Einstein, who did not believe in a personal God, nevertheless said that "God does not play dice with the universe."[9] But he also said of the universe, "The fact that it is comprehensible is a miracle."[10] By "comprehensible" Einstein meant that it could be explored profitably through theories and experiments, such that it might yield knowledge—not mere speculation or opinion. Knowing the universe at the sophisticated level of physics and cosmology is not easy, but progress can and has been made, particularly concerning the confirmation of the big bang theory (as addressed in chapter 4). Einstein's wonderment surfaces the matter of what philosophers call "the intelligibility of the universe."[11] It is one thing to verify the big

---

7. Stephen Hawking and Leonard Mlodinow, *The Grand Design* (New York: Bantam, 2010), 5. For a critique of Hawking, see John C. Lennox, *God and Stephen Hawking: Whose Design Is It Anyway?* (Oxford: Lion Hudson, 2011).

8. See J. P. Moreland, *Scientism and Secularism: Learning to Respond to a Dangerous Ideology* (Wheaton, IL: Crossway, 2018).

9. On Einstein's worldview and its relationship to Christianity, see Alister McGrath, *A Theory of Everything (That Matters): A Brief Guide to Einstein, Relativity, and His Surprising Thoughts on God* (Carol Stream, IL: Tyndale, 2019).

10. Albert Einstein, "Physics and Reality" (1936; repr., *Daedalus* 132 [Fall 2003]: 24). Einstein may not have been a realist about nature (we can know nature as it is in itself), but he did believe that its intelligibility was attributable to some kind of divine order.

11. For an excellent treatment of this topic with special attention to the history of Western science, see Melissa Cain Travis, "A Glorious Resonance: The Intelligibility of Nature and the

bang cosmology (and be open to its replacement by another theory); it is quite another to ask why it is that human beings can know anything at all about the vast and complicated universe. Here theism has much to offer, as can be argued philosophically and by consulting the history of science. First, to philosophy.

Contrary to Einstein, it is not incomprehensible that the universe is comprehensible if that universe was created and designed by God—an infinite and personal being who desires that we know God's world. Genesis teaches that male and female were created in God's image and likeness and placed on earth to procreate and develop culture by exercising their unique abilities to know and cultivate the world (Gen. 1–2; Pss. 8; 36:9). They were designed to know God, themselves, and the cosmos.

The other alternative is bleak. A quintessential description of the atheistic understanding of humanity's place in the cosmos was given by Bertrand Russell (1872–1970) in "A Free Man's Worship" in a marvelously long and eloquent sentence, which will be abbreviated here:

> That Man is the product of causes which had no prevision of the end they were achieving; that his origin, his growth, his hopes and fears, his loves and his beliefs, are but the outcome of accidental collocations of atoms . . .—all these things, if not quite beyond dispute, are yet so nearly certain, that no philosophy which rejects them can hope to stand. Only within the scaffolding of these truths, only on the firm foundation of unyielding despair, can the soul's habitation henceforth be safely built.[12]

Yet if "Man is the product of" nonrational and impersonal forces, and if his identity can be reduced to mere matter configured by chance, then he has little chance of knowing reality, let alone finding a safe habitation for his nonexistent soul. Many reasons could be cited, but I will limit myself to two before making a positive case for the intelligibility of the universe from the history of science.

Imago Dei," in *The Story of the Cosmos*, ed. Paul Gould and Daniel Ray (Eugene, OR: Harvest House, 2019).

12. Bertrand Russell, *Mysticism and Logic and Other Essays* (n.p.: Delhi Open Books, 2021), 50–51, Kindle.

First, consider human knowing. If humans are undesigned, then all of their capacities must be thoroughly explained through antecedent and unknowing material causes, "which had no provision of the ends they were achieving," according to Russell. On this view, it is sheer dumb luck that human beings have attained present levels of knowledge and that the earth holds a uniquely privileged position to observe the rest of the universe scientifically.[13] Some atheist philosophers, such as Hawking, simply assert or presuppose an objective knowledge of the world without God. Russell himself, despite his dour metaphysic, pursued truth in science and morality.[14] But others more realistically realized they cannot do so. Charles Darwin wrote this to a friend: "But then with me the horrid doubt always arises whether the convictions of man's mind, which has been developed from the mind of the lower animals, are of any value or at all trustworthy. Would any one trust in the convictions of a monkey's mind, if there are any convictions in such a mind?"[15] As atheist and Darwinist philosopher Richard Rorty (1931–2007) put it, "The idea that one species of organism is, unlike all the others, oriented not just toward its own increased prosperity but toward Truth, is as un-Darwinian as the idea that every human being has a built-in moral compass—a conscience that swings free of both social history and individual luck."[16] Nevertheless, Rorty, while foreswearing access to Truth, still presented his ideas as *true*, otherwise he would have nothing to say or write. Yet if we accept his worldview, we have no reason to believe his statements to be true. He is thus hoisted by his own petard.[17]

Schaeffer put this well:

If we are going to live in this world at all, we must live in it acting on a correlation of ourselves and the thing that is there, even if one

---

13. See Guillermo Gonzales and J. Wesley Richards, *Privileged Planet: How Our Place in the Cosmos Was Designed for Discovery* (Washington, DC: Regnery, 2020).

14. On Russell, see Douglas Groothuis, "Bertrand Russell: An Atheist Philosopher Christians Should Know," *Christian Research Journal* 41, no. 3 (August 7, 2020), https://www.equip.org/article/bertrand-russell-an-atheist-philosopher-christians-should-know/.

15. "Charles Darwin to W. Graham, July 3, 1881," in *The Life and Letters of Charles Darwin*, ed. Francis Darwin (1897; repr., Boston: Elibron, 2005), 1:285.

16. Richard Rorty, "Untruth and Consequences," review of Paul Feyerabend's autobiography, *Killing Time*, in *New Republic*, July 31, 1995, 36.

17. On Richard Rorty, see Groothuis, *Truth Decay*, 43–44, 104–5, 187–92, 197–202.

has a philosophy that there is no correlation. There is no other way to live in this world. That is true for everybody, even . . . the man who says there is no correlation. It does not matter a bit. He lives in this world on the basis of his experience that there is a correlation between the subject and the object. He not only lives that way, he has to live that way. . . . That is the way the world is made.[18]

But Rorty is not alone on his self-inflicted petard. Materialist Patricia Churchland joins him:

Boiled down to essentials, a nervous system enables the organism to succeed in . . . feeding, fleeing, fighting, and reproducing. The principal chore of nervous systems is to get the body parts where they should be in order that the organism may survive. . . . Improvements in sensorimotor control confer an evolutionary advantage . . . and enhance the organism's chances of survival. Truth, whatever that is, definitely takes the hindmost.[19]

Thus, the atheist is left with two equally objectionable outcomes. Either we have no objective knowledge (Rorty), or we have inexplicable knowledge without a creator-designer (Hawking). Both alternatives are unacceptable philosophically. Christianity has a better answer.

Second, consider how the universe operates in relation to human knowers. Given an uncreated and undesigned universe, we find no reason why human subjects should gain knowledge of objective realities. It would all be happenstance. But how likely would it be for a naturalistic world to kick up beings who possess knowledge far transcending what is needed for mere survival (which is all Darwinism expects)? Take the relation of mathematics to the objective world. Eugene Wigner (1902–95) wrote a frequently cited essay titled "The Unreasonable Effectiveness of Mathematics." But why consider it *unreasonable* when mathematics works so well in science and technology? It all has to do with worldview.

---

18. Francis A. Schaeffer, *He Is There and He Is Not Silent*, rev. and updated ed. (Carol Stream, IL: Tyndale, 2001), 61.

19. Patricia Churchland, "Epistemology in an Age of Neuroscience," *Journal of Philosophy* 84 (1987): 548–49, emphasis in original.

We will interact with Wigner below, but first consider a comment by philosopher of mathematics, the aforementioned Bertrand Russell:

> Mathematics, rightly viewed, possesses not only truth, but supreme beauty—a beauty cold and austere, like that of sculpture, without appeal to any part of our weaker nature, without the gorgeous trappings of painting or music, yet sublimely pure, and capable of a stern perfection such as only the greatest art can show. The true spirit of delight, the exaltation, the sense of being more than man, which is the touchstone of the highest excellence, is to be found in mathematics as surely as in poetry.[20]

Mathematics for the atheist Russell was "more than Man," meaning it had an objective power and even a "beauty" that called forth reverence. One need not be a Pythagorean philosopher to agree.[21] Moreover, he found beauty, but as an atheist he could assign no Artist to that grand task (as we did above). But what is it about reality that accounts for the truth, knowability, and beauty of mathematics? On a materialistic view, it is a brute fact that beings who were not designed to know mathematics just happen—sheer dumb luck again—to have epistemic contact with (that is, knowledge of) this realm. This world of mathematics is not reducible to matter since it traffics in abstractions. The Pythagorean theorem, for example, applies to every possible material object and is not reducible to any one of them or to all of them. The principles of addition and subtraction apply to any material state that can be enumerated.

Yet this more-than-human realm of mathematics is knowable by human beings. Further, mathematics gives us the tools to design machines, send people to the moon and back, and build computers with processing powers far beyond the ken of any woman or man.

Let us return to Eugene Wigner. After reflecting on the nature of mathematics and its relation to physics, Eugene Wigner wrote "The Unreasonable Effectiveness of Mathematics in the Physical Sciences."

---

20. Russell, *Mysticism and Logic and Other Essays*, 63, Kindle; https://users.drew.edu /~jlenz/br-ml-ch4.html.

21. Pythagoras was a pre-Socratic Greek philosopher who believed the ultimate reality was mathematical.

He spoke of "the two miracles of the existence of laws of nature and of the human mind's capacity to divine them."[22]

What Wigner meant by "miracles" is not what the Christian means. He meant that these facts are unexpected and, in fact, "unreasonable," *given a naturalistic worldview*—that is a world without design. A Christian accounts for the laws of nature and our ability to "divine them" as gifts of the Divine, who ordered the universe in this way. Once again, Schaeffer captured this:

> The God who is there made the universe, with things together, in relationships. Indeed, the whole area of science turns upon the fact that he has made a world in which things are made to stand together, that there are relationships between things. So God made the external universe, which makes true science possible, but he has also made man and made him to live in that universe. He has not made man to live somewhere else. So we have three things coming together: God, the infinite-personal God, who made the universe; and man, whom he made to live in that universe; and the Bible, which he has given us to tell us about that universe. Are we surprised that there is a unity between them? Why should we be surprised?[23]

The second point in the intelligibility as design argument is historical. Although many contemporary scientists (such as Hawking, Dawkins, and Wigner) do not operate according to a Christian worldview, it was precisely that worldview that gave birth to modern science, beginning in the later Middle Ages and on into "the scientific revolution." Whether you appeal to great scientists such as Newton, Galileo, Kepler, Francis Bacon, Boyle, Faraday, or Pascal, the leaders in modern science took the universe to be orderly, knowable, and worthy of exploration. On that basis, they charted their courses and made their discoveries.[24] Several concepts propelled their work.

---

22. Eugene Wigner, "The Unreasonable Effectiveness of Mathematics in the Natural Sciences," *Communications in Pure and Applied Mathematics* 13, no. 1 (February 1960), https://www.maths.ed.ac.uk/~vlranick/papers/wigner.pdf.

23. Schaeffer, *He Is There and He Is Not Silent*, 59–60.

24. On Pascal's contribution, see Douglas Groothuis, "Scientist and Philosopher of Science" in *On Pascal* (Belmont, CA: Wadsworth, 2003); and William R. Shea, *Designing Experiments and*

First, modern science broke from the Greek idea that nature could be approached *a priori* on the basis of rational principles that required no empirical verification. Aristotle, while an empiricist, was the authority for premodern scientists (called *natural philosophers*) and theologians, whose ideas sometimes hindered the work of actually finding out how nature worked. As Stephen C. Meyer notes,

> Invoking considerations of logical necessity—and often Aristotle's authority—some medieval theologians and philosophers asserted that the universe must be eternal; that God could not create new species; that God could not have made more than one planetary system; that God could not make an empty space; that God could not give planets noncircular orbits; and many other such propositions.[25]

Blaise Pascal was a philosopher of science as well as a scientist whose experimental work affirmed that questions such as whether "nature abhors a vacuum" must be settled empirically, not by assumptions about how nature should work. Pascal rejected an overly personalized notion of nature ("nature abhors a vacuum," etc.) in favor of a more mathematical and empirically-based perspective. His experiments helped produce the syringe, the concept of a hydraulic pump, and the basic principles of hydrostatics (including Pascal's principle regarding the pressure distribution of enclosed fluids).[26]

As Meyer explains, the Christian worldview pushed them in another direction by "asserting the contingency of nature upon the will of a rational God."[27] They agreed with the Greeks that "nature exhibited an underlying order. Nevertheless, they thought this natural order had been impressed on nature by a designing mind with a will—the mind and will of the Judeo-Christian God."[28] Therefore, if you wanted to know

Games of Chance: The Unconventional Science of Blaise Pascal (Canton, MA: Science History Publications/USA, 2003).

25. Stephen C. Meyer, *Return of the God Hypothesis* (New York: HarperOne), 34, Kindle. Meyer supplies ample documentation for each of these ideas.

26. Donald Adamson, *Blaise Pascal: Mathematician, Physicist and Thinker about God* (New York: St. Martin's Press, 1995), 32–33.

27. Meyer, *Return of the God Hypothesis*, 34–35.

28. Meyer, 35.

what God had done in nature, you need to find out through empirical investigation. As Robert Boyle explained, "The job of the natural philosopher was not to ask what God must have done, but what God actually did. Boyle argued that God's freedom required an empirical and observational approach, not just a deductive one."[29]

Second, the modern scientists were confident they could explore nature and find its mechanisms because it is *intelligible*. As philosopher Alfred North Whitehead argued, "There can be no living science unless there is a widespread instinctive conviction in the existence of an *Order of Things*. And, in particular, of an *Order of Nature*."[30] He attributed this conviction among the pioneers of modern science to the "medieval insistence upon the rationality of God."[31] In the words of the astronomer Johannes Kepler (1571–1630), "God wanted us to recognize" natural laws and made that possible "by creating us after his own image so that we could share in his own thoughts."[32]

Three metaphors, all rooted in the Bible, also encouraged scientific work: nature as God's book, the cosmos as clockwork, and the notion of natural laws governing nature.

Several early church theologians referred to both nature and the Bible as *two books to be read*. This is rooted primarily in Psalm 19:1–4 (already cited) and Romans 1:20: "For since the creation of the world God's invisible qualities—his eternal power and divine nature—have been clearly seen, being understood from what has been made, so that people are without excuse."

Augustine and Thomas Aquinas used the metaphor of God's two books as well. Francis Bacon is often and aptly cited regarding this: "To conclude, therefore, let no man out of weak conceit of sobriety, or in ill applied moderation, think or maintain, that a man can search too far or be too well studied in the book of God's word, or in the book of God's works."[33]

---

29. Meyer, 35. Meyer oddly omits Pascal from his account.
30. Alfred North Whitehead, *Science in the Modern World* (New York: Free Press, 1925), 3–4; quoted in Meyer, *Return of the God Hypothesis*, 36, emphasis in original.
31. Whitehead, *Science in the Modern World*, 3–4.
32. Meyer, *Return of the God Hypothesis*, 36.
33. Francis A. Schaeffer, *How Should We Then Live? The Rise and Decline of Western Thought and Culture*, L'Abri 50th Anniversary ed. (Wheaton, IL: Crossway, 2009), locs. 1654–55, Kindle.

Added to the two-books metaphor was the idea of nature as clockwork or more generally as a machine constructed by a master engineer. Robert Boyle developed this idea at length, which influenced many scientists. The parts of nature worked together to form orderly patterns of activity, whether that be planetary motion or any other natural system. As Meyer notes, "Boyle's analogy, likening God to a skilled watchmaker, expressed a common reverence for both the ingenuity and the regularity of divine activity as manifest in the natural world. The mechanical philosophers celebrated the regular concourse of nature as a consequence of God's ingenious design of various mechanistic processes."[34]

Just as a good mechanic can divine the workings of an engine for which he has no operating manual, the mechanical philosophers investigated the machinery of nature through investigation and theorizing, confident that answers could eventually be found as to its working. If it was a mechanism, then it had a maker; and if it had a maker, the maker's mind was imprinted on the mechanism, and that rationality could be discovered and harnessed through the minds of the made (the mechanical philosophers).

The third idea that inspired modern science was that of natural law. Given the contemporary deference to science and the idea of natural laws explaining the way the world regularly works, it may seem odd to think that this concept as a scientific category came about fairly recently, as world history goes. However, neither Aristotle nor Plato understood the workings of the world as law governed. Muslim philosophers stressed Allah's absolute will, which could not be limited by laws. Meyer notes that this notion helped science in that they could not deduce the workings of nature from rationalistic first principles. "They instead realized that they would need to observe nature in order to discover its lawlike regularities."[35] The idea of a law of nature assumed a "reliable divine oversight," which stimulated the application of mathematics to describe the regularities of nature. This "fostered unprecedented technological advance. Only a few centuries after Newton characterized the universal law of gravity, human beings harnessed this knowledge to put men on the moon."[36]

---

34. Meyer, *Return of the God Hypothesis*, 55.
35. Meyer, 59.
36. Meyer, 59.

INTELLIGENT DESIGN: COSMIC FINE-TUNING

In his essay "On Atheism," the philosopher Francis Bacon wrote of the testimony of the cosmos to God. "For while the mind of man looketh upon second causes scattered, it may sometimes rest in them, and go no further; but when it beholdeth the chain of them, confederate and linked together, it must needs fly to Providence and Deity."[37]

Bacon maintained that the atheist's mind may rest on various particular events in nature and not venture further afield to consider its Author. It is a kind of conceptual squint, isolating the part from the whole. But if one considers the larger and interlinked system, he must see the mind of God at work in God's world. Although God's design can be seen in the smallest things—such as molecular machines and in the information in DNA—we will start by considering "the chain of secondary causes," which are "confederate and linked together."

Design arguments may appeal to the cosmos as a whole or to parts within it. We begin with conditions of the universe that must be just right for there to be conscious embodied life. All life, whether human or otherwise, can exist only within a particular range of contingencies. As Pascal noted, "Man is only a reed, the weakest in nature, but he is a thinking reed. There is no need for the whole universe to take up arms to crush him: a vapour, a drop of water is enough to kill him. But even if the universe were to crush him, man would still be nobler than his slayer, because he knows that he is dying and the advantage the universe has over him. The universe knows none of this."[38]

Note two points. First, we know what the universe does not. In that is our nobility. In fact, our knowledge of the universe has increased dramatically in the past fifty years concerning the finely balanced factors needed to make life possible. Second, we are "a reed, the weakest in nature," which means the fragility of our lives given our context. Once we exist, we are fragile, if noble. But for us to come to exist in the first place required a vast range of fine-tuned factors, each of which was unlikely and when understood as "confederate and linked together" was

---

37. Francis Bacon, *The Essays*, 84, Kindle.
38. Blaise Pascal, *Pensées* (New York: Penguin, 2017), 66, Kindle.

even more unlikely. Just as "a vapour, a drop of water" is enough to kill us once we exist, a few small changes in the configuration of the cosmos would have forbidden us from coming to exist at all.

In the 1970s, physicists started speaking of "anthropic coincidences"—the confederacy of cosmic contingencies necessary for humans to exist. Meyer summarizes this by referring to our "Goldilocks universe," "where the fundamental forces of physics have just the right strengths, the contingent properties of the universe have just the right characteristics, and the initial distribution of matter and energy at the beginning exhibited just the right configuration to make life possible."[39]

None of these variables had to be what they are; that is, they are contingent states of affairs. But they are all specified for allowing life in the cosmos. (Thus far, the only known life in the universe is on earth, but that is not a component of this argument.) Thus, there are only two explanations for this "Goldilocks universe": (1) it is there by chance, sheer dumb luck (again), or (2) it was designed by a mind that selected each of the many contingencies in order to facilitate life. The first explanation might be likely if the odds permitted it, but they do not. Each of the variables is extremely unlikely to occur by chance, and the total of all the variables is even more unlikely to occur by chance. Meyer puts this into perspective concerning just one necessary factor, the cosmological constant, which is "the energy density of space that contributes to the outward expansion of space in opposition to gravitational attraction."[40]

Robin Collins says that if the "cosmological logical constant were not fine-tuned to within an extremely narrow range—one part in 10 to the 53rd or even 10 to the 120th of its 'theoretically possible' range of values—the universe would expand so rapidly that all matter would quickly disperse, and thus galaxies, stars, and even small aggregates of matter could never form."[41]

Given these odds, the hypothesis that all of this happened by chance does not have a chance. It is far more rational to infer that the fine-tuning

39. Meyer, *Return of the God Hypothesis*, 207–8.
40. Meyer, 240.
41. Robin Collins, "The Teleological Argument," in *The Routledge Companion to Philosophy of Religion*, ed. Chad Meister and Paul Copan (New York: Routledge, 2007), 352. See also Meyer, *Return of the God Hypothesis*, 240.

is there because there is a fine-tuner.[42] We can eliminate the idea of several fine-tuners as explaining the universe, since simple explanations are preferred to more complex explanations, all things considered.

Having argued for design from knowledge gained from cosmology and physics, we can move to the vexed domain of biology. Is there evidence for a designer in biological life, or did Darwin defeat Deity?

DARWINISM AND DESIGN

The subject of Darwinism, design, and the Bible is a vexed and multifaceted topic—one we cannot adequately address here. Nonetheless, we can clarify a few issues and make a few essential points that will take the hot air out of the claim that Darwinism has defeated the design argument and refuted the Bible.

Darwin and honest Darwinists take the theory of evolution through natural selection as a *designer substitute*. Darwin thought nature to be too cruel and wasteful to evidence the hand of God.[43] So he took matters into his own hands and devised a theory to explain the development of species through a mindless process. Darwinism in principle says nothing about how the first life on earth came about. However, Darwin claimed that all life comes from a "common ancestor." He ventured some speculations about the first life but nothing more. Darwin claimed to discover the mechanism by which nature generates new species. Nature selects those organisms with the functions necessary for survival. Over time organisms very gradually (incrementally) change through this thoroughly materialistic process such that new species emerge over vast periods of godless time.

Rather than write much about the copious errors and false promises of Darwinism, I will rather survey a few of its failures and give evidence from biology for intelligent design. First, the Darwinian "tree of life" has not been found to exist. Darwin claimed that all species evolved from

---

42. For a more developed version of this argument, see "The Design Argument: Cosmic Fine Tuning," in Douglas Groothuis, *Christian Apologetics: A Comprehensive Case for Biblical Faith*, 2nd ed. (Downers Grove, IL: IVP Academic, 2022).

43. Cornelius Hunter, *Darwin's God: Evolution and the Problem of Evil* (Eugene, OR: Wipf and Stock, 2019).

one common ancestor and that the fossil record confirms this. It does not, as even many Darwinists will admit.[44] Paleontologist Stephen Jay Gould developed a theory called *punctuated equilibrium* to address this problem. Since the fossil records reveal long periods of stasis (no major changes) and then sudden emergence of species, Gould could not affirm the traditional Darwinist view of slow, incremental change.[45] However, he offered no biological mechanism by which these punctuations could be explained.

The Cambrian explosion reveals that in a geologically short period of time new organisms emerged with no evidence of a long, gradual evolutionary heritage. It is called biology's *big bang*. Darwin was aware of this issue in his own day but thought that time would reveal evidence to confirm his theory against the explosion. No such evidence has been forthcoming, and instead, the Cambrian explosion is better established as biology's big bang than it was in Darwin's day. This has been conclusively argued by Stephen C. Meyer in *Darwin's Doubt*.[46] When I (Doug) debated atheist Professor Michael Tooley in 2014 on intelligent design versus Darwinism, he dismissed the Cambrian explosion by saying he had seen something on television that explained it.[47] However, there is no such evidence that harmonizes it with Darwinism.

Second, there is no known genetic mechanism that could explain the increase in genetic information needed for evolution from simpler to more complex forms of life. This was highlighted long ago by mathematician Murray Eden, who argued that Darwinian evolution was mathematically impossible. Even in 1976, long before the intelligent design movement took off, Schaeffer noted that the statistical problems with Darwinism had

been pointed out by Murray Eden (1920–) in the 1967 article "Heresy in the Halls of Biology—Mathematicians Question Darwin"

44. See Jonathon Wells, "Darwin's Tree of Life," *Icons of Evolution: Why Much of What We Teach about Evolution Is Wrong* (Washington, DC: Regnery, 2002).

45. Stephen Jay Gould, "Evolution's Erratic Pace," *Natural History* 86 (1977): 14.

46. Stephen C. Meyer, *Darwin's Doubt: The Explosive Growth of Animal Life and the Case for Intelligent Design* (New York: HarperOne, 2014).

47. "War of the Worldviews: Intelligent Design versus Darwinian Evolution," August 2, 2014, https://www.youtube.com/watch?v=omv6rbRhJLQ.

(*Scientific Research*, November 1967). This problem was also dealt with in a more technical way in Eden's article "Inadequacies of Neo-Darwinian Evolution as a Scientific Theory," which appeared in *Mathematical Challenges to the Neo-Darwinian Interpretation of Evolution* (1967). Statistical studies indicate that pure chance (randomness) could not have produced the biological complexity in the world out of chaos, in any amount of time so far suggested. "Has there been enough time for natural selection, as it is seen through the eyepieces of Darwinism or Neo-Darwinism to operate and give rise to the observed phenomena of nature? No, say these mathematicians."[48]

In two recent and extensively documented books, Stephen C. Meyer has abundantly shown that these problems have only gotten worse since Schaeffer's prescient 1976 remarks about Eden's work.[49] Propaganda to the contrary, the case for Darwinism is weakening and the case for intelligent design is only getting better, as we will further argue below.

We will limit the case for design from biology to one area: molecular machines. In 1996, biochemist Professor Michael Behe rocked the biological world with his book *Darwin's Black Box*, in which he argued that Darwinism could not explain the intricate workings of the cell.[50] The book was widely reviewed, unlike books from the earlier creationist movement that were typically only read and reviewed in Christian circles.[51] Here was a bona fide biochemist challenging Darwinism in a book published by a New York publisher, and he was a Roman Catholic

---

48. Schaeffer, *How Should We Then Live?*, locs. 1750–56.

49. See Meyer, *Return of the God Hypothesis*, chs. 10–15.

50. Michael Behe, *Darwin's Black Box: The Biochemical Challenge to Evolution*, 2nd ed. (New York: Free Press, 2006).

51. Creationism, for all its cogent criticisms of Darwinism, did not advance a credible philosophy of science or develop an approach to new scientific evidence that would significantly challenge Darwinism and advance a theistic alternative in the public square. The intelligent design movement generally agrees with creationism in its critique of Darwinism but does not appeal directly to the Bible as evidence for design in nature, but confirms the biblical teaching that the cosmos is designed. It remains neutral on matters of the age of the earth and the issue of the extent of Noah's flood. On the intelligent design movement, see Thomas Woodward, *Doubts about Darwin: A History of Intelligent Design* (Grand Rapids: Baker, 2007). Two key books in the creationist movement are Duane Gish, *Evolution: The Fossils Still Say No!* (California: Institute for Creation Research, 1985) and Henry Morris, *Scientific Creationism*, 2nd ed. (Green Forest, AR: Master Books, 1974).

who found nothing in his religion that would motivate him to challenge Darwinism. It was science that caused him to change his mind.[52] Behe gives several examples from biology of what he calls "irreducible complexity," a reality unaccounted for by Darwinism. He defines it like this:

> By irreducibly complex I mean a single system composed of several well-matched, interacting parts that contribute to the basic function, wherein the removal of any one of the parts causes the system to effectively cease functioning. An irreducibly complex system cannot be produced directly (that is, by continuously improving the initial function, which continues to work by the same mechanism) by slight, successive modifications of a precursor system, because any precursor to an irreducibly complex system that is missing a part is by definition nonfunctional.[53]

The most well-known example of irreducible complexity—but not the only one—is called the *bacterial flagellum*. It is a forty-component rotary motor attached to the back of a bacterium that is used to propel the bacterium around. It is rightly called a *molecular machine*, given its interactive component parts necessary for its function. However, this machine was made by no mortal.

What makes the flagellum irreducibly complex is that each of its forty parts—involving a stator, a rotor, a u-joint, etc.—is necessary for its function. Take one away and it loses its function as a motor. But what of it? Listen to Behe: "An irreducibly complex biological system, if there is such a thing, would be a powerful challenge to Darwinian evolution. Since natural selection can only choose systems that are already working, then if a biological system cannot be produced gradually it would have to arise as an integrated unit, in one fell swoop, for natural selection to have anything to act on."[54]

---

52. Behe read the first edition of Michael Denton's book, *Evolution: A Theory in Crisis* (New York: Adler and Adler, 2002), which convinced him of the scientific weaknesses of Darwinism. For a video account of Behe's change of mind, see "Revolutionary," https://revolutionarybehe .com. Denton does not take a religious viewpoint but appeals only to scientific evidence. He has also written *Evolution: Still A Theory in Crisis* (Seattle, WA: Discovery Institute, 2016).

53. Behe, *Darwin's Black Box*, 49.

54. Behe, 49–50.

The common mousetrap illustrates irreducible complexity. Take away any of its few components and it fails to catch mice. But the flagellum is vastly more complex, with about forty different component parts.

The flagellum motor could not have evolved part-by-part, since all the parts are needed for its function in the cell and to give it a selective advantage—that is, a function conducive to its survival. If so, there is no plausible evolutionary pathway for its emergence. A better explanation is that the flagellum motor was intelligently designed with the end in view. But evolution, as Darwin saw it, has no end in view, since nature is mindless until animal minds appear. But no animal or human mind designed the flagellum, which is literally a living motor.

Numerous Darwinists have flailed away at Behe's argument ever since it appeared, and Behe has dutifully responded to every one of the counterarguments upon each one's arrival. This is well documented in Behe's book *A Mousetrap for Darwin: Michael J. Behe Responds to His Critics*.[55] The bacterial flagellum has become a kind of poster child for the intelligent design movement, and its luster has not faded. Nor is it the only star on the horizon.

As it stands, any irreducibly complex organism is a refutation of Darwinism, since the latter does not offer any credible way that an unguided and gradual process could produce something in that category. As Darwin himself wrote, "If it could be demonstrated that any complex organ existed, which could not *possibly* have been formed by numerous, successive, slight modifications, my theory would absolutely break down. But I can find no such case."[56]

If by "possibly" Darwin means "likely," then we have found a counterexample to his claim. If he meant "logically possible," then he rendered his theory unfalsifiable, since some broadly possible scenario can be conceived—even in the teeth of all existing evidence. If it is

55. Michael J. Behe: *A Mousetrap for Darwin: Michael J. Behe Responds to His Critics* (Seattle, WA: Discovery Institute, 2020).

56. Charles Darwin, *The Origin of Species*, ch. 6, p. 189 (London: Langham, 1859). Facsimile available at "The Complete Works of Charles Darwin Online," Darwin Online, http://darwin-online.org.uk/, emphasis added. We have chosen to cite the first of the five editions because later works incorporate some aspects of Lamarkianism, which are no longer favored by contemporary Darwinists. We owe this insight to William Dembski.

unfalsifiable, it is not a serious scientific theory, since science trades on contingent explanations.

That a designing mind was involved in some way is a far better explanation for the complexity and fine-tuning we find in nature than a series of undirected causes. The argument is not meant to refute every aspect of evolutionary theory—for example, it says nothing about a common ancestor—but it does introduce intelligence into the biological world and thus releases it from the naturalistic stranglehold it has experienced for too long. Let biology breathe!

Space forbids much discussion of the argument for design from the information encoded in DNA. We will mention that the information contained in and exchanged in the DNA in a living cell far exceeds the capacities of the most powerful computer. Since no one could imagine a computer coming about without a designer, then we are justified in positing a designer for the information in DNA as well. When information is present, we reliably infer design given our uniform experience of such. By information, I mean a specified or functional pattern that communicates a meaning.[57] A bunch of leaves strewn on a lawn is complex but bears no information. However, if we see leaves arranged to spell out "Douglas Loves Kathleen," we spot both complexity and specification, because a message is conveyed that requires intelligence for its formation. Clouds can be majestic in beauty. We might even see something like a face or some other object in a cloud. But once any image gets more specific, we infer a designer. We can discriminate a suggestive outline in a cloud from a case of skywriting, for example. The first commercial skywriting message—"DAILY MAIL"—was done in 1922 for the British newspaper of that name. Even if someone had not seen the airplane writing this message, no one would infer that his message had appeared because of the unguided atmospheric conditions.[58] The information contained in DNA far exceeds any simple sentence, although those messages use a different alphabet.[59] Thus it has an Author.

---

57. For much more detail, see Stephen C. Meyer, *The Signature in the Cell* (New York: HarperOne, 2009), ch. 4.

58. See Stephan Wilkinson, "The Sky Is Their Canvas: The Lost Art of Skywriting," HistoryNet, December 11, 2017, https://www.historynet.com/the-skys-their-canvas.htm.

59. See Groothuis, *Christian Apologetics*, 311–15. The most thorough development of this information argument is Meyer, *Signature in the Cell*.

DESIGN, UGLINESS, AND EVIL

Chapter 6, "The Moral Argument," looks at the problem of evil in more detail, but a few points in relation to the design argument are helpful. The problem of evil concerns the relationship of an all-good and all-powerful God and the existence of objective evil. Can a theist rationally affirm that God's existence is compatible with so much evil in the world? An all-good God would want to eliminate it. An all-powerful God could eliminate it. If this is so, then why is there evil? Several strategies have been advanced. For our purposes, let us consider three points about the argument from design in relationship to the existence of evil.

First, if we have good arguments for design—from this chapter and elsewhere—these arguments do not lose their force in the face of evil, both human (crime, cruelty, racism) and natural (earthquakes, plagues, forest fires). The task becomes reconciling the existence of God with the existence of evil. Nevertheless, evidence of design remains in place. There is beauty in the world, which indicates an artist. The cosmos is intelligible, which requires an epistemic agent at its core. The universe is fine-tuned, which requires a fine-tuner. Biology reveals not a Darwinian story, but intelligent design. Yet there is so much suffering and waste in the world.

Second, inferring design is a fundamental and intuitive response to many events we experience.[60] Even atheist Richard Dawkins defines biology as "the study of living things that give the appearance of having been designed for a purpose."[61] This intuition can be supported by the detailed arguments for design, but it is as strong as the sense of the existence of real evil in the world. Thus, instead of denying design because of evil, it is more rational to work out a theory in which both design and evil cohere. This is precisely what Christian philosophers have worked out in several ways over the last two thousand years.[62]

---

60. Douglas Axe develops this intuitive sense of design (among other things) in his book *Undeniable: How Biology Confirms Our Intuition That Life Is Designed* (New York: HarperOne, 2016).

61. Richard Dawkins, *The Blind Watchmaker* (New York: Norton, 1986), 1.

62. I (Doug) have done so in detail in my chapter "The Problem of Evil," in *Christian Apologetics*.

Third, the crucial move in reconciling design with evil is the Christian doctrine of the fall. While God is still on the throne, the world has gone wrong because of a rebellion against the Creator that has led to the estrangement of humans from God, from themselves, and from each other (Gen. 3). This breakage in relationships is the ultimate cause of evils. Love is lost, and cruelty abounds. In this sense, the world is abnormal—not as it was originally designed to be. Thus, we find ugliness, selfishness, cruelty, and all manner of venality. As Pascal went to great and brilliant lengths to show, nature is corrupt and needs redemption.[63] But corruption can only be understood in light of an original good, a benevolent game plan or design. Thus, an appropriate design is foundational to the very idea of corruption and evil. C. S. Lewis made this point.

You can be good for the mere sake of goodness: you cannot be bad for the mere sake of badness. You can do a kind action when you are not feeling kind and when it gives you no pleasure, simply because kindness is right; but no one ever did a cruel action simply because cruelty is wrong—only because cruelty was pleasant or useful to him. In other words badness cannot succeed even in being bad in the same way in which goodness is good. Goodness is, so to speak, itself: badness is only spoiled goodness. And there must be something good first before it can be spoiled.[64]

The Christian narrative of creation, fall, redemption, and consummation makes better sense of evil in our world than any other worldview, however many difficulties remain.[65]

---

63. Many of the fragments of *Pensées* make this point. Pascal wrote that his principle apologetic task was to show that nature and human nature are corrupt and that there is a Redeemer proved by Scripture who can rectify this condition. See Groothuis, "Deposed Royalty," in *Christian Apologetics*.

64. C. S. Lewis, *Mere Christianity*, C. S. Lewis Signature Classics (London: HarperCollins, 2012), 21, Kindle.

65. On living through unexplained evils, see Douglas Groothuis, *Walking through Twilight: A Wife's Illness—A Philosopher's Lament* (Downers Grove, IL: InterVarsity, 2017). A classic lament by a Christian is C. S. Lewis, *A Grief Observed* (New York: HarperCollins, 2001). See also Psalms 22; 39; 88; and 90.

DESIGN CONFIRMED BY GOD'S FINGERPRINTS

We began this chapter by claiming that the argument from design finds God's fingerprints all over his creation. Our dusting for these finger-prints found that design is evident in (1) the beauty of nature, (2) the intelligibility of nature (needed for science), (3) cosmic fine-tuning, and (4) molecular machines and the information in DNA. Along the way, Darwinism was found inadequate to explain all of biology (especially the fossil record and the Cambrian explosion), and that key features of biology were better explained by intelligent design. And despite the ugliness and evil in the world, design remains a settled fact with which we must account.

Whatever else we may say of this ancient, vast, and mysterious cosmos, we must agree with Paul that life is a divine gift.

> We are bringing you good news, telling you to turn from these worthless things to the living God, who made the heavens and the earth and the sea and everything in them. In the past, he let all nations go their own way. Yet he has not left himself without testimony: He has shown kindness by giving you rain from heaven and crops in their seasons; he provides you with plenty of food and fills your hearts with joy. (Acts 14:15–17)

Not only should we recognize God's design in his world, but we ought to be grateful and give thanks for it. The essence of atheism is not glorifying God or giving thanks to him for his good world. As Paul warned, "For although they knew God, they neither glorified him as God nor gave thanks to him, but their thinking became futile and their foolish hearts were darkened" (Rom. 1:21).

STUDY QUESTIONS

1. Why might the argument from beauty have more existential punch than the fine-tuning argument?
2. How do we know the universe is fine-tuned for life?

3. Would life on other planets refute the fine-tuning argument?
4. How do we address the skeptic's response, "Who designed the Designer?"

SUGGESTED READING

Adamson, Donald. *Blaise Pascal: Mathematician, Physicist and Thinker about God.* New York: St. Martin's Press, 1995.

Axe, Douglas. *Undeniable: How Biology Confirms Our Intuition That Life Is Designed.* New York: HarperOne, 2016.

Behe, Michael. *Darwin's Black Box: The Biochemical Challenge to Evolution.* 2nd ed. New York: Free Press, 2006.

_____. *A Mousetrap for Darwin: Michael J. Behe Responds to His Critics.* Seattle, WA: Discovery Institute, 2020.

Darwin, Charles. *The Life and Letters of Charles Darwin.* Edited by Francis Darwin. 1897. Repr., Boston: Elibron, 2005.

_____. *The Origin of Species.* 189. London: Langham, 1859. Facsimile available at "The Complete Works of Charles Darwin Online," Darwin Online. http://darwin-online.org.uk/.

Dawkins, Richard. *The Blind Watchmaker.* New York: Norton, 1986.

_____. *River Out of Eden.* New York: Basic Books, 1996.

Denton, Michael. *Evolution: A Theory in Crisis.* 3rd ed. New York: Adler and Adler, 2002.

_____. *Evolution: Still A Theory in Crisis.* Seattle, WA: Discovery Institute, 2016.

Dillard, Annie. *Holy the Firm.* New York: HarperCollins e-books. Kindle edition.

Gish, Duane. *Evolution: The Fossils Still Say No!* California: Institute for Creation Research, 1985.

Gonzales, Guillermo, and J. Wesley Richards. *Privileged Planet.* Washington, DC: Regnery Gateway, 2020.

Gould, Stephen Jay. "Evolution's Erratic Pace." *Natural History* 86 (1977).

Groothuis, Douglas, *Christian Apologetics: A Comprehensive Case for Biblical Faith,* 2nd ed. Downers Grove, IL: IVP Academic, 2022.

_____. *On Pascal.* Belmont, CA: Wadsworth, 2003.

_____. *Truth Decay.* Downers Grove, IL: InterVarsity, 2000.

Hawking, Stephen. *The Grand Design.* New York: Bantam, 2012.

Hunter, Cornelius. *Darwin's God: Evolution and the Problem of Evil.* Eugene, OR: Wipf and Stock, 2019.

McGrath, Alister. *A Theory of Everything (That Matters): A Brief Guide to Einstein, Relativity, and His Surprising Thoughts on God.* Carol Stream, IL: Tyndale, 2019.

Meyer, Stephen C. *Return of the God Hypothesis: Three Scientific Discoveries That Reveal the Mind behind the Universe.* New York: HarperOne, 2021.

———. *The Signature in the Cell.* New York: HarperOne, 2009.

Moreland, J. P. *Scientism and Secularism: Learning to Respond to a Dangerous Ideology.* Wheaton, IL: Crossway, 2018.

Morris, Henry. *Scientific Creationism.* 2nd ed. Green Forest, AR: Master Books, 1974.

Pascal, Blaise. *Pensées.* New York: Penguin, 2017. Kindle edition, 66.

Russell, Bertrand. "A Free Man's Worship." Bertrand Russell Society, 1996. https://www3.nd.edu/~afreddos/courses/264/fmw.htm.

Sagan, Carl. *Cosmos.* New York: Ballentine, 2013.

Schaeffer, Francis. *He Is There and He Is Not Silent.* Carol Stream, IL: Tyndale House. Kindle edition.

———. *How Should We Then Live? The Rise and Decline of Western Thought and Culture.* L'Abri 50th Anniversary ed. Wheaton, IL: Crossway, 2009. Kindle edition, locs. 1654–55.

Scruton, Roger. *Beauty: A Very Short Introduction.* Very Short Introductions. New York: Oxford University Press. Kindle edition.

Wigner, Thomas Eugene, "The Unreasonable Effectiveness of Mathematics," *Communications in Pure and Applied Mathematics* 13, no. 1 (February 1960). https://www.maths.ed.ac.uk/~v1ranick/papers/wigner.pdf.

Woodward, Thomas, *Doubts about Darwin: A History of Intelligent Design.* Grand Rapids: Baker, 2007.

PART 3

THE CHRISTIAN STORY

IS TRUE

CHAPTER 8

THE BIBLE'S
TRUSTWORTHINESS

Our world is filled with distrust, suspicion, and of course, bias. Whether it's about scientific research, government initiatives, or celebrity gossip, our culture suffers from a credibility gap. This may not be what one would expect, especially considering that information is more easily accessed than ever, with the world's databases of news and factoids accessible through devices we keep in our pockets. Even so, it is still common to doubt what one hears on the news. This credibility gap is even more tragic when we start considering cultural attitudes toward the Bible. Once generally respected by many in Western culture, today the Bible is often neglected, derided, and vilified. The Bible is seen as being racist, homophobic, misogynistic, narrow, and outdated in its approach to life and spirituality.[1] Perhaps the Bible contains some insights about the moral life, but for the average person outside the household of faith, the Bible may only be opened briefly at a wedding or a funeral.

We lament this credibility gap both in public affairs and with respect to the Bible, but we see a pathway to showing others the truth of the

---

1. For an excellent set of responses to accusations that are leveled against Christianity, see Rebecca McLaughlin, *Confronting Christianity: 12 Hard Questions for the World's Largest Religion* (Wheaton, IL: Crossway, 2019). See also Douglas Groothuis, "Distortions of Christianity—or the God I Don't Believe In," in Douglas Groothuis, *Christian Apologetics: A Comprehensive Case for Biblical Faith*, 2nd ed. (Downers Grove, IL: IVP Academic, 2022).

Bible, to helping them be open to its claims, and to encouraging them to reach out for the Lord whose story is told in its pages. We believe that even today there are good reasons to trust the Bible. Now our particular beliefs about the Bible go beyond its general trustworthiness. Though we have reasons for trusting that the biblical manuscripts were originally inerrant, a belief in this kind of inerrancy is not required to show that the Bible is trustworthy.[2]

In a cultural moment when knowledge is so often reduced to scientific claims, Christians need to learn why Christian truth claims are reliable, especially those delivered to us through biblical revelation. This chapter will explain how the Bible is a source of historical knowledge, particularly by showing how the Bible is reliable in its manuscript transmission, its external corroboration, and its internal evidence. It will also supply you with evidence that the biblical records are as reliable as or more reliable than other ancient historical sources. Apologetically, we believe that being able to show this kind of reliability can undercut someone's initial skepticism about using the Bible as a historical document, and it can open people up to considering whether the message of the Bible, particularly the message of the gospel, is true. We will start by explaining the goals of such an inquiry and then discuss separately reasons why the Old Testament and the New Testament records are reliable historical documents.

The big disclaimer that we offer regarding all of this is that the Bible is a richly diverse set of ancient documents from different authors, genres, and time periods. It is impossible to give a chapter-length treatment of all of the lines of evidence for either testament, and in fact, entire scholarly works (some even multivolume) are dedicated to the reliability of even a single book of the Bible. So what you will read in the following pages is an overview of some of the key lines of evidence for trusting in the Bible and some of the examples we have found most helpful in our apologetic ministries. After all, the goal for most apologetic purposes does not need to be showing how every verse in the Bible is reliable. Instead, we want to show that there is enough historical

---

2. A classic evangelical statement on inerrancy is The Chicago Statement on Biblical Inerrancy (1978): https://www.etsjets.org/files/documents/Chicago_Statement.pdf.

reliability in the Bible's key claims to warrant a closer look at the claims of the Christian worldview in general, and to the claims and credentials of Jesus Christ and the relationship we may have with him in particular.

WHAT ARE WE TRYING TO SHOW ABOUT THE BIBLE?

As the above disclaimer suggests, the purpose of this chapter is not to give you comprehensive evidence for every apologetic issue that might need to be raised about the Bible. Again, this chapter would spill over into an encyclopedia. Instead, think again about what we are trying to do when we do apologetics. Apologetics is about defending and commending the faith, and ultimately our faith is in Jesus Christ rather than in the Bible. However, this distinction can be misleading. Yes, our faith is in Jesus Christ, but the definitive revelation of Christ is the Bible. While Christ is revealed to our hearts reliably through the Holy Spirit and in the church, what we think about Jesus must be measured against the Bible's record of him. Further, because the Son has been ministering since creation, we must see the entire Bible as the revelation of Christ, from the creation to the new heavens and the new earth. This means that the broader story of the Bible (both Testaments) is one that we should learn from, meditate on, and allow to minister to our lives. In apologetics, this means that we need to develop the ability to show how the Bible is generally a reliable set of documents that is worth learning from and listening to. Further, the Bible is not just a spiritual document that teaches people about the moral life. The Bible is a historical document that recounts God's work among God's people. It can be investigated for its claims about broader reality, not just about personal ethics.

Though we are both inerrantists, we do not think that proving inerrancy is required to show that the Bible is historically reliable, for this level of proof is not required to trust the records of any other ancient document. It would be unfair to hoist upon the Bible a burden of proof that we do not require for, say, the sources that recount the life and times of Julius Caesar. We can know a good deal about Caesar reliably without the requirement of inerrancy in the sources. Finally, since the task of apologetics is to point people to Jesus by defending and commending the Christian worldview, we need to help those around us to accept that the Bible is a generally reliable historical witness. In so doing, we can help them to rationally accept the truth claims made in the Bible about Jesus. Believing that the Bible's records are without error is not required for this task.

That said, we have found that sometimes people do raise very specific criticisms or counterclaims to certain issues in the Bible. Since we cannot provide a handbook on all of these issues, we hope that what follows will inspire you to read more on the subject, and we suggest starting with works that we reference in this chapter. In what follows, we will defend the reliability of the Old Testament and then the New Testament, and we have different goals for each section. Because of the relative age of the Old Testament documents, our approach is to show that the Old Testament documents we have today are part of a reliable tradition of transmission, the history of which can be traced back thousands of years. In addition, we will explore a sample of the kinds of archaeological evidence that corroborates key elements of the Old Testament historical record. Regarding the New Testament, our aims are more ambitious. We will show that the New Testament documents have been reliably transmitted, providing modern scholars with a high degree of confidence as to the content of the original manuscripts. Subsequently, we will explain the New Testament's internal marks of authenticity, elements that show that what we read in our modern Bibles is likely what was originally written. Finally, we will explore external corroboration for some key historical details contained in the New Testament. This chapter will provide a more general overview to the New Testament's reliability, and the following chapter will focus on the life of Jesus Christ and the records of the Gospels, showing more specifically that the accounts about Jesus in the Bible are true.

THE RELIABILITY OF THE OLD TESTAMENT

For many scholars, the discussion about the reliability of the Old Testament begins in the postexilic communities of Jews living in Palestine in the fifth through the third centuries BCE. The story told about these people is that of a small group of people struggling to find a sense of identity in a world being dominated by the power struggle between the Persian Empire to the east and the Greek powers to the west. These Jews started compiling an imagined history of their past in the lands of Palestine that legitimized their claims to the land and their particularities as a people unique from their neighbors. In so doing, they relied on oral traditions, legends, and their imaginations to cobble together what eventually took shape as the Hebrew Bible (what Christians refer to as the Old Testament), with its origin stories of the children of Israel, its wisdom writings, and its prophetic literature. This is the so-called minimalist view.[3] It entails that the Hebrew Bible is primarily fiction, an imagined national history used to legitimize the status of a people over and against their powerful neighbors. Much is at stake here. Consider the Old Testament's focus on the chosen people Israel, set apart from among their neighbors for a universal purpose. Consider the revelation of God's moral and judicial standard revealed in the Law and the Prophets. Consider the prophecies about the Messiah to come in relation to the promises given to Abram (Gen. 12:1–3), the word given to Moses (Deut. 18:15), the promise spoken over the royal house of David and Solomon (2 Sam. 7:12–16), the foreshadowing of the suffering servant (Isa. 53), and the prediction of the Son of Man (Dan. 7:13–14).

On the other hand, there is a more skeptical view that the Bible is simply legendary. Appealing to no particular set of evidence, this perspective gains credence from popular books or from TV documentaries about the Bible. These works usually have titles like *The True History of the Israelites, Hidden Secrets about Jesus,* or *The Books Banned from the Bible.* The mere existence of these kinds of books, articles, and programs contributes to a general cultural sense that the Bible is legendary. This denigrates the importance of whether we even understand what the text says in favor of the spiritual power or legendary appeal of what the text does. Consider popular writer Karen Armstrong's reinterpretation of the Bible: "These stories were not historical in our sense, because they

---

3. See K. A. Kitchen, *On the Reliability of the Old Testament* (Grand Rapids: Eerdmans, 2003), 2; see also Yosef Garfinkel, "The Birth & Death of Biblical Minimalism," in *Biblical Archaeology Review* 37, no. 3 (May/June 2001), https://www.baslibrary.org/biblical-archaeology -review/37/3/6.

were *more* than history."[4] It was not until modern times that scientific precision made us look at religious texts as things to be evaluated as historically reliable. "In their desire to produce a wholly rational, scientific faith . . . Christian fundamentalists have interpreted scripture with a literalism that is unparalleled in the history of religion."[5] So the story goes, we should let the Bible be what it has always been, a text that helps us to develop a moral life, a set of myths that explain how humans in the past thought about themselves and the good life. The value of the Bible in such an approach will be varied, for some may find the Bible personally helpful, and some may find it strange and outdated. Both of these conclusions would invalidate the Old Testament as a historical document and would ultimately cancel its ability to speak to humanity today in the cosmic sense in which, we believe, God intends it. So why should we trust the Old Testament?

Bibliographic Evidence

The first reason we should trust the Old Testament has to do with the nature of the Old Testament documents themselves. The books that make up the Hebrew Bible come to us via three key manuscript traditions that emphasized precision and care in the transmission of the texts, and the manuscript traditions themselves go far back into ancient history, showing that old traditions are not necessarily compromised with the passage of time. This should give us great confidence in approaching the Old Testament, not just as a source for modern spiritual seeking, but for reliable historical information. This is a necessary but insufficient test for historical reliability. It is necessary to establish that the text we have was accurately preserved for us, making possible further inquiry into more specific questions of historical reliability.

Indeed, the number and age of the manuscripts in each tradition is astounding for ancient literature. The first tradition, which forms the standard against which other traditions may be compared is the Hebrew-language Masoretic tradition. Scholars have more than three thousand full and partial manuscripts of the Masoretic Text of the Bible, the oldest of

---

4. Karen Armstrong, *The Case for God* (New York: Knopf, 2009), xi.
5. Armstrong, xv.

which dates back to the ninth century CE.[6] The second is a set of primarily Greek-language translations of the Hebrew Bible that go back to year 200 BCE.[7] This tradition is called the Septuagint (sometimes identified by the Roman numerals for seventy, LXX) and was used by Greek-speaking Jews around the Mediterranean. Scholars have more than two thousand full or partial manuscripts of the Septuagint. The third tradition comes to us from the religious communities located around the Dead Sea in Israel and are known as the Dead Sea Scrolls. These were discovered starting in the 1940s, and they provide an incredibly well-preserved record of the Hebrew Bible. Though comparatively fewer in number (230 manuscripts), these are very early manuscripts, dating to around 250 BCE.[8] Also discovered in the twentieth century were the texts from Masada, the site near the Dead Sea where Jewish zealots escaped after their failed revolt against the Romans in the 70s CE. They brought biblical texts with them, used for worship in the synagogue, and these provide another well-preserved sample. However, these are not the earliest recordings of the Hebrew Bible. Old Testament scholar Richard Hess describes a remarkable set of silver scrolls discovered by archaeologists in 1979:

> The earliest manuscript of any recognizable part of the Old Testament is a text of part of Numbers 6:24–26 found incised on two small silver scrolls discovered . . . during the excavation of Jewish burial sites at Ketef Hinnom, immediately southwest of the City of David in Jerusalem. . . . Although they were discovered in a burial context that dates from the years immediately before the destruction of Jerusalem in 586 BC, it is likely that the actual composition of these silver manuscripts should be assigned an earlier date, in the seventh century BC.[9]

---

6. Craig Blomberg, *Can We Still Believe the Bible? An Evangelical Engagement with Contemporary Questions* (Grand Rapids: Brazos, 2014), 28. See also Ellis R. Brotzman, *Old Testament Textual Criticism: A Practical Introduction* (Grand Rapids: Baker, 1994), 58; and Paul D. Wegner, *A Student's Guide to Textual Criticism of the Bible* (Downers Grove, IL: InterVarsity, 2006), 158–59.

7. Richard D. Hess, *The Old Testament: A Historical, Theological, and Critical Introduction* (Grand Rapids: Baker Academic, 2016), 14.

8. Hess, 29. See also Emanuel Tov, *Textual Criticism of the Hebrew Bible, Qumran, Septuagint: Collected Essays, Volume 3*, VTSup 167 (Leiden: Brill, 2019).

9. Hess, *Old Testament*, 10.

This finding is significant, for it speaks to the presence of worshipers of Yahweh living around Jerusalem and using the biblical texts in their worship prior to the exile. This does not exhaust the evidence, but it is a helpful sample.

The true significance of this number of manuscripts across various traditions is the power for scholars to employ comparative criteria to determine the likely original words contained in the earliest versions of historical texts. There are, of course, variants between the textual traditions, but the large number of manuscripts helps scholars to determine what the earliest readers of the Bible were likely reading. When you have hundreds of manuscripts, variants stand out, and places where the textual traditions are similar increase scholarly confidence in what the earliest text actually was. For example, one of the Dead Sea Scrolls is actually a well-preserved copy of the book of Isaiah. The text of this scroll, likely dating from the second or first century BCE, is strikingly similar to that of the Masoretic Text tradition from a thousand years later.[10] This proves that Jewish scholars had a long tradition of accurately copying texts and preserving the biblical message. When there are variations between the Masoretic Texts and other texts, most modern Bible translations provide footnotes explaining the variant tradition. In almost every case, these variations do not affect meaning or theology. Establishing a reliable biblical text is what the discipline of Old Testament textual criticism has arisen to address. Biblical scholar Paul Wegner describes why this is so important: "First and foremost, [Old Testament textual criticism] attempts to establish the most reliable reading of the text. Second, in cases where a definite reading is impossible to determine, it can help to avoid dogmatism. And third, it can help the reader better understand the significance of marginal readings that appear in various Bible translations."[11] As Hebrew scholar Bruce Waltke concludes, Old Testament criticism shows that 90 percent of the Old Testament texts are without major variations.[12] This means that we have a great deal of confidence

---

10. Blomberg, *Can We Still Believe the Bible?*, 29.

11. Paul D. Wegner, *The Journey from Texts to Translations: The Origin and Development of the Bible* (Grand Rapids: Baker Academic, 1999), 177.

12. Bruce K. Waltke, "Old Testament Textual Criticism," in *Foundations for Biblical Interpretation*, ed. David S. Dockery, Kenneth A. Matthews, and Robert B. Sloan (Nashville: Broadman & Holman, 1994), 157.

that when we open the Old Testament, we are reading the same message its earliest readers understood.

Archaeological Confirmations

There are many more reasons not to simply trust the Old Testament record but to believe in the truthfulness of the records themselves. In particular, there are many independent archaeological confirmations of a number of features of the Old Testament record that verify key details and confirm the Old Testament's credibility as a historical source. Here is a sample of important archaeological finds that corroborate the Old Testament. Hazor was a Canaanite city located in what is modern Tell el-Qedah, Israel. The book of Joshua records that the Israelites under Joshua captured the city and burned it (Josh. 11:10, 13). There is evidence at the modern Hazor archaeological site of a "massive conflagration in the thirteenth century [BCE]," which is in keeping with a traditional dating of the conquest of Canaan recorded in the Bible.[13] We do not find similar burn layers from this time in other Canaanite sites, and this is in keeping with the book of Joshua's recording of this conquest: "Yet Israel did not burn any of the cities built on their mounds—except Hazor, which Joshua burned" (11:13). There is additional corroborating evidence from Hazor as well. The king of Hazor named in the Bible is Jabin (Josh. 11:1), and his eventual successor is also named Jabin in Judges 4:2. This name is unique, and scholars think that it is related to the name of a distant predecessor at Hazor named Ibni-Adad, who is named in an eighteenth-century BCE record discovered in the archives found in Mari, Syria.[14] This evidence corroborates the Canaanite (that is, not influenced by Persian or Hellenistic contexts) provenance of the biblical history, and it undermines the minimalist claim that there was no ethnic or political group that could be called Israel until the eighth century BCE.

Another set of discoveries at the Tel Dan (or in Arabic, Tell el-Qadi) site in Israel corroborate the rule of kings of Israel and Judah as recorded in the books of 1 and 2 Samuel, 1 and 2 Kings, and 1 and 2 Chronicles.

---

13. Kitchen, *On the Reliability of the Old Testament*, 185.
14. Kitchen, 175, 184.

Discovered at the site more than one hundred years apart from one another are two stelae about three feet high and two feet wide each and made of black basalt from the ninth century BCE. The previously discovered Mesha stela tells of a rebellion of the Moabites against Israel after having been oppressed by "Omri, king of Israel" and Omri's son (or grandson). This seems to correspond with the biblical record in 2 Kings 3:4–27.[15] Later in the inscription, the stele also mentions that Mesha, king of Moab, also fought against what is likely recorded as "the House of David." While the reading is disputed, it is corroborated by the more recent discovery of the Tel Dan stele at the same site, which much more clearly records the phrase "the House of David."[16] Until these discoveries, Old Testament minimalists claimed that David was a mere legend, or at best a local chieftain warrior, and they claimed that Israel did not develop a national identity until the postexilic period of the fifth–third centuries BCE. However, these discoveries not only corroborate aspects of the biblical rebellion of the Moabites, but they show that the house of David was at least strong enough to oppose another, albeit local, political power in the ancient Near East, and was known by regional powers as early as the ninth century BCE.

Third, there are the archaeological discoveries that revolve around conflict between the Assyrian king Sennacherib (d. 681 BCE) and the Judahite king Hezekiah (c. 741–687 BCE). Archaeologists have found clay prisms that record the annals of Sennacherib and his siege of Jerusalem. The same events are recorded in 2 Kings 18–19; 2 Chronicles 32; and Isaiah 36–37. In addition, the Babylonian Chronicle from the seventh or sixth centuries corroborates the conflict. In 2 Chronicles 32:3–4, 30, the Bible describes Hezekiah blocking off and rerouting the water supply around Jerusalem so that the people in the city could survive a prolonged siege. Evidence of this, what is now known as Hezekiah's Tunnel, was discovered by archaeologists in the nineteenth century CE,

---

15. André Lemaire, "'House of David' Restored in Moabite Inscription," *Biblical Archaeology Review* 20, no. 3 (1994), https://www-baslibrary-org.dtl.idm.oclc.org/biblical-archaeology-review/20/3/2.

16. "'David' Found at Dan," *Biblical Archaeology Review* 20, no. 2 (1994), https://www-baslibrary-org.dtl.idm.oclc.org/biblical-archaeology-review/20/2/1.

and it dates to the same period. Interestingly, both Sennacherib's prism and the biblical record describe their respective monarchs appealing to divine authority in their quests, Sennacherib to Ashur and Hezekiah to Yahweh, while the Babylonian Chronicle presents a more straightforward record of the events without the mention of divinities. Sennacherib's prism depicts Assyria prevailing while the Bible depicts that Hezekiah paid tribute to Sennacherib before the angel of the Lord killed the whole Assyrian army.

Some differences in how these events were recorded reveals a common objection to reading the Bible as history. Clearly the biblical texts have a perspective about God's authority and presence in the world. One might even say that the biblical texts are biased toward belief in God, toward the validity of his laws, and with a theocentric view of history. Does this mean that the events described in the Bible did not happen as they are recorded in the Bible? Does the presence of a particular perspective rule out the Bible as a historical source? Of course not; historians do not discount the annals of Sennacherib simply because those records make reference to the god Ashur. Let us let you in on a secret that all historians have known for generations: *all historical accounts have bias.* There is no such thing as a bias-free accounting of anything, and the different theological emphases of Sennacherib's prism and the biblical accounts of Hezekiah simply corroborate that fact. Modern scholars typically attempt to be aware of their biases and presuppositions, but this does not mean that bias is absent from their work. Ancient writers normally did not state their biases, but they were aware of them. As readers today, we should try to detect bias in what we are reading, but primarily, we should simply try to assess the factuality of the claims made in what we are reading. In this case, with multiple lines of verification of the biblical events, the basic details of the Bible's recording of the conflict between Assyria and Judah are confirmed.

These archaeological confirmations are important to suggesting that the Old Testament is reliable, but these are just representative examples of an ever-growing body of evidence that the historical record matches the Old Testament texts. Consider these additional confirmations from K. A. Kitchen's *On the Reliability of the Old Testament.*

1. The relatively short period in which the Midianite people appear in other ancient records. This group likely only existed in the thirteenth and twelfth centuries BCE, so "if the Exodus-Numbers-Deuteronomy and Judges narratives had only been invented many centuries later (e.g., in the sixth to third centuries), nobody would ever have heard of the Midianites, to be able to write stories about them."[17]

2. Terms like *Shankhar/Shangar* in Joshua 7:21. Referring to the origin of a robe taken by Achan as illicit plunder from Jericho, this is often translated "Babylonia" or "Shinar," and was a term uniquely used in the "sixteenth to thirteenth centuries, not later, and is a mark of authenticity."[18] The term would not have fit a document written later.

3. The authenticity of names from the second millennium BCE as reported in the Bible, such as group names Horites/Hivites, Perizzites, and Girgashites, as well as the personal names Rahab, Japhia, Jabin, Yabni-Adad, Horam, and Adoni-sedeq. These were real names used at the time, not later inventions.

4. Evidence of military and territorial conquests from landless tribal groups like the Apiru, whose exploits are recorded in the fourteenth-century BCE Amarna letters. Similar to the landless Israelites, such groups were able to conquer limited territories in Levant despite their rootless status and the presence of established powers like the Hittites and the Egyptians.

5. Extensive Iron Age I (1200–1000 BCE) and II (1000–586 BCE) evidence of the Philistine cities of Gath, Ashdod, Ekron, Ashkelon, and Gaza.

6. Contemporary cultural analogues for Solomon's temple, palace, and revenues. For example, Solomon is said to have received 666 talents (around 50,000 pounds or 25 tons) of gold in revenues annually in 1 Kings 10:14. This is a pittance compared to 383 tons of gold and silver the Egyptian king Osorkon I gave to Egyptian gods and temples within four years of his accession to the throne.[19]

---

17. Kitchen, *On the Reliability of the Old Testament*, 214.
18. Kitchen, 177.
19. Kitchen, 134.

7. Proof of horse breeding in Egypt before, during, and after Solomon's reign and horse trade with Egypt in 1 Kings 10:28–29. This has been called "royal propaganda" by some skeptics, but mention of horses from Egypt exists in a number of different sources from different times and places.[20]

8. The existence of Shishaq, king of Egypt, who "harbored Jeroboam (rebel against Solomon) and invaded Canaan in the fifth year of Rehoboam king of Judah (1 Kings 11:40; 14:25)."[21] A stela found at Megiddo records his conquest in Canaan.

9. Corroboration of the existence of Ahab, son of Omri, king of Israel in the records of the Assyrian king Shalmaneser III from 853 BCE.

10. At least four different inscriptions from different sites (Arslan Tash, Nimrud, Eritria, and Samos) which mention Hazael king of Aram, who is recorded as an enemy of Israel in multiple places in 2 Kings.

11. Two bullae (tokens to authenticate a formal letter) from the personal seals of "Berechiah [= Baruch], son of Neriah the scribe," which is the name of Jeremiah's scribe (Jer. 32:12; 16; 43:1–7; 45).[22]

A vast number of confirmations are recorded in Kitchen's impressive work. This list merely starts to paint a picture of an Old Testament that accurately represents the time periods reported therein.

Countering Ethical Objections

Finally, an additional popular set of objections to the Old Testament's spiritual reliability is briefly worth considering. Well-meaning people have taken issue with the Old Testament's presentation of people at the margins of Jewish society. The Old Testament seems to justify slavery, the denigration of women, and the condemnation of homosexuals. Here are some summary comments on these important issues.

---

20. Kitchen, 115. See a skeptical denial of the possibility of the Solomonic trade in Egyptian horses in Paul S. Ash, *David, Solomon and Egypt: A Reassessment* (Sheffield, UK: Sheffield Academic Press, 1999), 119–22.

21. Kitchen, 10.

22. Kitchen, 21.

First, slavery in the Old Testament was different from chattel slavery as practiced in places like the antebellum United States. As Paul Copan shows at length, "Israel's laws [regarding slavery] provided safety nets for protection," and a slave was typically an "indentured servant who voluntarily sold himself to live in another's household to pay off his debts."[23] Despite the fact that Israel sometimes disobeyed God's laws, there were serious considerations in the law of Moses meant to protect slaves from being mistreated by their masters, considerations completely absent from other ancient law codes.[24]

Second, while it would be foolish to deny the fact that Israelite society was patriarchal and sexist, the Old Testament laws attempt to limit the ability for women to be trafficked, abused, and discarded by ensuring proper protection, respect, and economic consideration. Moreover, Genesis claims that women are equal to men and made in the image of God (Gen. 1:26–28). By comparison, even many centuries later, Plato was teaching that a wicked man would be reborn as a woman.[25] Even so, regarding slaves and women, Israelite society did not provide (nor does the Hebrew Bible prescribe) a level of equality that we are comfortable with in the modern West.[26] The reason for this is related to the nature of revelation. The Bible reveals God's will over time, so God's perspective on issues like gender, race, economics, and freedom is made more explicit throughout the biblical record. It is likely that the Israelite recipients of the Old Testament would not have been able to accept the revolutionary nature of God's full plan and revelation.[27]

Third, homosexual sex (and not homosexuality[28]) is condemned in

---

23. Paul A. Copan, *Is God a Moral Monster? Making Sense of the Old Testament God* (Grand Rapids: Baker, 2011), 139.

24. Copan, 147.

25. Plato, *Timaeus 42B*, trans. Francis McDonald Cornford (London: Routledge, 1937), 144.

26. Tom Holland argues persuasively that our comfort level on these issues is directly related to the way in which the Judeo-Christian worldview has determined Western sympathies. See Tom Holland, *Dominion: How the Christian Revolution Remade the World* (New York: Basic Books, 2019), 142–43, 273–77, 308–9, 383–86, 409–12, 429–34, and 524–33.

27. This is William Webb's argument in *Slaves, Women and Homosexuals: Exploring the Hermeneutics of Cultural Analysis* (Downers Grove: InterVarsity, 2001).

28. While this distinction may seem strange to some in North American culture, there is a big difference between prevailing attitudes about sex and gender and the biblical picture of sexuality. For example, most North Americans uncritically think that having sexual attraction toward a particular group entails that someone ought to be sexually active with members of

the Old Testament, but it was in the context of a unique understanding of the design of sex for the purpose of procreation within marriage. Most importantly, the covenant that God made with Israel was voluntarily accepted by the Israelites, the people binding themselves to God's laws about homosexuality willingly (Ex. 24:7). There is more to say about these issues with respect to the reliability of the New Testament, the topic to which we turn next.

THE RELIABILITY OF THE NEW TESTAMENT

With the Old Testament, we established that we should generally respect the documents as historical sources, and with the New Testament, we essentially argue the same thing. However, because the New Testament contains the records of Jesus' life in the four canonical gospels, we think that trusting these sources is of utmost importance. Of course, the Old Testament is equally the word of God, yet because the New Testament contains the records of the life and ministry of Jesus of Nazareth, we will give this extra apologetic attention. This section will bleed over into the next chapter where we will consider the particular claims and credentials of Jesus of Nazareth. But for now our goals are threefold. First, we will talk about the genre of the Gospels and how they can be viewed as historical. Second, we will show that the New Testament documentary record is reliable with a large number of manuscripts reflecting a documentary tradition that can be traced to the first century CE. Third, we will show that internal features of the New Testament documents support using them as historical records of the events that they purport to describe. Finally, we will show that external sources corroborate the New Testament documents, as well.

We begin this discussion on the topic of the genre of the Gospels. In recent years, some skeptics have rejected the historicity of the Gospels. Instead of seeing the Gospels as sources that can tell us a great deal about

---

that group. This kind of thinking is blatantly absurd when one considers someone who has sexual attraction to children. For a good overview of this topic, see McLaughlin, *Confronting Christianity*, ch. 9.

the history of Jesus and his earliest followers, these skeptics argue that the Gospels are legendary texts, much like hero stories. In some ways, this is deeply embedded in the popular consciousness. Many lay people in Western contexts hold some conviction that the Gospels are legends written by Christians perhaps many, many years after the life of Jesus of Nazareth.[29] This cultural phenomenon is often backed by appeal to the fact that Gospels record certain events and sayings of Jesus' life differently in different places. To some, each canonical Gospel reads like a completely different work of historical fiction. However, this skepticism is also result of *both* the methodological naturalism that seeks to undermine the supernatural worldview required for Jesus' miracle working and resurrection *and* a postmodern concern about how truth claims in stories supposedly always seek to exert a kind of political control over others.[30] While we think that the evidence on the age and number of the New Testament documents and the ways in which the documents show signs of reliability are vital for showing that we can trust the New Testament (all of which will be laid out in the following), it is important to answer this particular skeptical challenge with a discussion on the genre of the Gospels in particular. Are the Gospels more like historical fiction or more like biographies?

Thankfully, New Testament scholar Craig Keener has responded to this challenge in recent years by affirming that the Gospels show definitive signs of belonging the genre of biography, and therefore, would not have been seen as legendary historical fictions by their earliest readers. Keener shows that most ancient novels were about two romantic lovers of legend, not a single historical figure.[31] Importantly, there are no historical novels from the same time period of the life of Jesus, and the few extant historical novels that we have knowledge of were often written hundreds of years after the lives of those they describe (unlike the Gospels, which were written very soon after the events on which they

---

29. While mostly a popular phenomenon, the charge has also been expressed in more formal ways. For example, Randel Helms, *Gospel Fictions* (New York: Prometheus, 1989).

30. For more on the postmodern critique of truth and truth's relation to power, see Shepardson, *Who's Afraid of the Unmoved Mover?*, 59–62; and Groothuis, *Truth Decay*, 98–100.

31. Craig Keener, *Christobiography: Memory, History, and the Reliability of the Gospels* (Grand Rapids: Eerdmans, 2019), 41.

report).[32] Moreover, the Gospel writers used other historical sources to compile their accounts, such as Luke's and Matthew's use of Mark's text and Luke's interest in Mary's firsthand knowledge of the events of Jesus' life. Luke even includes an historical introduction unlike anything else in ancient novels (1:1–4). Keener concludes that the Gospels are more like ancient biographies in that they are "clustered around historical intention, certainly where they narrated about an individual based on prior sources."[33] This does not mean that ancient biographies are like modern ones. Ancient biographies were not as concerned with chronology, reporting the subject's words verbatim, or attempting to avoid historical bias. But this is simply a difference in cultural standards on what a biography is, and the Gospels (and any other ancient biography for that matter) should be assessed according to the standards of their own time.

Keener also argues that John's Gospel, so often misidentified as an example of the skewed agenda of the early church in reconstructing the life of Jesus, is remarkably similar to the Synoptic Gospels in scores of ways. For example, the Gospels all record Jesus riding into Jerusalem on a colt (Matt. 21:7; Mark 11:7; Luke 19:35; John 12:14) while people shouted, "Blessed is [he] who comes in the name of the Lord" (Matt 21:9; Mark 11:9; Luke 19:38; John 12:13).[34] While John may be unique stylistically for a first-century CE biography, "his work remains much closer to biography than to a novel," especially given its correspondence with other biographies like the Synoptics.[35] Thus we agree that "in contrast to the position of radical skeptics that burden of proof rests on any claim in the Gospels, a more historically probable starting point is that these biographies written within living memory of Jesus do in fact succeed in preserving many of Jesus's acts and teaching."[36] Let us now go

---

32. Keener, 44–49.

33. Keener, 67. For a comparative investigation of the life of the Roman Emperor Otho (as narrated by Suetonius, Tacitus, and Plutarch) and Jesus (in the Synoptic Gospels), see 271–84.

34. For 103 points of similarity, see Keener, 356–61. There are some minor differences; for example, while John records Jesus as finding a donkey (12:14), the Synoptics record that Jesus' disciples acquired a colt (Matt. 21:1–7; Mark 11:1–7; Luke 19:28–35).

35. Keener, 364.

36. Keener, 497.

deeper into that historical evidence, starting with the New Testament manuscripts themselves.

The next line of evidence needed to show the reliability of the New Testament is the bibliographic test. Do we have reason to believe that the New Testament documents were transmitted in a reliable fashion so that the texts we have are approximately what the original readers and hearers would have had? Related to this is the age of the New Testament texts. Were the New Testament texts written close enough to the events of the New Testament so as to diminish the likelihood that the records had not been influenced by the development of legends or at least that the documents could have been written by eyewitnesses or those who had access to eyewitness testimony? We will take these questions in turn. Regarding the manuscripts, we have more than 5,300 manuscripts of the Greek New Testament and more than 20,000 manuscripts from various other ancient languages.[37] This means that, through textual criticism, scholars have a large amount of data with which to separate what was most likely to have been in the original manuscripts from variants added in by later scribes. Reconstructing the original message of the New Testament is much easier when you have so much comparative data to go from in such a large body of manuscript evidence. Consider by comparison the Gospel of Thomas. Of this text, we have only "one complete fourth-century [CE] manuscript and fragments from three second-century [CE] texts."[38] This means that recovering the message of the original New Testament is much easier than recovering the message of the original Gospel of Thomas. The fact that there are so few manuscripts that date so late for the Gospel of Thomas suggests that it was never widely used by the earliest Christians and that what it records about Jesus likely reflects a tradition that was far removed from the actual events of Jesus' life.

The variations in the manuscripts are important. Variations in one text were often passed along to later texts, so technically some individual words may vary from manuscript to manuscript. However, New

---

37. Blomberg, *Can We Still Believe the Bible?*, 16; Blomberg, *The Historical Reliability of the New Testament* (Nashville: B&H Academic, 2016), 613. Since the publication of these works, Blomberg has revised this estimate down from 5,700.

38. Blomberg, *Can We Still Believe the Bible?*, 36.

Testament scholars have so many manuscripts to use in comparison that it is easy to isolate where variants are anomalies that do not challenge a consensus view of what the earliest manuscripts said, and where the variants may reveal genuine ignorance of what the originals said. With that in mind, the reader should be comforted that only 6 percent of the New Testament language is in any serious doubt as to its basic original reading.[39] Of the variants, "Less than 3 percent of them are significant enough to be presented in one of the two standard critical editions of the Greek New Testament. Only about a tenth of 1 percent are interesting enough to make their way into footnotes in most English translations. It cannot be emphasized enough that *no orthodox doctrine or ethical practice of Christianity depends solely on any disputed wording.*"[40]

The great number of manuscripts is important for trusting the New Testament records, but the age of those manuscripts (when they were written and how much time passed between the biblical events and the time of those events being recorded) is vitally important as well. The events of the New Testament most likely take place between the year 7 BCE with the conception and birth of Jesus and mid-90s CE with John's visions recorded in Revelation. Moreover, all of the New Testament documents can be dated to have been written easily within the first century CE, with Revelation likely being the latest, written around 81–96 CE.[41] The oldest manuscript we have of the New Testament dates to the early second century CE. Recording a fragment of the Gospel of John, the "Rylands Papyrus . . . is thought to be dated to about A.D. 125 to 150 . . . the interval between its authorship and extant manuscript evidence is thus very short."[42] The "interval between" is what ought to be noted. The time taken for legends to develop is typically no less than two generations but can take much longer. For example, the earliest records we have of Alexander the Great's life date to five hundred years after his death, but those records show no signs of legendary and miraculous embellishments. However, the records that date to a thousand years

---

39. Paul D. Wegner, *A Student's Guide to Textual Criticism of the Bible* (Downers Grove, IL: InterVarsity, 2006), 39.

40. Blomberg, *Can We Still Believe the Bible?*, 27. Emphasis in original.

41. D. A. Carson and Douglas J. Moo, *Introduction to the New Testament*, 2nd ed. (Grand Rapids: Zondervan, 2009), 708.

42. Carson and Moo, 40–41.

after his death are where the embellishments start to show up. As Craig Blomberg concludes, "When we realize that the Gospels were written between thirty and sixty years after the death of Jesus, the likelihood of the miraculous encroaching in the Gospels where it didn't originally exist becomes slim."[43] There are many other ancient manuscripts of partial books and codices of complete books and collections of books as well. For example, the Chester Beatty collection includes portions of the books of Matthew, Mark, Luke, John, Acts, and many of the Pauline Epistles, and the fragments in this collection date to around 200–250 CE. The Bodmer collection contains large portions of John, a copy of Jude, and portions of Luke that date between 175 and 300 CE.[44]

Reliable manuscripts are necessary to have a New Testament that we can show to be trustworthy, but we can also show that internal features of the New Testament documents confirm its trustworthiness. Consider the many countercultural teachings of Jesus. Regarding families, Luke 14:26 records Jesus saying, "If anyone comes to me and does not hate father and mother, wife and children, brothers and sisters—yes, even their own life—such a person cannot be my disciple." It would have been highly unlikely for a religious leader to teach something like this in Jesus' day. The Judaism of the period was family oriented at its core. The inclusion of this statement indicates that Luke would not have felt at liberty to make Jesus' words more appealing, which gives modern readers that much more of a reason to trust it.[45] In fact, Jesus was known for his difficult teaching. John 6 records a sermon at the synagogue in Capernaum where Jesus claimed that eating his flesh and drinking his blood is required for everlasting life. Recognizing how this teaching was frustrating to his hearers, John recorded, "From this time many of his disciples turned back and no longer followed him" (John 6:66). The fact that his disciples would abandon him certainly does not paint Jesus in a good light.[46]

It is not merely the embarrassment at Jesus' losing many of his disciples that makes us trust the New Testament's account here. Of the

---

43. Blomberg, *Historical Reliability of the New Testament*, 440.
44. Wegner, *Student's Guide to Textual Criticism*, 257–59.
45. Blomberg, *Historical Reliability of the New Testament*, 134.
46. Blomberg, *Historical Reliability of the New Testament*, 203.

ones who remained, one of his key disciples, Judas Iscariot, betrayed Jesus. The fact that Jesus would have allowed the one who would betray him into his inner circle would have been incredibly embarrassing. That is, to the readers of the Gospels in Jesus' day, such an invention would have been counterproductive to the message of Jesus' identity as the Son of God. Would not the Son of God have been wise enough to keep his enemies further removed? This is not to say that Jesus did not have good reason for allowing Judas to be a member of the Twelve. Rather, it is unclear why Jesus' followers would have invented Judas when his presence could seem to undercut Jesus' wisdom and skill as a leader. Moreover, the Gospels all recount that nearly all of the male disciples abandoned Jesus at his trial and crucifixion. Again, this would have been an embarrassing detail to invent about Jesus unless it was true. In fact, if the disciples were attempting to fabricate a hoax for the purpose of setting themselves up as the rightful heirs to Jesus' legacy after his death, it would be counterproductive for them to paint themselves in such a negative light. This is underscored by the fact that all of Jesus' remaining disciples were willing to suffer and die for their Christian testimony, and many did indeed give their lives in this way.[47]

We will share more on this in the next chapter, but here are some other potentially counterproductive teachings and events in the New Testament:

1. "The Gospel writers would not have invented Jesus' baptism by John because it creates the problem of his apparently having to repent of sin."[48]
2. Following Peter's rebuke of Jesus, "But when Jesus turned and looked at his disciples, he rebuked Peter. 'Get behind me,

---

47. Gary Habermas argues that this is key to supporting the historicity of the resurrection of Jesus, as well, which we will see in chapter 10. See Habermas, "The Case for Christ's Resurrection," in *To Everyone an Answer: A Case for the Christian Worldview*, ed. Francis J. Beckwith, William Lane Craig, and J. P. Moreland (Downers Grove, IL: IVP Academic, 2004), 196: "There is the oft-acknowledged precept that those who are willing to die for a cause genuinely believe in it." See also Sean McDowell, "Did the Apostles Really Die as Martyrs for Their Faith?," in *Christian Research Journal* 39, no. 2 (2016), http://www.equip.org/PDF/JAF1392.pdf.

48. Blomberg, *Historical Reliability of the New Testament*, 307. Blomberg continues, "Yet all the Synoptics agree that the baptism was the occasion of identifying Jesus as both the

Satan!' he said. 'You do not have in mind the concerns of God, but merely human concerns'" (Mark 8:33).

3. Jesus' saying, "But about that day or hour no one knows, not even the angels in heaven, nor the Son, but only the Father" (Mark 13:32). One would think that the Son of God would be privy to such knowledge.

4. Peter and the disciples' insistence that they would never deny Jesus followed by their betrayal.

One final set of evidence shows that the New Testament documents are reliable—the great support outside the Bible for the details contained in the Bible. Just as with the Old Testament, ancient histories and modern archaeological discoveries are the apologist's allies here. First, there are many ancient witnesses that speak of Jesus and the earliest Christians. While not sympathetic with Christians' theological claims, the ancient historians Tacitus, Suetonius, Pliny the Younger, and Josephus all confirm key accounts of Jesus and his followers, including Jesus' setting in Judea, prophetic claims, that he was reported to have been a miracle worker, his crucifixion under Pontius Pilate, and his followers' belief that he had risen from the dead. Take Tacitus, for example. In speaking of the great fire that broke out in Rome (in 64 CE), his *Annals* confirm some key details about the New Testament narrative.

> Nero fastened the guilt and inflicted the most exquisite tortures on a class hated for their abominations, called Christians by the populace. Christus, from whom the name had its origin, suffered the extreme penalty during the reign of Tiberius at the hands of one of our procurators, Pontius Pilatus, and a most mischievous superstition, thus checked for the moment, again broke out not only in Judaea, the first source of the evil, but even in Rome, where all things hideous and shameful from every part of the world find their centre and become popular.[49]

Messiah and the Suffering Servant by the heavenly voice's allusions to Psalm 2:7 and Isaiah 42:1, respectively."

49. Tacitus, *The Annals* 15:44, trans. Alfred John Church and William Jackson Brodribb, Internet Classics Archive, http://classics.mit.edu/Tacitus/annals.11.xv.html.

Of course, these historians would not have agreed with the New Testament's unique claims about Jesus' divine identity, a topic to which we will return, but the fact that Jesus' life and ministry are corroborated by these witnesses is helpful in showing that key elements of the Bible are trustworthy.

The second line of external evidence for the New Testament are the many archaeological discoveries that confirm the biblical accounts. Pontius Pilate's prefecture has been confirmed in ruins at Caesarea in Israel. On a stone commissioned "to honor his imperial benefactor, the emperor Tiberius,"[50] there appears the partial inscription: "Pontius Pilate . . . Prefect of Judea." To the date of its discovery in the 1960s, evidence of Pilate had not appeared in the archaeological record, but only in written records. However, further confirmation of his existence was confirmed in 2018 when researchers deciphered the name of Pilate on a copper-alloy ring that had been unearthed in 1968–69 at the Herodium site southeast of Bethlehem.[51] Another discovery is what most scholars think is the Pool of Bethesda that forms the setting for one of Jesus' healings in John 5:1–15. John's account tells of a pool "surrounded by five covered colonnades" (v. 2), and this is exactly what can be seen today. Scholars believe that this was a site for ritual immersion by pilgrims to Jerusalem.[52] Finally, some scholars have doubted whether a crucifixion victim would have been given the kind of burial that Joseph of Arimathea gives to Jesus in the Gospels. John Dominic Crossan famously claims, "In normal circumstances, the soldiers guarded the body until death and thereafter it was left for carrion crow, scavenger dog, or other wild beasts to finish the brutal job."[53] However, Crossan acknowledges that it may have been possible that the Roman soldiers guarding Jesus' body took it down from the cross themselves and buried it in a shallow grave. Either way, though, Crossan says, "The dogs were waiting."[54] If this were truly

---

50. Robert R. Cargill, "First Person: Was Pontius Pilate's Ring Discovered at Herodium?," *Biblical Archaeology Review* 45, no. 2 (March/April 2019), https://www-baslibrary-org.dtl.idm .oclc.org/biblical-archaeology-review/45/2/7.

51. Cargill, "First Person."

52. Blomberg, *Historical Reliability of the New Testament*, 200.

53. John Dominic Crossan, *Jesus: A Revolutionary Biography* (San Francisco: HarperSan Francisco, 1994), 153.

54. Crossan, 154.

the case, then this would undercut the New Testament accounts that Jesus was given a proper Jewish burial, and thereby, the accounts' overall reliability. However, we now know that at least sometimes, crucifixion victims' bodies were handled with respect and care after their deaths. There are, of course, many accounts of crucifixion victims' remains being treated as Crossan suggests, but the counterexamples show that it is possible that events in the New Testament records happened as described. An ossuary, or ceremonial burial box for the bones of the deceased, has been found northeast of Jerusalem, containing the remains of a first-century crucifixion victim named "Jehohanan," who received a proper Jewish burial, in contradiction to Crossan's claim.[55] In addition, *The Digest of Justinian*, written toward the end of the third century CE, quotes the Roman jurist Paulus's *Sententiae*, which states that "the bodies of executed persons are to be granted to any who seek them for burial."[56] Though the *Digest* is late, "the tradition he hands on may be much earlier."[57]

These things, of course, do not prove the reliability of the New Testament beyond a shadow of a doubt, but that has never been our goal. Instead, the reliability of the Bible is useful for the apologist in showing that the Christian worldview is rational. The examples provided show that we can trust the biblical sources as historical sources, and this should prompt the truly open-minded person into further consideration of those sources' claims. In this regard, there is much to support the Christian who seeks to show that there is ample evidence to believe the Christian worldview. Even better, the ample evidence presented here is just a small sample of the "embarrassment of riches" that can be found by the one who wants to find out the truth of the Bible.[58] Our hope is

---

55. Alan Watson, trans. *The Digest of Justinian*, vol. 4 (Philadelphia: University of Pennsylvania Press, 1998), 377; quoted in John Granger Cook, "Crucifixion and Burial," *New Testament Studies* 57, no. 2 (April 2011): 203.

56. Cook, "Crucifixion and Burial," 196.

57. Cook, 196. For the full collection of texts relevant to Jesus' crucifixion, see David W. Chapman and Eckhard J. Schnabel, *The Trial and Crucifixion of Jesus: Texts and Commentary* (Carol Stream, IL: Tyndale House, 2019).

58. J. Ed Komoszewski, M. James Sawyer, and Daniel B. Wallace, *Reinventing Jesus: How Contemporary Skeptics Miss the Real Jesus and Mislead Popular Culture* (Grand Rapids: Kregel, 2006), 75. This phrase, which the authors apply to the New Testament texts, surely applies to the evidences that we outline here.

that the earnest student of apologetics will follow the footnotes in this chapter to continue studying this vast topic that we have started to outline here. But before doing so, we must turn our attention to the key character in the Bible's story of God's redemption: Jesus Christ, and his claims and credentials.

STUDY QUESTIONS

1. Why is it important for apologetics to argue for the Bible's reliability?
2. Must we argue for the inerrancy of the Bible to do good apologetics? Explain your answer.
3. What are the basic logical stages in defending the reliability of the Bible?
4. How do you respond to the allegation that since the Bible contains miracle claims, it cannot be true?

SUGGESTED READING

Armstrong, Karen. *The Case for God.* New York: Knopf, 2009.

Biran, Avraham. "'David' Found at Dan." *Biblical Archaeology Review* 20, no. 2 (1994). https://www-baslibrary-org.dtl.idm.oclc.org/biblical-archaeology -review/20/2/1.

Blomberg, Craig. *Can We Still Believe the Bible? An Evangelical Engagement with Contemporary Questions.* Grand Rapids: Brazos, 2014.

_____. *The Historical Reliability of the New Testament: Countering the Challenges to Evangelical Christian Beliefs.* Nashville: B&H Academic, 2016.

Brotzman, Ellis R. *Old Testament Textual Criticism: A Practical Introduction,* 58. Grand Rapids: Baker, 1994.

Cargil, Robert R. "First Person: Was Pontius Pilate's Ring Discovered at Herodium?" *Biblical Archaeology Review* 45, no. 2 (March/April 2019). https://www -baslibrary-org.dtl.idm.oclc.org/biblical-archaeology-review/45/2/7.

Carson, D. A., and Douglas J. Moo. *Introduction to the New Testament,* 267. Grand Rapids: Zondervan, 2005.

"The Chicago Statement on Biblical Inerrancy" (1978). https://www.etsjets.org /files/documents/Chicago_Statement.pdf.

Cook, John Granger. "Crucifixion and Burial." *New Testament Studies* 57, no. 2 (April 2011): 203.

Copan, Paul A. *Is God a Moral Monster? Making Sense of the Old Testament God.* Grand Rapids: Baker, 2011, 139.

Crossan, John Dominic. *Jesus: A Revolutionary Biography.* San Francisco: HarperSanFrancisco, 1994.

Garfinkel, Yoseph. "The Birth & Death of Biblical Minimalism." *Biblical Archaeology Review* 37, no. 3 (May/June 2001). https://www.baslibrary.org /biblical-archaeology-review/37/3/6.

Groothuis, Douglas. "Distortions of Christianity—or the God I Don't Believe In." In Douglas Groothuis, *Christian Apologetics: A Comprehensive Case for Biblical Faith.* 2nd ed. Downers Grove, IL: IVP Academic, 2022.

Habermas, Gary. "The Case for Christ's Resurrection." In *To Everyone an Answer: A Case for the Christian Worldview,* edited by Francis J. Beckwith, William Lane Craig, and J. P. Moreland. Downers Grove, IL: IVP Academic, 2004.

Hess, Richard D. *The Old Testament: A Historical, Theological, and Critical Introduction.* Grand Rapids: Baker Academic, 2016.

Kitchen, K. A. *On the Reliability of the Old Testament.* Grand Rapids: Eerdmans, 2003.

Komoszewski, J. Ed, M. James Sawyer, and Daniel B. Wallace. *Reinventing Jesus: How Contemporary Skeptics Miss the Real Jesus and Mislead Popular Culture.* Grand Rapids: Kregel, 2006.

Lemaire, André. "'House of David' Restored in Moabite Inscription." *Biblical Archaeology Review* 20, no. 3 (1994). https://www-baslibrary-org.dtl.idm. oclc.org/biblical-archaeology-review/20/3/2.

McDowell, Sean. "Did the Apostles Really Die as Martyrs for Their Faith?" *Christian Research Journal* 39, no. 2 (2016). http://www.equip.org/PDF /JAF1392.pdf.

McLaughlin, Rebecca. *Confronting Christianity: 12 Hard Questions for the World's Largest Religion.* Wheaton, IL: Crossway, 2019.

Plato. *Timaeus.* Translated by Francis McDonald Cornford. London: Routledge, 1937.

Sloan, Robert B., David S. Dockery, and K. A. Mathews. *Foundations for Biblical Interpretation.* Nashville: Broadman & Holman, 1994, 157. Cited in Paul D. Wegner, *The Journey from Texts to Translations: The Origin and Development of the Bible.* Grand Rapids: Baker Academic, 1999.

Tacitus. *The Annals*, 15:44. Translated by Alfred John Church and William Jackson

Brodribb. Internet Classics Archive. http://classics.mit.edu/Tacitus/annals.11
.xv.html.

Tov, Emanuel. *Textual Criticism of the Hebrew Bible, Qumran, Septuagint:
Collected Essays, Volume 3*. Supplements to Vetus Testamentum, vol. 167.
Leiden: Brill, 2019.

Waltke, Bruce K. "Old Testament Textual Criticism." In *Foundations for Biblical
Interpretation*, edited by David S. Dockery, Kenneth A. Matthews, and
Robert B. Sloan. Nashville: Broadman & Holman, 1994.

Watson, Alan, trans. *The Digest of Justinian*. Vol. 4. Philadelphia: University of
Pennsylvania Press, 1998.

Wegner, Paul D. *The Journey from Texts to Translations: The Origin and
Development of the Bible*. Grand Rapids: Baker Academic, 1999.

_____. *A Student's Guide to Textual Criticism of the Bible*. Downers Grove, IL:
InterVarsity, 2006.

CHAPTER 9

THE TRUTH ABOUT JESUS

Whatever you make of him, Jesus of Nazareth has been the most influential—and controversial—person in world history. He is the founder of the world's largest religion, which is growing most dramatically in the two-thirds world.[1] The mark of Jesus is found everywhere—in church architecture, statuary, literature, ethics, and in a thousand philanthropic organizations inspired by him. Nonreligious people often cry out, "Oh Jesus!" or "Christ!" in distress or to show their contempt.[2] Jesus' teachings are commonplace even when people fail to trace their origins. We hear of "good Samaritans," "turning the other cheek," "practicing what you preach," "the blind leading the blind," and more. Since the beginning of Christianity, with the martyrdom of Stephen (Acts 7), followers of Jesus have given their all and even their very lives in service to Jesus Christ. Were they deceived?

Influence, nevertheless, is not the same as objective truth. False ideas can go a long way, century after century. Islam may be the fastest-growing religion today and might eclipse Christianity in numbers in a

---

1. See Phillip Jenkins, *The Next Christendom*, 3rd ed. (New York: Oxford University Press, 2011).

2. *New Yorker* magazine, a thoroughly secular magazine, had on its November 14, 2016, cover an image of a newspaper being held by a subway commuter with the headline "Oh, Sweet Jesus, Please God, No" after the election of Donald Trump. Bruce and Carolyn Winfrey Gillette, "A Hymn-Prayer for the Election," HuffPost, updated November 8, 2016, https://www.huffpost.com/entry/a-hymn-prayer-for-the-election_b_581e1ae0e4b0102262411806.

few decades.[3] But that does not make Islam true. Placebos can also effect cures. Thus, the question comes down to, how can we know the truth about Jesus, and why should we care to?

TRUTH CONSIDERED

If we want to know the truth about Jesus, we have to get clear on the nature of truth itself. Given people's penchant for claiming something as "my truth" or "my lived experience" as the basis for reality, we need to explore the truth about the truth.

First, we should distinguish *beliefs* from *truth*. As a child, I believed in Santa Claus. My belief, though understandable, was false; it was untrue. It was true that I believed in Santa Claus, but there was no corresponding entity (St. Nick in the popular image) to make that belief true. Anytime we admit that we were wrong in one of our beliefs, we must then admit to the distinction between belief and truth.

Second, the significance or profundity of one's experience does not make that experience the basis for objective reality. I may feel terribly slighted by a comment made about me, go into paroxysms of anger, and feel deeply offended by the comment. Yet none of my subjective responses means that the person who made the comment was trying to insult me. It could be that I simply misunderstood his comment, and he meant no offense. In this case, the statement "You offended me" is true; but the statement "You meant to offend me" is false.

Third, the beneficial results stemming from a belief do not, in themselves, make a belief true. You may think that you lost $500 in cash and attribute this to your sloppiness and irresponsibility. This shocks you into reforming your life such that you become a successful businessperson. Later you find out that your roommate stole the money from you. Thus, a false belief was instrumental in a good result.[4] Similarly, while a Christian's testimony to how Jesus has worked in their life is a significant

---

3. Michael Lipka and Conrad Hackett, "Why Muslims Are the Fastest-Growing Religious Group," Pew Research Center, April 6, 2017, https://www.pewresearch.org/fact-tank/2017/04/06/why-muslims-are-the-worlds-fastest-growing-religious-group.

4. See Winfried Corduan, *No Doubt about It* (Nashville: Broadman & Holman, 1997), 60–61.

part of apologetics, it cannot bear the entire weight, since it is *possible* that belief in Jesus confers some psychological or other benefits without Christianity itself being true.

These three points converge on the idea that a true statement is one that corresponds to or reflects reality, and a false belief is one that fails to correspond to or reflect reality. As Aristotle put it, "To say of what is that it is not, or of what is not that it is, is false, while to say of what is that it is, and of what is not that it is not, is true; so that he who says of anything that it is, or that it is not, will say either what is true or what is false."[5]

To believe with all one's heart that the earth is flat is to believe a false statement, since the earth is round. To joyfully and confidently believe that you are the handsomest man in the world when mirrors repeatedly crack at the sight of your visage is to hold a false belief—like it or not. But we have another issue to consider.

Someone might admit to what I just wrote but affirm that *in matters of religion or spirituality* we cannot apply this understanding of truth. Just as moral relativists claim that morality is relative to their own subjective values—even if there are objective truths like gravity and the multiplication table—some people claim that religious or spiritual values are relative and depend on subjective wants and needs. On this understanding, Christianity can be "true for you," Buddhism be "true for me," and Islam "be true for someone else." Is this right?

Of first concern is that every religion claims to be objectively, absolutely, and universally true and of the utmost importance for human beings. There isn't a whiff of relativism or subjectivism to be sniffed. The Buddha's first sermon was on the "Four Noble Truths," not "The four interesting ideas you might find helpful if you so choose." The confession that makes one a Muslim is "There is one God and Muhammad is his prophet," not "Islam might be for you. Try it out." And so it goes for all religions. To make the worldview claims of religions merely subjective or relative does not do justice to the religions themselves. One should be honest about this.

Further, all religions cannot be true because they make different

---

5. Aristotle, *Metaphysics* 4.7.

claims about reality and the religious life. Just as I cannot claim that both Anchorage and Juneau are the capitals of Alaska (Juneau is the capital), neither can I claim that Muhammad is a prophet and that Jesus is God incarnate. This is because Muhammad taught that Jesus is not God, and Jesus himself claimed to be God, as we will see. Even more, some religions, unlike Christianity and Islam, deny the very existence of a personal God. Buddhism teaches that the ultimate reality is an impersonal state called *nirvana*, and Taoism asserts it is "the Tao that cannot be named." While Christianity and Judaism emphasize the significance of prayer (since there is a God who hears and acts on prayer), Buddhism and Taoism do not, since their sense of ultimate reality is impersonal, not personal.[6]

Christianity claims to be a revelation from the one true God. Christianity, among all the religions of the world, has always emphasized teaching, preaching, creeds, confessions, catechisms, and apologetics— all concerned with the truth of who God is, what God has done, and how we should respond. As Paul said about the resurrection of Christ, "If Christ has not been raised, our preaching is useless and so is your faith. More than that, we are then found to be false witnesses about God, for we have testified about God that he raised Christ from the dead" (1 Cor. 15:14–15). Far from resting in the positive effects of believing a comforting falsehood, Paul addressed the implications of Christ having not been resurrected. "If Christ has not been raised, your faith is futile; you are still in your sins. Then those also who have fallen asleep in Christ are lost. If only for this life we have hope in Christ, we are of all people most to be pitied" (vv. 17–19).

There is no reason, *a priori*, to assume that there is no truth available to us when it comes to the ultimate claims of religion about the ultimate reality, the human condition, and salvation. But many have opted for a kind of "post-truth" understanding of religion in which individuals cobble together their own version of spirituality in a fact-free manner.[7] But the proof of the pudding is in the eating. If we find good, sufficient,

---

6. That may not stop individual Buddhists and Taoists from praying, though, since human beings often sense their need for transcendent help, even if their worldview forbids it.

7. See Tara Isabella Burton, *Strange Rites: New Religions for a Godless World* (New York: Public Affairs, 2020).

and existentially compelling reasons to take the biblical account of Jesus Christ to be true, then all self-styled spirituality goes up in a cloud of unholy smoke.

Second, we should be concerned that the claims of Christianity are consequential since they address the basics of one's existence, now and forever. If Christianity is true, then God has an absolute claim on our lives, we are sinners before a holy God, and we need to repent, believe the gospel, and live wholeheartedly for the cause of Christ, his church, and his kingdom. Eternity itself is at stake, since Jesus said that he came to give us eternal and abundant Life (John 3:16; 10:10). It is only prudent, then, for someone to consider thoughtfully investigating Christianity. After Paul preached at Athens, we read that "when they heard about the resurrection of the dead, some of them sneered, but others said, 'We want to hear you again on this subject'" (Acts 17:32). Those at all interested in the identity of Jesus should pursue knowledge about him since he said, "Now this is eternal life: that they know you, the only true God, and Jesus Christ, whom you have sent" (John 17:3).

Third, as Francis Schaeffer has argued, many have given up on reason to provide a unified worldview that gives meaning to life. Instead of pursuing truth through reason and evidence, many simply take a blind leap of faith to believe something—anything—that gives a sense of meaning, comfort, or belonging.[8] We are creatures of hope, but hope without truth is pointless. The claim of this book—and so many others, including the books of Schaeffer—is that no one need give up his or her intellect in the pursuit of meaning, since meaning and truth align in Jesus Christ. Christianity gives answers that satisfy the whole person, heart and mind. Jesus came to take away our sins, not to take away our minds (Matt. 22:37–40).[9]

Having tried to clear up the question of truth and its pertinence to life, we will now consider how we might learn the facts about Jesus and their significance. We begin with our sources of knowledge.

---

8. See Francis A. Schaeffer, *How Should We Then Live? The Rise and Fall of Western Culture* (1976; repr., Wheaton, IL: Crossway, 2005); Schaeffer, *Escape from Reason* (1968; repr., Downers Grove, IL: InterVarsity, 2006); Schaeffer, *The God Who Is There* (1968; repr., Downers Grove, IL: InterVarsity, 2020).

9. See Douglas Groothuis, "Jesus: Philosopher and Apologist," *Christian Research Journal* 25, no. 2 (2002), https://www.equip.org/article/jesus-philosopher-and-apologist.

JESUS: BASIC FACTS

We have already argued for the reliability of the Bible in broad strokes. Before going on, I will review and add to the case. When it comes to the identity of Jesus, we are thrown back to history as our primary source of knowledge. As the apostle John said of Jesus, "The Word became flesh and made his dwelling among us. We have seen his glory, the glory of the one and only Son, who came from the Father, full of grace and truth. . . . The one and only Son, who is himself God and is in closest relationship with the Father, has made him known" (John 1:14, 18).

The God that Jesus claimed to know and reveal to humanity is a God who created the world and who acts in space-time actuality. While other religions, particularly Taoism and Hinduism, trade in mystical aphorisms and sacred mythologies, the Bible is anchored in facts about people, places, and things in the material world. It sticks its neck out into the fields of war, peace, politics, people, family, famine, harvest, life, death, and everything else under the sun.

The Gospels are our primary sources on the life of Jesus, although the rest of the New Testament contributes as well. While the Gospels contain accounts of miracles, they are not written in the style of myths or legends.[10] If natural theology does its work, we should allow the possibility of miracles, since there is a supernatural creator, designer, and lawgiver who might deign to intervene in his creation for his purposes. Furthermore, if miracle stories are attested by several sources (as they are in the Gospels), if they fit into a coherent narrative plot (as they do in the Gospels), and if they are written by eyewitness to the events or by those who consulted eyewitnesses (as were the Gospels), then we have good reason to trust them.

Some biblical scholars of yesterday and today have tried to de-mythologize the Gospels by eliminating any supernatural elements. A naturalized or desupernaturalized Jesus is then reduced to being a moral teacher and martyr. Since we should not rule out the supernatural in principle (given natural theology), this is an artificial and unwarranted

---

10. Craig L. Keener, "Comparison of Early Christian with Other Ancient Accounts," *Miracles: The Credibility of the New Testament Accounts*, vol. 1 (Grand Rapids: Baker Academic, 2011).

move. Moreover, the supernatural is thickly interwoven into the stories about Jesus. His origin is supernatural (the virginal conception), the events around his birth are supernatural, his ministry of healing, exorcism, and prophecy is supernatural, and his resurrection from the dead is supernatural. This led Schaeffer to write, "The rationalistic theological liberalism of the nineteenth century was embarrassed by and denied the supernatural, but still tried to hold on to the historic Jesus by winnowing out of the New Testament all the supernatural elements."[11] However, this effort failed. "The rationalistic theologians could not separate the historic Jesus from the supernatural events connected with him. History and the supernatural were too interwoven in the New Testament. If one retained any of the historical Jesus, one had to keep some of the supernatural. If one got rid of all the supernatural, one had no historical Jesus."[12] Since there is abundant evidence for the existence of Jesus in history, this desupernaturalizing or demythologizing effort suffers a fatal flaw.

Nevertheless, in recent years, due largely to unreliable internet sources, some claim that Jesus never existed. This is called *mythicism*. While the theory was entertained in liberal German scholarship in the nineteenth century, few New Testament scholars even entertain the idea today. The exception is freelance scholar Richard Carrier.[13] On the face of it, it is extremely unlikely that the entire literature of the New Testament would be based on a falsehood, particularly when it offers historical claims related to the known geography, culture, and politics of ancient Palestine. The existence of Jesus is also verified by numerous sources outside of the New Testament.[14] Even the agnostic

---

11. Francis A. Schaeffer, *How Should We Then Live? The Rise and Decline of Western Thought and Culture*, L'Abri 50th Anniversary ed. (Wheaton, IL: Crossway, 2009), locs. 2134–36, Kindle.

12. Schaeffer, *How Should We Then Live?*, locs. 2142–44. For an in-depth defense of the reliability of the Gospels along with their miracles, see Craig L. Blomberg, *The Historical Reliability of the Gospels*, 2nd ed. (Downers Grove, IL: IVP Academic, 2007).

13. On this theory and Carrier's argument in particular, see the New Testament scholar Larry Hurtado's essay "Why the 'Mythical Jesus' Claim Has No Traction with Scholars," *Larry Hurtado's Blog*, December 2, 2017, https://larryhurtado.wordpress.com/2017/12/02/why-the -mythical-jesus-claim-has-no-traction-with-scholars.

14. See Murray Harris, *Three Crucial Questions about Jesus* (Grand Rapids: Baker, 1994). The first of these questions is "Did Jesus exist?"

critic of Christianity, Bart Ehrman, has defended the existence of Jesus in ancient history.[15] The attempts to mythicize Jesus rely on artificially cobbling together various ideas from non-Christian religions.[16]

Having made a case for the nature and importance of truth and for the existence and supernatural character of Jesus, we are ready to consider his claims, credentials, and achievements and to put these in comparative perspective with those of other religious teachers.

JESUS' INCOMPARABLE LIFE

Jesus' résumé is best understood when considered through the narrative of his life. We will isolate and explain several claims and events in Jesus' life, but it behooves the reader to work through the Gospels themselves to experience the Jesus who emerges there. Each gospel has a somewhat different emphasis since each was written by a different person and to a different audience. For example, the Gospel of Mark emphasizes Jesus as a man of action and does not feature the longer teachings we find in the other three gospels, particularly in John. But each gospel fulfills a purpose, and the fourfold witness is stronger than anything less. Thus, I advise anyone interested in Jesus to pick up the Gospels and read carefully.

These are the basic contours of Jesus' story. He was born of a virgin to fulfill a prophecy (Isa. 7:14; Matt. 1:22–23), and the events around his birth were filled with angelic interventions. But Jesus labored in obscurity as a carpenter until about age thirty when he began his public ministry, after being heralded by the prophet John the Baptist, who said of him, "Look, the Lamb of God, who takes away the sin of the world!" (John 1:29). We read that after Jesus was baptized by John, "he went up out of the water. At that moment heaven was opened, and he saw the Spirit of God descending like a dove and alighting on him. And a voice

---

15. Bart Ehrman, *Did Jesus Exist? The Historical Argument for Jesus of Nazareth* (New York: HarperOne, 2013).

16. See Craig L. Blomberg, "Jesus of Nazareth: What Historians Can Know about Him and Why It Matters," in Douglas Groothuis, *Christian Apologetics: A Comprehensive Case for Biblical Faith*, 2nd ed. (Downers Grove, IL: IVP Academic, 2022).

from heaven said, 'This is my Son, whom I love; with him I am well pleased'" (Matt. 3:16–17).[17] Thus, the Trinity is indicated.

Jesus was then led into the wilderness where he successfully resisted the temptations of the devil, who wanted to deter him from his rightful ministry (Matt. 4:1–11; Luke 4:1–13). He began his public ministry by echoing John the Baptist (Matt. 3:2): "Repent, for the kingdom of heaven has come near" (see also Matt. 4:17). Later Jesus quoted from Isaiah and declared his purpose in the synagogue in Nazareth:

> "The Spirit of the Lord is on me,
>> because he has anointed me
>> to proclaim good news to the poor.
> He has sent me to proclaim freedom for the prisoners
>> and recovery of sight for the blind,
> to set the oppressed free,
>> to proclaim the year of the Lord's favor."

> Then he rolled up the scroll, gave it back to the attendant and sat down. The eyes of everyone in the synagogue were fastened on him. He began by saying to them, "Today this scripture is fulfilled in your hearing." (Luke 4:18–21)

Jesus is no ordinary figure and is far more than a prophet on the same level as John the Baptist or any Old Testament prophet. He fulfilled prophecy and understood himself to be the Messiah. When the imprisoned John the Baptist later questioned Jesus' credentials, Jesus assured John that he was the Messiah.

> When John, who was in prison, heard about the deeds of the Messiah, he sent his disciples to ask him, "Are you the one who is to come, or should we expect someone else?"

---

17. John's baptism was for repentance, so he was surprised when Jesus wanted to be baptized. Nevertheless, Jesus said it was right. See Matthew 3:1–7. Scripture affirms that Jesus was perfectly righteous and never sinned (2 Cor. 5:21; Heb. 4:15; 1 Peter 2:22). We never see Jesus admitting fault, apologizing, or feeling guilt.

Jesus replied, "Go back and report to John what you hear and see: The blind receive sight, the lame walk, those who have leprosy are cleansed, the deaf hear, the dead are raised, and the good news is proclaimed to the poor. Blessed is anyone who does not stumble on account of me." (Matt. 11:2–6)

These credentials single Jesus out as the Messiah. But what does it mean to be the Messiah? Jesus fulfilled these prophecies and others but also achieved more than was expected, though he did not politically liberate the Jews from their Roman domination. He did claim to liberate human beings from bondage to sin, death, and the devil.

Jesus operated outside the religious establishment of the Jews but gained a following through his teaching, preaching, and miracles. His inner circle was limited to twelve men, one of whom betrayed him. He stirred controversy wherever he went—not by showmanship, but through the honesty, intelligence, and courage of his teaching and interactions. He scandalized some by associating with the down-and-out (prostitutes) and the up-and-out (tax collectors). He feared no one, hated no one; and was never intimidated, out-argued, or backed into a corner. It was said of him, "He has done everything well" (Mark 7:37).

After about three years of ministry, neither the Jewish religious establishment nor the Roman government could endure Jesus any longer. He was deemed a heretic by the Jews and a threat to the government by the Romans. He was neither, but on that basis, he was tried, sentenced to death, and crucified between two common criminals. He died. He was buried. But Christianity is based on the reality that he rose again from the dead as the Lord of life. We dedicate chapter 10 to this topic. That is the story in broad outline. Now let us consider some of Christ's specific claims and what we can make of them.

JESUS' CLAIMS

Jesus' moral teachings resonate throughout the world, even the most radical ones that are seldom obeyed: "Love your enemies." "Pray for those who persecute you." "Turn the other cheek." But his words cannot be limited to moral conduct. He spoke much about his own identity in relation to his teachings. Because of this, we cannot separate the man from the message. Given the reliability of the Gospels, we should take all of what Jesus said as true and worthy of respect. Consider some of his statements about himself.

Jesus went to Capernaum and "preached the word" in a house jammed with listeners. Four men carried a paralyzed man to Jesus but could not reach him because of the crowd. Undaunted, "they made an opening in the roof above Jesus by digging through it and then lowered the mat the man was lying on" (Mark 2:4). Jesus then surprised everyone (again):

> When Jesus saw their faith, he said to the paralyzed man, "Son, your sins are forgiven."
>
> Now some teachers of the law were sitting there, thinking to themselves, "Why does this fellow talk like that? He's blaspheming! Who can forgive sins but God alone?"
>
> Immediately Jesus knew in his spirit that this was what they were thinking in their hearts, and he said to them, "Why are you thinking these things? Which is easier: to say to this paralyzed man, 'Your sins are forgiven,' or to say, 'Get up, take your mat and walk'? But I want you to know that the Son of Man has authority on earth to forgive sins." So he said to the man, "I tell you, get up, take your mat and go home." He got up, took his mat and walked out in full view of them all. This amazed everyone and they praised God, saying, "We have never seen anything like this!" (Mark 2:5–12)

Jesus discerned their thoughts and responded, not by denying he had the power to forgive sins, but by demonstrating his supernatural and divine authority by healing the paralytic. C. S. Lewis captured the significance of this.

> Now unless the speaker is God, this is really so preposterous as to be comic. We can all understand how a man forgives offences against himself. You tread on my toes and I forgive you, you steal my money and I forgive you. But what should we make of a man,

himself unrobbed and untrodden on, who announced that he forgave you for treading on other men's toes and stealing other men's money? . . . Yet this is what Jesus did. He told people that their sins were forgiven, and never waited to consult all the other people whom their sins had undoubtedly injured. He unhesitatingly behaved as if He was the party chiefly concerned, the person chiefly offended in all offences.[18]

Lewis went on to say that this "makes sense only if He really was the God whose laws are broken and whose love is wounded in every sin."[19]

Later in Mark, chapter 2, Jesus got into a dispute about the keeping of the Sabbath. Jesus ended his response by saying, "The Sabbath was made for man, not man for the Sabbath. So the Son of Man is Lord even of the Sabbath" (Mark 2:27–28). The meaning may not be obvious, but Jesus was making a titanic statement. It is *God* who established the Sabbath. Only God is the Lord of the sabbath. "By the seventh day God had finished the work he had been doing; so on the seventh day he rested from all his work. Then God blessed the seventh day and made it holy, because on it he rested from all the work of creating that he had done" (Gen. 2:2–3). Since no mere human is the Lord of the Sabbath, Jesus was claiming that he is God, the one who made the Sabbath for man. As such, he has the authority to rule on its observance. We are not told the response of his interlocuters, but they must have known the implication.

One more of Jesus' claims to deity will suffice. In a nasty dispute where Jesus was accused of being "a Samaritan and demon-possessed," he capped off the argument by saying:

Your father Abraham rejoiced at the thought of seeing my day; he saw it and was glad."

"You are not yet fifty years old," they said to him, "and you have seen Abraham!"

---

18. C. S. Lewis, *Mere Christianity*, C. S. Lewis Signature Classics (London: HarperCollins, 2012), 24, Kindle.
19. Lewis, 24.

"Very truly I tell you," Jesus answered, "before Abraham was born, I am!" At this, they picked up stones to stone him, but Jesus hid himself, slipping away from the temple grounds. (John 8:56–59)

Jesus was not only claiming to have *existed before Abraham*. He was claiming to have existed *as God* before Abraham. His disputants picked up stones because they deemed Jesus to be blaspheming, claiming to be God. This is because "I am" is the divine name God used for himself when he revealed himself to Moses in the burning bush.

Moses said to God, "Suppose I go to the Israelites and say to them, 'The God of your fathers has sent me to you,' and they ask me, 'What is his name?' Then what shall I tell them?"

God said to Moses, "I AM WHO I AM. This is what you are to say to the Israelites: 'I AM has sent me to you.'" (Ex. 3:13–14)

Moreover, Jesus, during his earthly ministry, accepted worship on several occasions. After Jesus walked on the water, "those who were in the boat worshiped him, saying, 'Truly you are the Son of God'" (Matt. 14:33). After Jesus healed a blind man, he asked the man if he believed in the Son of Man (Jesus). He responded, 'Lord, I believe,' and he worshiped him" (John 9:38). After Jesus was resurrected, "the eleven disciples went to Galilee, to the mountain where Jesus had told them to go. When they saw him, they worshiped him; but some doubted" (Matt. 28:16–17). Only God is to be worshiped (Matt. 4:9–10), so when Jesus accepted worship, he was affirming that he was God. No small thing, that.[20]

Thus far we know that Jesus claimed to be the Messiah, that he worked miracles, that he claimed to forgive sin, and that he said he was the God who revealed himself to Moses. Before we speak more about his purpose "to seek and to save the lost" (Luke 19:10) and "to give his life as a ransom for many" (Matt. 20:28; Mark 10:45), we need to ponder what kind of man would make such extraordinary claims.

---

20. For an academic study of this issue, see Ray Lozano, *The Proskynesis of Jesus in the New Testament* (London: T&T Clark, 2021).

ASSESSING JESUS' CLAIMS

When faced with this evidence, we are left with only a few options for interpretation. First, we can deny Jesus made these claims; they are merely legendary. If so, we can dismiss them as fiction. But we have already ruled that out, given the nature of our sources. The next options assume that Jesus made these statements. If so, he was either right or he was wrong in making them about himself. Let us consider the option of his being wrong first.

If Jesus claimed to be divine and was not, we have only two basic options about his character. Either (1) he was self-consciously lying about himself or (2) he was deceived about his own identity. Consider each in turn.

What evidence might convince us that Jesus was lying? First, we need to identify a motive for such a horrendous lie. Why would a mere man in a militantly monotheistic culture claim to be God? As Lewis wrote,

> Among Pantheists, like the Indians, anyone might say that he was a part of God, or one with God: there would be nothing very odd about it. But this man, since He was a Jew, could not mean that kind of God. God, in their language, meant the Being outside the world, who had made it and was infinitely different from anything else. And when you have grasped that, you will see that what this man said was, quite simply, the most shocking thing that has ever been uttered by human lips.[21]

If Jesus lied about his identity, he would have been a bad man. But the evidence is that, while he was controversial, Jesus was a compassionate and righteous man who associated with the lowly, fed the masses when they were hungry, healed the sick, cast out demons, and more. This counts against him lying about who he was. More on this below.

Jesus did not gain any worldly benefit by claiming to be divine. He was poor. "Foxes have dens and birds have nests, but the Son of Man

---

21. Lewis, *Mere Christianity*, 24.

has no place to lay his head" (Luke 9:58). He didn't even have a wife or children, which was common in his day. He was betrayed by his followers, he was scorned, and he was crucified between two criminals. No one in their right mind would claim any divine prerogatives in ancient Palestine. So we must cross off this option. But maybe he was not in his right mind.

A few sad souls have suffered from great delusions, giving themselves undeserved metaphysical compliments of various kinds. However, thinking oneself to be the creator of the universe when one is not is surely the worst kind of mental disorder. We would not expect someone so deluded to exhibit the clarity of thought and intention of action we find in Jesus of Nazareth. Jesus' own family thought he might be out of his mind at one point (Mark 3:21), but this was early in Jesus' ministry and did not reflect their settled opinion. Some of Jesus' detractors said he was demon possessed, as we saw above (John 8:48–52), but again, this did not fit the composed and rational character we find in the Gospels.

Considering other religious leaders, it may be difficult to determine whether a God-claimant is deluded or is lying (or some combination of both). For example, the New York minister Father Divine (née George Baker), claimed to be God outright. He died in 1965 and was not resurrected.[22] Rev. Sun Myung Moon, who founded the Unification Church, claimed to be the "Lord of the Second Advent" (that is, the second coming of Christ).[23] He died in 2012 and was not resurrected. Whether they—and others like them—were deceived or deceiving (or a combination of both), we can confidently affirm that Jesus Christ is not among their ilk.

Therefore, if we have ruled out (1) that Jesus' claims were legendary (he never made them), (2) that he was a liar, and (3) that he was mentally deranged, then the remaining option is that he was indeed who he said he was, the Lord. Put another way, believing Jesus' words in the Gospels is the best explanation given all the evidence. As C. S. Lewis famously wrote,

---

22. J. Gordon Melton, "Father Divine," *Encyclopaedia Britannica*, last updated February 25, 2022. https://www.britannica.com/biography/Father-Divine.

23. Editors of *Encyclopaedia Britannica*, "Sun Myung Moon," *Encyclopaedia Britannica*, last updated January 10, 2022, https://www.britannica.com/biography/Sun-Myung-Moon.

You must make your choice. Either this man was, and is, the Son of God: or else a madman or something worse. You can shut Him up for a fool, you can spit at Him and kill Him as a demon; or you can fall at His feet and call Him Lord and God. But let us not come with any patronising nonsense about His being a great human teacher. He has not left that open to us. He did not intend to.[24]

THE WORK OF JESUS

Jesus did not come simply to declare his identity, to heal the sick, to cast out demons, to receive worship, and to teach a moral system. He came to rescue and redeem people who were lost and needing salvation. We mentioned that he claimed the authority to forgive sin. But just how did he make this possible? The subject of Jesus' saving work is vast and deep, but we can only focus on some crucial points related to his death.[25]

The Gospels give a disproportionate amount of their narratives to the events leading to Jesus' death—and for good reason, since Jesus' death was really the purpose of his life. While death is the sad end to most people's lives, Jesus' death was the reason he lived, why he came into the world. Jesus taught on many subjects, but he also taught on his fate. At least three times, Jesus spoke of his coming death. Consider one: "The Son of Man must suffer many things and be rejected by the elders, the chief priests and the teachers of the law, and he must be killed and on the third day be raised to life" (Luke 9:22; see also Matt. 17:22–23; 20:17–19; Mark 9:30–32; 10:32–34; Luke 9:43–45; 18:31–34). Jesus had to rebuke Peter when he questioned Jesus' statement about Jesus' death.

> Jesus began to explain to his disciples that he must go to Jerusalem and suffer many things at the hands of the elders, the chief priests and the teachers of the law, and that he must be killed and on the third day be raised to life.

24. Lewis, *Mere Christianity*, 24.
25. See John Stott's modern classic *The Cross of Christ* (Downers Grove, IL: Inter-Varsity, 1986).

Peter took him aside and began to rebuke him. "Never, Lord!" he said. "This shall never happen to you!"

Jesus turned and said to Peter, "Get behind me, Satan! You are a stumbling block to me; you do not have in mind the concerns of God, but merely human concerns." (Matt. 16:21–23)

After responding to the repentance of a corrupt tax collector, Jesus said, "The Son of Man came to seek and to save the lost" (Luke 19:10). He also spoke of giving his life for that cause. As part of his teaching on serving others, Jesus offered himself as the ultimate example:

"Whoever wants to become great among you must be your servant, and whoever wants to be first must be your slave—just as the Son of Man did not come to be served, but to serve, and to give his life as a ransom for many." (Matt. 20:26–28)

In John 14–17, Jesus gave a long and loving discourse on the meaning of his death and what would come after. He summed this up by saying, "I came from the Father and entered the world; now I am leaving the world and going back to the Father" (16:28). But what exactly did his death mean? What did it accomplish?

The key is found in Isaiah's prophecy that the Messiah would suffer in his redemptive work for humanity.

> Surely he took up our pain
>   and bore our suffering,
> yet we considered him punished by God,
>   stricken by him, and afflicted.
> But he was pierced for our transgressions,
>   he was crushed for our iniquities;
> the punishment that brought us peace was on him,
>   and by his wounds we are healed. (Isa. 53:4–5)[26]

---

26. Michael L. Brown argues against Jewish critics that this passage refers to the Messiah. See *Jewish Objections to Jesus* (Grand Rapids: Baker, 2003), 40–85.

New Testament authors quote at least seven specific verses from Isaiah 53 (Isa. 53:1, 4, 5, 6, 8, 9, 11) that were fulfilled by Christ. Consider just two:

"He himself bore our sins" in his body on the cross, so that we might die to sins and live for righteousness; "by his wounds you have been healed." For "you were like sheep going astray," but now you have returned to the Shepherd and Overseer of your souls. (1 Peter 2:24–26)

Also:

This was to fulfill what was spoken through the prophet Isaiah:

"He took up our infirmities
and bore our diseases." (Matt. 8:17)

While Jesus spoke of the necessity of his death for our salvation, it was his apostles, especially Paul, who explained its meaning most fully. Therefore, I will appeal to some of his teaching.

Although he had first persecuted the church, Paul was accredited and authorized as an apostle by Jesus himself when Jesus encountered Paul on the road to Damascus (Acts 9). Paul would do more to spread and explain Christianity than any other teacher in the early church. Consider his works about the death of Christ. In his most detailed account of God's ways with humanity (Romans), Paul wrote, "For all have sinned, and come short of the glory of God; being justified freely by his grace through the redemption that is in Christ Jesus: whom God hath set forth to be a *propitiation* through faith in his blood, to declare his righteousness for the remission of sins that are past, through the forbearance of God" (Rom. 3:23–25 KJV, emphasis added).

I have used the King James Version because it best emphasizes Jesus' death as *propitiation*, a term the New International Version translates as "sacrifice of atonement." Propitiation means that Jesus, though sinless, took the punishment that we deserve through his suffering and death.[27] This is exactly what Isaiah 53:4–5 (quoted above) teaches. Since God's wrath is revealed against human sin (Rom. 1:18–21), that wrath must be assuaged somehow. Jesus Christ, God's only Son, offered himself to God in our place. As Paul also wrote, "God made him who had no sin to be sin for us, so that in him we might become the righteousness of God" (2 Cor. 5:21). Jesus did not become a sinner, but a sinless substitute for our sin. He bore our sins and gave us his righteousness (1 Cor. 1:30; Phil. 3:9).

There are more dimensions to the atoning work of Christ, but propitiation is at the heart of it. Christ also delivers us from the power of Satan (Col. 2:15), unites us to himself (Rom. 5:11–21), pays our debt (Luke 7:36–50; 1 Cor. 7:23), and much more.[28] There is no greater demonstration of God's love than the atoning work of Jesus Christ, who laid down his life of his own volition in agreement with the Father and the Holy Spirit (John 10:15).

But Jesus' life and death cannot be understood apart from his resurrection from the dead, which vindicated his mission. As Paul said, Jesus "was a descendant of David, and who through the Spirit of holiness was appointed the Son of God in power by his resurrection from the dead: Jesus Christ our Lord" (Rom. 1:3–4). This is so significant that we dedicate a whole chapter to this claim.

RESPONDING TO JESUS

We can know the truth about Jesus. This chapter has tried to chart the way step-by-step. But there is more. We must come to Jesus on Jesus' terms. A Buddhist reveres Buddha as teacher and model. Muslims honor Muhammad as the final prophet. Hindus may select one of Hinduism's many gods to worship, none of whom is a savior. Jews try to follow the law of Moses. But Jesus calls us to believe in him alone to be born

---

27. For a thorough defense of propitiation, biblically, theologically, and philosophically, see William Lane Craig, *Atonement and the Death of Christ* (Waco, TX: Baylor University Press, 2020).

28. For a fuller treatment, see Stott, *The Cross of Christ*; and Groothuis, "The Atonement: Stating It Properly," and "The Atonement: Defending It," in *Christian Apologetics*.

again. As he told Nicodemus, "Very truly I tell you, no one can see the kingdom of God unless they are born again" (John 3:3). The way of being born again is simply the way of faith, of believing in what Jesus has accomplished through his life, death, and resurrection. Jesus continued in his discussion with Nicodemus:

> "Just as Moses lifted up the snake in the wilderness, so the Son of Man must be lifted up, that everyone who believes may have eternal life in him."
> For God so loved the world that he gave his one and only Son, that whoever believes in him shall not perish but have eternal life. For God did not send his Son into the world to condemn the world, but to save the world through him. Whoever believes in him is not condemned, but whoever does not believe stands condemned already because they have not believed in the name of God's one and only Son. This is the verdict: Light has come into the world, but people loved darkness instead of light because their deeds were evil. (John 3:14–19)

All apologetic enterprise should lead to Jesus Christ and confirm Christians in their faith in Christ. This is no game, but a matter of life or death, heaven or hell, salvation or damnation. The truth about Jesus is the truth that sets us free. "To the Jews who had believed him, Jesus said, 'If you hold to my teaching, you are really my disciples. Then you will know the truth, and the truth will set you free'" (John 8:31–32).

STUDY QUESTIONS

1. How does Jesus differ from other religious teachers, according to the Bible?
2. What are the salient truths about Jesus that make him unique and matchless in his identity?
3. Explain the "God or a bad man" argument.
4. What is the apologetic significance of Jesus' death on the cross?

SUGGESTED READING

Aristotle. *Metaphysics* 4.7.

Blomberg, Craig L. *The Historical Reliability of the Gospels*. 2nd ed. Downers Grove, IL: IVP Academic, 2007.

_____. "Jesus of Nazareth: What Historians Can Know about Him and Why It Matters," esp. 439–40. In Douglas Groothuis. *Christian Apologetics: A Comprehensive Case for Biblical Faith*. 2nd ed. Downers Grove, IL: IVP Academic, 2022.

Brown, Michael L. *Jewish Objections to Jesus*. Grand Rapids: Baker, 2003.

Burton, Tara Isabella. *Strange Rites: New Religions for a Godless World*. New York: Public Affairs, 2020.

Corduan, Winfried. *No Doubt about It: The Case for Christianity*. Nashville: Broadman & Holman, 1997.

Craig, William Lane. *Atonement and the Death of Christ*. Waco, TX: Baylor University Press, 2020.

Editors of *Encyclopaedia Britannica*. "Sun Myung Moon." *Encyclopaedia Britannica*. Last updated January 10, 2022. https://www.britannica.com/biography/Sun-Myung-Moon.

Ehrman, Bart. *Did Jesus Exist? The Historical Argument for Jesus of Nazareth*. New York: HarperOne, 2013.

Groothuis, Douglas. *Christian Apologetics: A Comprehensive Case for Biblical Faith*. 2nd ed. Downers Grove, IL: IVP Academic, 2022.

Harris, Murray. *Three Crucial Questions about Jesus*. Grand Rapids: Baker, 1994.

Hurtado, Larry. "Why the 'Mythical Jesus' Claim Has No Traction with Scholars." *Larry Hurtado's Blog*. December 2, 2017. https://larryhurtado.wordpress.com/2017/12/02/why-the-mythical-jesus-claim-has-no-traction-with-scholars.

Jenkins, Phillip. *The Next Christendom*. 3rd ed. New York: Oxford University Press, 2011.

Lipka, Michael, and Conrad Hackett. "Why Muslims Are the Fastest-Growing Religious Group." Pew Research Center. April 6, 2017. https://www.pewresearch.org/fact-tank/2017/04/06/why-muslims-are-the-worlds-fastest-growing-religious-group.

Lozano, Ray. *The Proskynesis of Jesus in the New Testament*. Edinburgh: T&T Clark, 2021.

Melton, J. Gordon. "Father Divine." *Encyclopaedia Britannica*. Last updated February 25, 2022. https://www.britannica.com/biography/Father-Divine.

Schaeffer, Francis A. *Escape from Reason*. 1968. Repr., Downers Grove, IL: InterVarsity, 2006.

_____. *The God Who Is There*. 1968. Repr., Downers Grove, IL: InterVarsity, 2020.

_____. *How Should We Then Live? The Rise and Decline of Western Thought and Culture*. L'Abri 50th Anniversary ed. Wheaton, IL: Crossway, 2009. Kindle edition.

Stott, John. *The Cross of Christ*. Downers Grove, IL: InterVarsity, 1986.

CHAPTER 10

THE RESURRECTION
OF JESUS

There is but one religion that is nothing without the resurrection of its founder. Buddha and Lao Tzu are deemed sages; Muhammad a prophet; Krishna an avatar; Bahá'u'lláh a manifestation of God. Jesus of Nazareth, however, is hailed by his followers as the slain and risen Lord and Savior of the world. World religions may claim various miracles, but none claims what Christianity claims about Jesus. Without an empty tomb and a risen Lord, there would be no Christianity, no church, no world outreach, and no billions of followers. As the apostle Paul said,

> And if Christ has not been raised, our preaching is useless and so is your faith. More than that, we are then found to be false witnesses about God, for we have testified about God that he raised Christ from the dead. . . . And if Christ has not been raised, your faith is futile; you are still in your sins. Then those also who have fallen asleep in Christ are lost. If only for this life we have hope in Christ, we are of all people most to be pitied.
>   But Christ has indeed been raised from the dead, the firstfruits of those who have fallen asleep. (1 Cor. 15:14–20)

Thus, any apologetic for Christianity worth its salt needs to explain and defend the resurrection of its founder. To that we turn.

GOD AND MIRACLES

Skeptics often deny the resurrection of Jesus or any miracle on the basis that miracles simply do not occur. The world, they say, is not like that, but consists of only material states organized by invariant natural laws. We addressed this claim in a previous chapter, but we need to briefly revisit the charge in light of the resurrection. If we can establish that a supernatural God exists through natural theology, then that God may work miracles. As creator of the universe, he has the power to do so. Any miracle God causes is done not randomly but for his purposes. Miracles do not violate any natural law (as David Hume put it), but, rather, supplement the natural order with a supernatural cause, such as Jesus turning water into wine or God raising Jesus from the dead.[1]

While no one is performing miracles today on the order of what Jesus purportedly did, there are many credible accounts of miracles in recent history. Journalist and apologist Lee Strobel makes a compelling argument for this in his book *The Case for Miracles*, in which he investigates numerous reports of healing and divine deliverance.[2] If miracles are occurring today, there is no reason to forbid them from occurring two thousand years ago, provided we have enough evidence to support the claims.

If someone believes in God, but not in Jesus' resurrection, the apologist can move directly to the constructive evidence for this miracle. If the unbeliever is an atheist or agnostic, it may be better to give arguments for God before presenting the evidence for the resurrection. However, even an agnostic or atheist might find the argument for Jesus' resurrection so compelling—apart from traditional natural theology—that they embrace the claim that God raised Jesus from the dead.

In some strange cases, an atheist might grant the resurrection and remain an atheist. Os Guinness recounted such a case in a recorded lecture.[3] After an atheist coworker of mine (Doug's) heard a Josh

---

1. See Craig L. Blomberg, "Don't All the Miracles Make the Bible Mythical?" in *Can We Still Believe in the Bible?* (Grand Rapids: Brazos, 2014).

2. Lee Strobel, *The Case for Miracles* (Grand Rapids: Zondervan, 2018). See also the two-volume scholarly work by Craig Keener, *Miracles: The Credibility of the New Testament Accounts* (Grand Rapids: Baker Academic, 2011).

3. This was given at the Swiss L' Abri ministry sometime in the 1970s, but we do not have the exact reference.

McDowell lecture on the resurrection, he granted that Jesus did rise from the dead, but that had no effect on him. "Weird things happen," he said. This is irrational, since if one accepts the event, it makes sense to accept the biblical understanding of the event—God raised Jesus from the dead. Nevertheless, these kinds of cases show that natural theology may be a needed philosophical prelude for using the resurrection as an apologetic.

THE MEANING OF THE RESURRECTION

Since religions claim various miracles, we ought to consider the meaning of the resurrection according to the Bible. It is not an anomaly in an otherwise naturalistic universe, nor is it in the same category as miracles claimed by other religions. For example, various miracles are attributed to the Buddha, but these were written hundreds of years after his death, and none speak of his resurrection. He died and attained nirvana, never to reincarnate again—end of story. The Qur'an makes no claim that Muhammad worked miracles, although they appear in later writings (hadith). Nevertheless, they have no salvific significance and are not well founded historically. The resurrection of Christ is in another category entirely. Everything hinges on it, and it is well established in history, as we will see.

Before going further, we should distinguish the resurrection of Jesus and its implications from the doctrines of karma and reincarnation. Hinduism and Buddhism affirm (although with some differences in metaphysics) that people and animals are part of the wheel of samara in which they are born, die, and are reborn (or reincarnated). This wheel of birth and death is cyclical and futile. Some part of the person continues from life to life according to their good or bad karma. However, the goal of Hinduism and Buddhism is to escape from the bounds of earthly embodiment and to reach nirvana (disembodied enlightenment). Unlike Jesus, no figure in Hinduism or Buddhism is a model of physical resurrection or promises his followers a resurrected body at the end of history. History is, rather, a mistake to be transcended through mystical experience. Jesus, however, is a participant in history and through his own resurrection promises a new world of renewed and embodied existence for his followers at the final resurrection (1 Cor. 15).[4]

Although Jesus' disciples were slow to understand, he predicted his death and resurrection several times in the Gospels. "He then began to teach them that the Son of Man must suffer many things and be rejected by the elders, the chief priests and the teachers of the law, and that he must be killed and after three days rise again" (Mark 8:31; see also Matt. 17:22; Luke 9:22). He spoke of the manner of his death (rejected and killed) and the timing of his rising again (three days). This was specific and risky. If it did not happen in this way, Jesus would be discredited. Jesus also spoke more indirectly. We read that after he had kicked the money changers out of the temple,

> the Jews then responded to him, "What sign can you show us to prove your authority to do all this?"
>
> Jesus answered them, "Destroy this temple, and I will raise it again in three days."
>
> They replied, "It has taken forty-six years to build this temple, and you are going to raise it in three days?" But the temple he had spoken of was his body. After he was raised from the dead, his disciples recalled what he had said. Then they believed the scripture and the words that Jesus had spoken. (John 2:18–22)

So, we find that Jesus specifically predicted his death and resurrection and claimed they demonstrated his authority. After his resurrection, Jesus further explained the relationship of his achievement to the mission of the church:

> "This is what is written: The Messiah will suffer and rise from the dead on the third day, and repentance for the forgiveness of sins will be preached in his name to all nations, beginning at Jerusalem. You are witnesses of these things. I am going to send you what

---

4. For more on Eastern thought in general, see James W. Sire, "Eastern Pantheistic Monism," in *The Universe Next Door: A Basic Worldview Catalog*, 6th ed. (Downers Grove, IL: InterVarsity, 2020).

my Father has promised; but stay in the city until you have been clothed with power from on high." (Luke 24:46–49)

Belief in Jesus' resurrection is, in fact, a condition for salvation. Paul said, "If you declare with your mouth, 'Jesus is Lord,' and believe in your heart that God raised him from the dead, you will be saved" (Rom. 10:9).

The most detailed explanation of the significance of Jesus' rising from the dead was given by Paul in 1 Corinthians 15. After speaking of the historical nature of Jesus' resurrection, Paul wrote that Jesus' individual resurrection is integrally tied to the general resurrection of his followers. His resurrection is "the firstfruits" of resurrection life. Death came through Adam, but resurrection comes through Jesus. Christ will reign "until he has put all his enemies under his feet. The last enemy to be destroyed is death" (15:25–26). In light of this glorious future, Paul encouraged his readers, saying, "Therefore, my dear brothers and sisters, stand firm. Let nothing move you. Always give yourselves fully to the work of the Lord, because you know that your labor in the Lord is not in vain" (15:58). Renowned New Testament scholar N. T. Wright, sums this up: "The resurrection of Jesus offers itself, to the student of history or science no less than the Christian or the theologian, not as on odd event within the world as it is but the utterly characteristic, prototypical, and foundational event within the world as it has begun to be. It is not an absurd event within the old world but the symbol and starting point of a new world."[5]

THE EVIDENCE FOR THE RESURRECTION

Some assert that the resurrection accounts in the New Testament are part of a larger pattern found in pagan, pre-Christian religions. Themes of dying and rising are tied to vegetative cycles. Christians simply dressed up these ideas and called it history. In this way, they try to reduce the

---

5. N. T. Wright, *Surprised by Hope: Rethinking Heaven, the Resurrection, and the Mission of the Church* (San Francisco: HarperOne, 2008), 67.

supernatural to the natural and the extraordinary to the ordinary. But the case fails. The deities of the pagan stories are, according to Bruce Metzger, "nebulous figures of an imaginary past" that were not meant to be historical.[6] J. N. D. Anderson observed, "There is all the difference in the world between the rising or re-birth of a deity which symbolizes the coming of spring (and the re-awakening of nature) and the resurrection 'on the third day' of an historical person."[7] C. S. Lewis noted at length that the elements of a natural religion (based on vegetative cycles) are absent from Judaism and the teachings of Jesus. The claim of a resurrection is supernatural and historical, not natural and mythic.[8] Further, the early church could have drawn no inspiration from mythical stories in their accounts of the risen Christ and the empty tomb. The mystery religions Christianity supposedly drew from were not well established during the time of Jesus or the early church.[9] Thus, the chronology is off.

In another way, the incarnation and resurrection fulfill the world's longing for redemption, a longing found in many of the world's myths and religions. C. S. Lewis wrote that God prepared the way for the gospel by sending "the human race what I call good dreams: I mean those queer stories scattered all through the heathen religions about a god who dies and comes to life again and, by his death, has somehow given new life to men."[10]

We must quote Lewis at greater length on this profound insight.

The heart of Christianity is a myth which is also a fact. The old myth of the Dying God, without ceasing to be myth, comes down from the heaven of legend and imagination to the earth of history. It happens—at a particular date, in a particular place, followed by

---

6. Bruce Metzger, *Historical and Literary Studies: Pagan, Jewish, and Christian* (Grand Rapids: Eerdmans, 1968), 13; quoted in James R. Edwards, *Is Jesus the Only Savior?* (Grand Rapids: Eerdmans, 2005), 136.

7. J. N. D. Anderson, *Christianity and Comparative Religion* (Downers Grove, IL: InterVarsity, 1971), 38.

8. C. S. Lewis, "Myth Became Fact," in *God in the Dock* (Grand Rapids: Eerdmans, 1979). Lewis argued that Jesus fulfilled the yearnings for redemption found in non-Christian myths, but that he did this through historical facts.

9. See Edwards, *Is Jesus the Only Savior?*, 135–36.

10. C. S. Lewis, *Mere Christianity*, C. S. Lewis Signature Classics (London: HarperCollins, 2012), 23, Kindle.

definable historical consequences. We pass from a Balder or an Osiris, dying nobody knows when or where, to a historical Person crucified (it is all in order) under Pontius Pilate. By becoming fact it does not cease to be myth: that is the miracle. I suspect that men have sometimes derived more spiritual sustenance from myths they did not believe than from the religion they professed. To be truly Christian we must both assent to the historical fact and also receive the myth (fact though it has become) with the same imaginative embrace which we accord to all myths. The one is hardly more necessary than the other.[11]

Having spoken of the historical nature of the Christian claim to Jesus' resurrection in relation to pagan stories, let us turn to the documentary evidence for the resurrection found in the New Testament.

Unless we simply presuppose the resurrection to have occurred, we need to infer its existence on the basis of surrounding facts. Certainly, the resurrection fits into the Christian worldview coherently, but the question as to its historical truth remains.

Our first concern is whether the New Testament documents have been accurately transmitted over time. In chapter 8, we answered that they were. In fact, the manuscript evidence for the New Testament is far better than for any piece of ancient literature. Thus, we need not fear that the original message was lost in translation or lost in transmission. The next question becomes whether what these sources say about Jesus' resurrection is true.

The next stage considers the general fitness of the documents. The Gospels read as historical accounts of the life of Jesus. Consider the prologue to Luke, with its concern for factual accuracy.

Many have undertaken to draw up an account of the things that have been fulfilled among us, just as they were handed down to us by those who from the first were eyewitnesses and servants of the word. With this in mind, since I myself have carefully investigated everything from the beginning, I too decided to write an orderly

---

11. C. S. Lewis, *God in the Dock* (New York: HarperOne), 66–67, Kindle.

account for you, most excellent Theophilus, so that you may know the certainty of the things you have been taught. (Luke 1:1–4)

While the gospel accounts differ in some details and in some of the chronological order, they agree on all the general themes of Jesus in his roles as teacher, prophet, miracle worker, and martyr, and as resurrected and ascended Lord. In fact, if the Gospels perfectly agreed in all details, we would fear collusion—a story too neat and simple to be historical. We addressed Jesus' claims in chapter 9; here we consider how the accounts of his resurrection in the Gospels fit the pattern of a supernatural figure who predicted his death and resurrection. As Stephen T. Davis points out, the Gospels agree that

> Jesus was dead, that he was buried in a tomb near Jerusalem supplied by a man named Joseph of Arimathea, that early on the day after the Sabbath certain women in the company of Jesus (among them Mary Magdalene) went to the tomb, that they found the tomb mysteriously empty, that they met an angel or angels, that the women were either told or else discovered that Jesus had been raised from the dead, and that Jesus subsequently appeared a number of times to certain of the women and certain of the disciples. There seem to be no resurrection texts that question any of these items.[12]

These resurrection accounts are not tacked onto the end of the Gospels but flow from the narratives. Without the resurrection, the accounts are hollow, pointless, cut off from their destiny. It is akin to the movie *Rocky* without Rocky Balboa winning the championship at the end.

Having laid a foundation for the basic historical reliability of the Gospels, let us proceed to consider seven reasons to believe that the resurrection occurred in space-time history.[13] We will address historical

---

12. Stephen T. Davis, *Risen Indeed: Making Sense of the Resurrection* (Grand Rapids: Eerdmans, 1993), 181.

13. I am here drawing much from Craig L. Blomberg, "A Positive Case for the Resurrection," in Carl Stecher and Craig Blomberg, *Resurrection: Faith or Fact? A Scholar's Debate between a Skeptic and a Christian* (Durham, NC: Pitchstone, 2019).

claims that are well established and use them as part of an overall case for the resurrection. We are not using the Bible to prove the Bible as in a circular argument. Each fact, we argue, is best explained by the resurrection of Jesus. When these facts are combined, their cumulative strength is greater than any one individual fact, as in a court of law when several competent witnesses agree on the same point.

First, women are listed as the first eyewitnesses of Jesus' resurrection according to the three gospels that mention witnesses (Matt. 28:1; Luke 24:10; John 20:1).[14] "No two Gospels give the identical list (though Mary Magdalene appears in all four), showing that the writers are not in collusion and possibly giving independent testimony at this point."[15] All four gospels list women as beholding the empty tomb. Today taking the testimony of female witnesses is nothing special, but women at that time in Israel were often not allowed to give testimony in a court of law. If the Gospel writers were fabricating an account of the resurrection, they would not have placed women in such a significant role as witnesses of the empty tomb. But they did. This is known as the "criterion of embarrassment" and "is one of the standard criteria of authenticity in historical-Jesus research (and elsewhere among classical historians)."[16] So given the low status of women as witnesses at that time, it is very unlikely that this sort of story would be made up against the facts.

Women were not then considered a threat to men, so they would have been allowed to stay at the cross, follow the soldiers to where Jesus was buried, and provide spices for his burial, just as all the Gospels claim (Matt. 27:56, 61; Mark 15:40–41, 47; Luke 24:55–56; John 19:25–27).

Second, we must consider why the early Christians, who were mostly Jews, would change their sacred and prescribed pattern of worship and rest on the seventh day of the week (the Sabbath, Ex. 20:8–11) and shift this to the first day of the week. Much of Jewish law concerned the proper observance of the Sabbath, and Jesus' teaching ministry addressed many questions about its nature and purpose (e.g., Mark 2:23–27). Yet after the death of Jesus, his followers began to "break

---

14. I have omitted the ending of Mark 16 because the appearances to witnesses occur in the disputed last verses.

15. Blomberg, "Positive Case for the Resurrection," 114.

16. Blomberg, 115.

bread" and collect gifts on Sunday, not Saturday (Acts 20:7–12; 1 Cor. 16:1–4; Rev. 1:10). Of course, Jesus rose from the dead on the first day of the week, Sunday (Matt. 28:1–10; Mark 16:1–8; Luke 24:1–2; John 20:1–10). Therefore, Blomberg writes,

> For the preceding three centuries [before Constantine legalized Christianity], Christians had to gather at their own peril. Even during the times when Rome was not officially persecuting them, they still had to carve out time after working a full day on Sunday (unless a local holiday happened to fall on that day). It does not seem likely that they would have created all this additional difficulty for themselves unless there was some fairly dramatic, objective, and foundational experience that actually occurred on a Sunday that they felt bound to commemorate on that day rather than any other day. A bodily resurrection, of course, would fit those criteria well, whereas it is much less clear that the alternatives to the resurrection suggested would do so.[17]

Third, unless Jesus rose from the dead victorious over the ignominy of his crucifixion, it is difficult to fathom why he was deemed Savior and Lord by his followers. Crucifixion was a scandalous and horrible way to be executed. "That Rome by 30 C.E. had crucified literally thousands of criminals and insurrectionists this way, at public crossroads as a deterrent to others, made Jesus' execution even more shameful than it was agonizing."[18] If Jesus had been killed in this manner and remained dead, he might be remembered as a brave martyr or wise teacher, but he would hardly be hailed as the Savior of the world. "Add in God's legal condemnation of such a victim [Deut. 21:23; Gal. 3:13], and it would have taken some spectacular event to convince Jesus' first followers to ignore all this and still declare him to be the Messiah and liberator of Israel. A bodily resurrection would do the trick, but it is hard to imagine what else could have provoked such a response."[19]

---

17. Blomberg, 116.
18. Blomberg, 117.
19. Blomberg, 117.

Fourth, considering that every other first-century messianic Jewish movement in Palestine had failed, why did the Jesus movement survive and thrive, even under intense persecution? Something made the Jesus movement stand out and hold up. And we know how the New Testament explains this—the resurrection of Jesus gave his followers hope and confidence to face adversity.

Fifth, without the resurrection, it is difficult to imagine why anyone would have become a Christian, especially in the first three centuries of the church in the Roman Empire. "This was the era in which believers were frequently persecuted for their faith, had no power base, and had nothing to gain economically or socially but often much to lose."[20] Jesus' teaching was radical in many ways, but what gave the Jesus movement its zeal and courage was its belief in and proclamation of his resurrection. It's emphasis on following Jesus in his manner of death (crucifixion, 1 Peter 2:21) would lack all sense and motivation had his followers not also believed in his resurrection. As C. S. Lewis noted, "The Resurrection is the central theme in every Christian sermon reported in the Acts. The Resurrection, and its consequences, were the 'gospel' or good news which the Christians brought."[21]

C. F. D. Moule wrote that "the birth and rapid rise of the Christian church *therefore remain an unsolved enigma for any historian who refuses to take seriously the only explanation offered by the Church itself.*"[22] Jewish New Testament scholar Pinchas Lapide called the resurrection reaction "the birth certificate of the church."[23]

Sixth, in 1 Corinthians 15, the apostle Paul distinguished the singular resurrection of Jesus (vv. 3–8) from a later resurrection of all the dead (vv. 9–58). The Jews of his day who believed in a resurrection (the Pharisees did; the Sadducees did not) awaited but one general resurrection at the end of history (Dan. 12:2). Since the Hebrew Bible does not make a clear distinction between these two resurrections, *something*

---

20. Blomberg, 118.
21. C. S. Lewis, *Miracles*, Collected Letters of C. S. Lewis (New York: HarperCollins, 2015), 234, Kindle.
22. C. F. D. Moule, *The Phenomenon of the New Testament* (Naperville, IL: Allenson, 1967), 13, emphasis in original. See pp. 1–20 for his entire argument.
23. Pinchas Lapide, *The Resurrection of Jesus* (Minneapolis: Fortress, 1985), 46.

earth-shaking had to occur to introduce this new idea. The resurrection of the coming Messiah was unexpected as well, so the Jews were in no way primed to believe it. That many Jews, such as Paul himself, ended up believing in the resurrection of Jesus and the later resurrection of the dead is remarkable (see his conversion in Acts 9). The best explanation is, of course, the resurrection of Jesus, which opened an entirely new chapter of history.[24]

Further, 1 Corinthians is accepted as a genuine Pauline epistle by all scholars and is dated earlier than the Gospels. The testimony Paul gave in the opening verses of chapter 15 about Jesus was very likely taken from an earlier creed or hymn of the church that affirmed the resurrection of Jesus. So this provides trustworthy evidence of the early Christians' belief in the resurrection.

Seventh, that "the same Jewish and Roman authorities who authorized Jesus' crucifixion never produced a body or pointed people to the tomb where his corpse still lay, even as claims of resurrection began to circulate within days of his death, suggests that his tomb really was empty."[25] Jesus' burial in Joseph of Arimathea's unused tomb is well established because it is reported in "the Synoptic (Mark 15:42–47 and parallels) and Johannine traditions (John 19:38–42) and so satisfies the criterion of multiple attestation."[26] Further, it is unlikely that anyone would make up such an unlikely story of a member of the elite Jewish Sanhedrin being a secret follower of Jesus.[27]

Both the Jewish and Roman authorities had reasons to squelch the resurrection claim, since both groups wanted Jesus dead and his followers to disband as had so many other messianic movements of that day. The Jewish authorities feared heresy, and the Romans feared insurrection. Yet we have no evidence that any body was produced to refute the resurrection claim. Rather, the tomb was empty, which is a necessary condition for the resurrection.

---

24. Blomberg, "Positive Case for the Resurrection," 118–19.
25. Blomberg, 119.
26. Blomberg, 120.
27. Blomberg, 120. See also William L. Craig, *Assessing the New Testament Evidence for the Historicity of the Resurrection of Jesus* (Edwin Mellen, 1989), 173–76.

One criticism of the resurrection grants that the tomb was empty but claims that someone stole Jesus' body from the tomb, thus leaving it empty. Who would do so, and for what reason?

The early Jewish apologetic against the Christians presupposed that Jesus' tomb was empty. Matthew wrote that the Jews spread the word that the disciples stole the body (Matt. 28:11–15). This is corroborated by Tertullian and Justin Martyr.[28] However, the disciples lacked both the motive and the means to steal Jesus' body. What good is a dead Messiah? There would be no motive to steal his body. Moreover, Matthew tells that the tomb was heavily guarded (Matt. 27:62–66), and it is unlikely that the disciples had the *means* to overpower the guards.

Some have argued that Jesus' tomb was raided by unknown grave robbers, since this was fairly common at that time. But this theory, too, would also have to overcome the guarding of the tomb objection. Moreover, grave robbers focused their attention on the graves of the wealthy, since they could steal expensive material left on the body of a rich corpse. Jesus had no such material riches on his person, having died naked and unadorned without any regalia.[29] Lastly, these far-fetched substitutes for the real resurrection of Jesus also fail to account for the strong testimony that the resurrected Jesus appeared to many people in different settings at different times.

The evidence is adding up for an empty tomb, a risen Jesus, and a church based on that world-changing fact. But what are the rival naturalistic or nonsupernatural theories?

Perhaps the most influential of the current anti-resurrection theories is the hallucination hypothesis.[30] This claims that the disciples had experiences they identified as being of the risen Jesus, but they were not veridical (that is, truth conveying); rather, the disciples were

---

28. Tertullian, *On Spectacles* 30; Justin Martyr, *Dialogue with Trypho* 108.

29. This paragraph is adapted from Douglas Groothuis, *Christian Apologetics: A Comprehensive Case for Biblical Faith*, 2nd ed. (Downers Grove, IL: IVP Academic, 2022), locs. 6073–75, Kindle.

30. Some have made the far-fetched and repeatedly refuted claim that Jesus never existed at all, and thus he was not resurrected. This is called *mythicism*. See a refutation from an agnostic New Testament scholar, Bart Ehrman, *Did Jesus Exist? The Historical Argument for Jesus of Nazareth* (New York: HarperOne, 2013).

deceived. This theory admits that there are several well-established reports of Jesus' resurrection, that they did not come long after Jesus death, and that they were sincerely made. So why should one think that the various reports of Jesus' resurrection would be based on a hallucination?

If we have laid a good groundwork for miracles through natural theology (there is a God who could work a miracle), then such a prejudice is unwarranted. Hallucinations are not the kind of events that would capture the events described by the Gospels and in Paul's first letter to the Corinthians. As Lapide wrote, "If the defeated and depressed group of disciples overnight could change into a victorious movement of faith, based only on autosuggestion or self-deception—without a fundamental faith experience—then this would be a much greater miracle than the resurrection itself."[31] By "fundamental faith experience," Lapide meant an experience of the resurrected Jesus. That is, the faith is based on fact. He said that "the resurrection belongs to the category of the truly real and effective occurrences, for without a fact of history there is no act of true faith."[32]

Moreover, the hallucination explanation cannot explain the empty tomb, which is well established historically. Further, if the experiences were merely hallucinations, the claims to resurrection could have been refuted by producing the dead body of Jesus, as mentioned above in point seven. But we have no record of that happening, as Blomberg said.

Before wrapping up this argument, we must note a common apologetic mistake that should be avoided about the resurrection. Many think that all of the apostles of Jesus, except Judas and John, died martyrs' deaths for their belief in Jesus and his resurrection. If so, this gives credence to the sincerity of their beliefs and to the likelihood that their beliefs about Jesus were true. However, the situation is more complicated, as Sean McDowell's research has shown in his excellent

---

31. Lapide, *Resurrection of Jesus*, 126.
32. Groothuis, *Christian Apologetics*, locs. 6036–38. For a critique of recent hallucination theories, see Joseph W. Bergeron and Gary R. Habermas, "The Resurrection of Jesus: A Clinical Review of Psychiatric Hypotheses for the Biblical Story of Easter," *Irish Theological Quarterly* 80, no. 2 (2015): 157–72.

book *The Fate of the Apostles*.[33] In brief, the claim that all the apostles except Judas (who betrayed Jesus and killed himself) and John died (who died a natural death at Patmos) martyrs' deaths is overstated. McDowell concludes:

Here is what I believe the historical record reveals:

Highest possible probability (9–10): Peter, Paul, James son of
  Zebedee, James brother of Jesus
More probable than not (7): Thomas
More plausible than not (6): Andrew
As plausible as not (5): Philip, Bartholomew, Matthew, James
  (son of Alphaeus), Thaddeus, Simon the Zealot, Matthias
Improbable (3): John.[34]

The witnesses of the resurrection were either *deceived* (believing in the resurrection when it did not happen) or *deceivers* (knowing it did not happen but saying it did). The chief explanation for how the witnesses could be deceived is the hallucination view, which we rejected. But could they have been deceivers? The witness of those apostles who were martyred for their faith is significant, since people do not give their lives *for what they know to be a lie*. Why would anyone die for the lie that Jesus rose from the dead when they knew he had not? How could that benefit them? Pascal sets this straight.

The hypothesis that the Apostles were knaves is quite absurd. Follow it out to the end and imagine these twelve men meeting after Jesus's death and conspiring to say that he had risen from the dead. This means attacking all the powers that be. The human heart is singularly susceptible to fickleness, to change, to promises, to bribery. One of them had only to deny his story under these

---

33. Sean McDowell, *The Fate of the Twelve Apostles: Examining the Martyrdom Accounts of the Closest Followers of Jesus* (New York: Routledge, 2018).

34. Sean McDowell, "Did the Apostles Really Die as Martyrs for Their Faith?," *Christian Research Journal* 39, no. 2 (2016), http://www.equip.org/PDF/JAF1392.pdf. This article summarizes the main conclusions of his book *The Fate of the Twelve Apostles*.

inducements, or still more because of possible imprisonment, tortures and death, and they would all have been lost.[35]

HE IS RISEN INDEED

On Easter Sunday, many worship leaders and pastors will say, "Christ is risen," and call for the response, "He is risen indeed!" We have affirmed this many times as Christians, as have tens of millions of others (in one way or another). In my (Doug's) church's worship, we affirm together the following three statements every Sunday:

Christ has died.
Christ has risen.
Christ will come again.

But this declaration of faith is also a confession of truth. In fact, that statement "Christ is risen" can be an item of knowledge (or justified, true belief) to be shared with unbelievers, given the arguments of this chapter and in many other books. Skeptics need not stifle our witness, since the evidence is in favor of an empty tomb, a risen Jesus, and a church militant and triumphant because of it.

STUDY QUESTIONS

1. What is the significance of Jesus' resurrection?
2. Do we need to assume the inerrancy of the New Testament to give a good apologetic for Jesus' resurrection?
3. What is the basic strategy of this chapter in defending the resurrection of Jesus?
4. Do you know of other apologetically solid ways to defend the resurrection of Jesus in history?

---

35. Blaise Pascal. *Pensées* (New York: Penguin, 2017), 97, Kindle.

SUGGESTED READING

Anderson, J. N. D. *Christianity and Comparative Religion.* Downers Grove, IL: InterVarsity, 1971.

Bergerson, Joseph W., and Gary R. Habermas. "The Resurrection of Jesus: A Clinical Review of Psychiatric Hypotheses for the Biblical Story of Easter." *Irish Theological Quarterly* 80, no. 2 (2015): 157–72.

Blomberg, Craig L. "Don't All the Miracles Make the Bible Mythical?" In *Can We Still Believe in the Bible? Answering Ten Contemporary Challenges to Christianity.* Grand Rapids: Brazos, 2014.

_____. "A Positive Case for the Resurrection." In Carl Stecher and Craig Blomberg, *Resurrection: Faith or Fact? A Scholar's Debate between a Skeptic and a Christian.* Durham, NC: Pitchstone, 2019.

Craig, William Lane. *Assessing the New Testament Evidence for the Historicity of the Resurrection of Jesus,* 173–76. Lewiston, NY: Edwin Mellen, 1989.

Davis, Stephen T. *Risen Indeed: Making Sense of the Resurrection.* Grand Rapids: Eerdmans, 1993.

Edwards, James R. *Is Jesus the Only Savior?,* 135–36. Grand Rapids: Eerdmans, 2005.

Ehrman, Bart. *Did Jesus Exist?* New York: HarperOne, 2012.

Groothuis, Douglas. *Christian Apologetics.* 2nd ed. Downers Grove, IL: InterVarsity, 2022.

Keener, Craig. *Miracles.* 2 vols. Grand Rapids: Baker Academic, 2011.

Lapide, Pinchas. *The Resurrection of Jesus: A Jewish Perspective.* Eugene, OR: Wipf and Stock, 2002.

Lewis, C. S. *Mere Christianity.* C. S. Lewis Signature Classics. London: HarperCollins, 2012. Kindle edition.

_____. "Myth Became Fact," in *God in the Dock.* Grand Rapids: Eerdmans, 1979.

McDowell, Sean. "Did the Apostles Really Die as Martyrs for Their Faith?" *Christian Research Journal* 39, no. 2 (2016). http://www.equip.org/PDF/JAF1392.pdf. This article summarizes the main conclusions of his book *The Fate of the Twelve Apostles.*

_____. *The Fate of the Twelve Apostles: Examining the Martyrdom Accounts of the Closest Followers of Jesus.* New York: Routledge, 2018.

Metzger, Bruce. *Historical and Literary Studies: Pagan, Jewish, and Christian.* Grand Rapids: Eerdmans, 1968.

Moule, C. F. D. *The Phenomenon of the New Testament.* Naperville, IL: Allenson, 1967.

Pascal, Blaise. *Pensées.* Edited by A. Krailsheimer. New York: Penguin, 1966.

Sire, James W. "Eastern Pantheistic Monism." In *The Universe Next Door: A Basic Worldview Catalog.* 6th ed. Downers Grove, IL: InterVarsity, 2020.

Strobel, Lee. *The Case for Miracles.* Grand Rapids: Zondervan, 2018.

Wright, N. T. *Surprised by Hope: Rethinking Heaven, the Resurrection, and the Mission of the Church.* San Francisco: HarperOne, 2008.

CHAPTER 11

APOLOGETICS IN LIFE
AND MINISTRY

I (Ike) have worked for many years in the software industry. The benefit of working in technology is that you meet people from all over the world with all kinds of experiences. This has given me the opportunity to use the arguments presented in this book in many different ways. When I was a new hire at one company, I was assigned the task of getting to know some of my coworkers in different departments. One such assignment was with a Muslim coworker who, through Western education and some hard life circumstances, had become disenchanted with Islam. During my conversation with this person, I shared about my interest in the Arabic philosopher Ya'qub ibn Ishaq al-Kindi (c. 800–870 CE), a polymath who lived in Baghdad during the growth of the House of Wisdom under the Abbasid caliphs al-Ma'mun (reigned 813–833 CE) and al-Mu'tasim (reigned 833–842 CE). A key work of his is *On First Philosophy*, an investigation into the existence and nature of God, which started a tradition in Arabic philosophy that was eventually revived by William Lane Craig in the *Kalām Cosmological Argument*.[1] I shared the same argument you learned in this book with this coworker, as well as

---

1. Ya'qub ibn Ishaq al-Kindi, *Al-Kindi's Metaphysics: A Translation of Ya'qub ibn Ishaq al-Kindi's Treatise "On First Philosophy" (fī al-Falsafah al-Ūlā)*, trans. Alfred L. Ivry (Albany: State University of New York Press, 1974). See also William Lane Craig, *The Kalām Cosmological Argument* (Eugene, OR: Wipf and Stock, 1979).

its origins in the same part of the world in which the coworker was born. My explanation was met with immediate gratitude and the opening of the door to talk about this person's disappointments with God.

In another instance, an intelligent coworker of mine discussed our interests over lunch, and I shared that I enjoy reading philosophy and theology. This coworker immediately started asking me skeptical questions about my belief in God and my Christian faith. I patiently answered the questions to the best of my ability and showed my openness to engage in these discussions in the future. Thereafter, this coworker would often explain books that he had been reading as well as share some of what was happening in his life. Eventually he told me that during the COVID-19 pandemic, he had started going to church, confessed his faith in Jesus, and started a treasured practice of receiving Communion. Though I had not known about it, there were others in his life who were talking to him about faith, and he shared with me that my ability to answer questions about the faith gave him confidence that he could intelligently investigate Christianity. He came out on the other side of his investigation as a brother in Christ.

As we near the end of this book, it is time to assess how apologetics will work in your unique set of circumstances. Apologetics is not just for gifted philosophers and academic theologians. The arguments and lines of evidence we provide here can and should be applied by earnest followers of Jesus in any profession or stage of life. In this chapter, we want to encourage you about the kind of impact you can have when you partner with the Holy Spirit to lovingly defend and commend the Christian worldview, an impact that can extend to your coworkers, family, friends, and neighbors, and to the ends of the earth. This means that we need to see where apologetics sits in relationship to evangelism and discipleship. We will explore those relationships in this chapter. We will also explain how to actually do apologetics. In this way, we would like to challenge the tendency to merely think about apologetics. This temptation is common, and we want to be careful to guide you, the student of apologetics, to start lovingly and sensitively taking the message of the truth and rationality of the Christian worldview to everyone whom God has placed within your sphere of influence.

One of the challenges any student has is in passing on what they have learned to others. It is easy to treat knowledge like a trophy. You learn something and place it up on the wall as a reminder to yourself of your achievement. However, the Christian life simply does not work that way. When we learn about God, we have not achieved something that is ultimately to our credit; instead, the knowledge of God is a gift we receive.[2] And the knowledge we gain is not something we keep to ourselves. The knowledge of God is meant to be passed along to others through evangelism and discipleship. Paul's instructions to Timothy are helpful here. "The things you have heard me say in the presence of many witnesses entrust to reliable people who will also be qualified to teach others" (2 Tim. 2:2).

These instructions entail a number of responses from the apologist. First, pay attention to those who have the responsibility of teaching you. After all, you are not the only one who may benefit from their sound instruction. Second, entrust what you have learned to others who will also be able to serve as reliable teachers of others. This means that Christians need to seek out people who are hungry for the truth and who are willing to develop the kind of character needed to train others in the Christian worldview. Third, expect that your apologetic study will not just impact you. Too often Christians fall in line with the rest of the culture in thinking that intellectual pursuits are solely for their own personal benefit. Surely apologetics has great personal benefit, as we will show in this chapter; however, the benefit is also for those who hear your message and will then entrust it to others. After all, Paul was claiming in his message to Timothy that four levels of evangelism and/or discipleship were happening: (1) Paul himself, (2) Timothy, (3) Timothy's students, and (4) the students of Timothy's students. This is an important reminder of the potential impact of godly instruction in any discipline and, of course for our purposes, apologetics in particular.

APOLOGETICS' RELATIONSHIP TO EVANGELISM

In chapter 1, we explained the biblical basis for apologetics and started to show how this relates to our partnership with the Holy Spirit in

---

2. See the section on revelation in Andrew I. Shepardson, *Who's Afraid of the Unmoved Mover?* (Eugene, OR: Pickwick, 2019), 126–36.

proclaiming the gospel. We believe that as we share the good news with others, we are being faithful to the biblical model when we bring explanations of the truth and rationality of the Christian worldview along with our proclamation of Jesus Christ, his crucifixion, and his resurrection. Indeed, evangelism often needs apologetics in some important ways.

First, apologetics can help the evangelist to awaken their audience to the importance of considering the Christian worldview. Think back to the moral argument. This argument states that morality requires God as the foundation for objective moral values and duties. For the person outside the household of faith, the realization that their sense of morality requires a divine foundation may help them to take seriously the possibility of the existence of God. Since people have an awareness of the moral law (Rom. 2:14–15) but have not necessarily thought about the foundation for moral values and duties, apologetics can reveal that belief in God is required to make sense of their moral intuitions. In addition, the moral argument is an occasion to consider how we all fall short of moral perfection. This may help the nonbeliever to recognize their need for the Savior.

Second, apologetics serves evangelism by helping the evangelist to respond to objections to the Christian worldview. Think back to our conversation on the relationship between Christianity and science. For someone who might object that Christianity is anti-science, we can point to the fact that there are a number of presuppositions required for doing science (the knowability of the external world, human cognitive reliability, mathematics, etc.) that Christianity uniquely supports and that naturalism puts in doubt. Answering the objection that Christianity is anti-science may be a key step in the evangelistic process of someone considering whether Christianity is true. In our experience, many people have presuppositions, concerns, or objections to Christianity. Even if they have not thought through all of their objections, most people who would not call themselves Christians have some thoughts about why they are not Christians. Why not do everything you can to be ready to respond to these objections? Now, it is also true that sometimes, people's objections to Christianity are more existential and personal than they are logical or philosophical. The approach that we recommend here is that apologetics may be required to respond to objections, but it may not be sufficient. In this way, evangelistic ministry is not a zero sum game where all you need is apologetics. Patient, personal connection, where you love someone in Jesus' name is always needed. We simply claim that sometimes loving someone in Jesus' name means providing rational answers to their objections.

Third, apologetics helps evangelists to explain and confirm the truth of the gospel, and this allows the one who hears the gospel to understand and accept the cognitive claims that Christianity makes as a prelude to genuine faith. A reminder of the nature of faith is in order. Christians have often understood faith as having multiple components of trust, belief, and knowledge. This tripartite picture of faith can be summed up in the Latin words *noticia*, *assensus*, and *fiducia*. *Noticia* is the intellectual component of faith whereby someone understands the Christian truth claims. *Assensus* is the emotional or convictional element whereby a person is able to say they believe Christianity is true. *Fiducia* is the side of faith that relates to the will whereby one is able to trust in Jesus as Savior and Lord. Apologetics is important, not because it causes someone to have faith but because it clears the intellectual ground for someone to be able to develop *noticia* and *assensus*. This seems to be partly what the writer of Hebrews was getting at when he said, "Without faith it is impossible to please God, because anyone who comes to him must believe that he exists and that he rewards those who earnestly seek him" (11:6). Apologetics can help someone to believe that God exists through natural theology and to believe that God rewards earnest seekers through establishing the reliability of the Bible.

Fourth, apologetics challenges the prevailing culture's worldview assumptions, and this allows Christianity to become a part of the culture's plausibility structure. A plausibility structure is comprised of all the beliefs a person may be willing to entertain as possibly true. For example, although you may never have seen her in person, your plausibility structure includes the belief that Beyoncé is a talented singer. However, your plausibility structure likely excludes the belief that Martians rigged the 2021 World Series through telepathic interference in game four. The way you may approach the Martian question is how some people view the idea that Jesus of Nazareth rose from the dead in Palestine roughly two thousand years ago. You are not really willing to entertain a belief in Martian telepathic interference in the same way that many are not willing to entertain a belief that a dead man rose. Apologetics, though, can challenge the worldview assumption that it is impossible for a dead man to rise. This is the case, too, with the culture's bias toward methodological naturalism, moral relativism, mythological/figurative readings of the Bible, and the idea that God speaks (revelation). Consider how important all of this is for evangelism. If you would like to share the good news that God was in Christ reconciling the world to himself, you would need your audience to believe that Jesus is a real person, and that the Bible reliably reports Jesus' claims to be God as well as his acts of dying and rising. None of this precludes God from directly certifying these truths to someone, but it could complement God's direct revelation. More on that in a moment.

Fifth, we live in a spiritual context in which the devil and the demons would love to deceive people into thinking that Christianity has no intellectual foundations. While we are not superstitious about the power and presence of the spiritual forces who oppose God, neither are we "unaware of [Satan's] schemes" (2 Cor. 2:11). We see apologetics as a weapon in our spiritual warfare against "the ruler of the kingdom of the air, the spirit who is now at work in those who are disobedient" (Eph. 2:2). He would try to make people think that religion poisons everything; that Christians are homophobic, racist, misogynistic, and bigoted; that understanding our origins does not require God; that morality does not require a divine foundation; and that the Bible is a bunch of childish stories. Explaining the truth and rationality of the Christian worldview rebuts the evil one with sound reasoning and exposes his lies for what they are. Therefore, Holy Spirit–empowered apologetics is a way to wage war for the kingdom of God against the kingdom of this present age. Apologetics again clears the ground for evangelism to proclaim the arrival of the true King by exposing the pretender to the throne as one who has been disarmed by Christ and made a public spectacle (Col. 2:15). If we look at apologetics this way, we must remember that our enemies are not those who disagree with us. We are not in a battle with atheists and pantheists. As Paul has reminded us, "Our struggle is not against flesh and blood, but against the rulers, against the authorities, against the powers of this dark world and against the spiritual forces of evil in the heavenly realms" (Eph. 6:12).

Indeed, apologists never attempt to take on the role of the Holy Spirit in the evangelistic task. Perhaps you have heard well-meaning Christians say things like, "Arguments never bring someone to Christ; only the Holy Spirit brings someone to Christ." Of course, we agree. However, this does not mean that apologists and other ordinary Christians play no role in how someone may eventually confess faith in Jesus. In fact, we argue that the Holy Spirit is necessary for any of our evangelistic and apologetic endeavors. Regarding evangelism generally, Jesus claims that he will send out the Holy Spirit "from the Father—the Spirit of truth who goes out from the Father—he will testify about me. And you also must testify" (John 15:26–27). We recognize that the Holy Spirit is sent first and speaks first, but that our testimony about Jesus ought to accompany his. And we need the Holy Spirit's presence to be effective in evangelism, for Jesus said, "You will receive power when the Holy Spirit comes on you; and you will be my witnesses" (Acts 1:8). Any effectiveness that we have in ministry is primarily due not to our cleverness but to the Holy Spirit's power. Moreover, the Holy Spirit instructs us, through the Scriptures and through his witness to our hearts, on what the gospel is: "But the Advocate, the Holy Spirit, whom the Father will send in my name, will teach you all things and will remind you of everything I have said to you" (John 14:26). The Holy Spirit is ultimately the one who convicts people of their sin (John 16:8–9) and breaks down the barriers that keep them from receiving Jesus (see Acts 8:26–40; 10:1–48; 15:22–29). So, when people claim that apologetics does not bring people to Christ and that only the Spirit can do this, we agree, but the same statement applies to evangelism generally.

Whether through classical apologetics or through a simple gospel presentation, the Holy Spirit is always the one who draws people to God. Yet no one would claim that we do not need simple gospel presentations. Since the ministry of apologetics is a biblical ministry (see chapter 1), we claim that the Holy Spirit uses apologetics to lead people to God in ways similar to his use of simple gospel presentations to lead people to God. Let's examine how this is so.

You will recall that Jesus refers to the Holy Spirit as "the Spirit of truth" (John 15:26). This means that the Holy Spirit has a unique ministry in certifying the truth about Jesus. In apologetics, we partner with the Holy Spirit in showing that God exists (a precondition for Jesus' identity as God), that the Scriptures are a reliable record of God's story, that the climax of God's story in the death and resurrection of Jesus is historically factual, and that key elements of God's story in Christ fit together into a cohesive whole. None of this takes over the role of the Holy Spirit. It is done in partnership with the Holy Spirit, and the Spirit's identity as the Spirit of truth ultimately certifies that what apologetics shows is actually the case.

Another doctrine of God supports apologetics' partnership with the Holy Spirit, as well: the doctrine of omnipresence. Apologetics trades on the fact that people can understand arguments and lines of evidence by using their minds to contemplate truth claims. Consider then what an argument is. It is not just something written down on a piece of paper or spoken by one person to another. When someone considers an argument, they have ideas that come to exist in the mind. Now ideas are not physical things; they are mental, nonphysical propositions. This is not dissimilar to God's nature. God is not a physical being. God is spirit and as such exists everywhere, including alongside apologetic arguments as they are entertained in our minds. Indeed, God's existence is a precondition for all rational thought, entailed by Paul's claims about the Son when he said that "all things have been created through him and for him . . . and in him all things hold together" (Col. 1:16–17). Here is an argument that sums up the Holy Spirit's relationship to apologetic arguments:

1. God is omnipresent.
2. God is omnipresent with the world of abstract ideas (i.e., arguments and propositions).
3. Apologetics is when logical argumentation is applied to propositions about God's revelation.
4. Apologetic arguments exist in minds.
5. God is omnipresent in minds.

Statement (1) is a classical doctrine of God universally recognized by the church, revealed in passages like Colossians 1. Statement (2) follows from (1). Statement (3) is in keeping with the account of apologetics that we developed in chapter 1. Statement (4) is supported by (3) and the account of arguments as mental things that we provided above. Statement (5) follows from (2) and (4).[3] Far from usurping the Holy Spirit's role, apologists depend on the Holy Spirit, especially his power, revelation, and presence, to make our efforts have any impact in evangelism at all.

APOLOGETICS' RELATIONSHIP TO DISCIPLESHIP

We champion a place for apologetics in how people come to confess Jesus as the Lord, but we also recognize that apologetics continues to play a role in how we follow Jesus moment by moment as his disciples. We see three key ways in which apologetics is related to discipleship. First, apologetics plays an important role in pre-Christian discipleship. This kind of discipleship goes hand in hand with evangelism, wherein seekers can begin to learn about Jesus and the Christian perspective on reality prior to confessing faith in Jesus. This is the kind of apologetics Jesus did with Nicodemus in John 3. Nicodemus did not understand Jesus' teaching about being born again, objecting that someone cannot be born when they are old. Jesus answered his objections and clarified the nature of the new birth as a spiritual birth. Nicodemus was not a follower of Jesus at this point, but Jesus was helping him to understand the nature of his message. Jesus even used the opportunity to challenge Nicodemus in his role as "Israel's teacher" (v. 10), helping him to understand that a different kind of authority exists in Christ for him to accept and proclaim. This seemed to work, because eventually Nicodemus venerated the crucified body of Jesus by assisting Joseph of Arimathea with the burial (John 19:39). This kind of discipleship for someone who is not yet a Christian is a key place where apologetics can do its work. North American culture has a place for interest in Jesus' life and ministry, particularly his ethical teaching, and good apologists

---

3. This argument is adapted from and more comprehensively defended in Andrew I. Shepardson, "The Spirit of Truth and the Unmoved Mover: The Presence of the Holy Spirit in Natural Theology," in *Quadrum* 2, no. 1 (July 2019): 44–59.

can use apologetics to help someone understand the cosmic and salvific nature of Jesus' ministry at a point where that same person may simply be attracted to Jesus' ethical teaching. In fact, good apologetics will show that Jesus' ethical teaching is tied to the kingdom of God and that one cannot separate Jesus' teachings from his kingdom mission, divine identity, and his death and resurrection.

Second, apologetics helps Christians to see that Christianity is true and not simply something that should be accepted without good reasons. Seeing the truth of Christianity helps Christians to start developing a lifestyle of faith seeking understanding. The truth and rationality of Christianity is encouraging, especially for Christians who are raised in a secular culture where truth claims are often reduced to scientific claims. When one can see that their faith has rational support, one is emboldened to study better and to share one's findings with others. As J. P. Moreland argues, "Discipleship unto the Lord Jesus is a thoughtful life."[4] This kind of life can pay dividends in many areas, but of course, for those of us interested in our discipleship, this can help with Bible study in particular. Westerners are trained to look at the world through secular lenses. When Christians study the Bible, this can negatively impact how they read and interpret it, perhaps causing them to miss the true significance of the biblical message. As Carl F. H. Henry argued, the biblical worldview will be "subject to alteration or displacement and its stern condemnation of false gods will be ignored. . . . Absolute truth about religious reality will be considered ugly dogmatism."[5] This seems to be exactly what happens when Christians start to miss the cosmic nature of the revelation of God in Christ and simply start to see Christianity as one religious preference among many in a world governed by reductively scientific versions of truth and rationality. Apologetics can challenge this. As Moreland claims, "Apologetics can focus attention on some of those secular structures, call them into question, and release the self to view the world in a way more compatible with a Christian worldview."[6] This makes reading the

---

4. J. P. Moreland, *Kingdom Triangle: Recover the Christian Mind, Renovate the Soul, Restore the Spirit's Power* (Grand Rapids: Zondervan, 2007), 132.

5. Carl F. H. Henry, *God, Revelation, and Authority*, 6 vols. (Wheaton, IL: Crossway, 1999), 2:25.

6. J. P. Moreland, *Scaling the Secular City: A Defense of Christianity* (Grand Rapids: Baker, 1987), 12.

Bible more fruitful and transformative in someone's life and gives greater confidence to the Christian as they minister to others.

Third, apologetics can help with some kinds of doubt. Think about what happens when one is confronted, often for the first time in high school or college, with the claims of Darwinism. The picture of reality painted by Darwinism pushes God to the edges, with all of the biological universe being the result of chance and necessity in a system that does not allow for divine design or intervention. This causes some young people to doubt if there is a place for God in how life has come to exist. The arguments that we provide in chapter 7 can help to assuage these doubts, giving the Christian confidence that the Christian worldview is true and the nature of the physical world actually shows evidence of divine design. This relief from doubt happened to me when I (Ike) first learned of the moral argument for the existence of God from the problem of evil. We discussed this argument in chapter 6. For many, the problem of evil is an intellectual and existential challenge. However, when I learned about the moral argument, I was convinced that my belief in God had rational support, and when I applied that argument to the existence of objective evil, I received further relief from my doubts through understanding the necessity of the existence of an objective evaluator to make sense of why some things are objectively evil. Apologetics can help to assuage some kinds of doubt, giving the Christian confidence in her convictions. However, while there are some kinds of doubt that can be addressed through studying apologetics, we recognize that humans are complex creatures who suffer doubt for various reasons and in various ways. Apologetics should not be used to address doubt like ibuprofen is used to address a headache. Prayerful care is needed to diagnose the cause of one's doubt and determine the best way forward.[7]

Good discipleship addresses the whole person, not just their capacity for rationality or their need for questions to be addressed. Yet apologetics has a role to play in someone's discipleship. Sadly, this is a neglected part of discipleship in many churches. We offer this book as one way to strengthen the church in hopes that leaders and teachers will take up

---

7. For an excellent resource in understanding various kinds of doubts, their causes, and cures, see Os Guinness, *God in the Dark: The Assurance of Faith beyond a Shadow of Doubt* (Wheaton, IL: Crossway, 1996).

the call to help those in their ministries to "always be prepared . . . to give the reason for the hope" they have (1 Peter 3:15) for the benefit of those inside the family of God (that is, in their own discipleship) and for those outside of God's family (evangelism).

HOW TO START DOING APOLOGETICS

Of course, our goals are bigger than simply equipping you with apologetic arguments. Our hope is that you take what you learn out into the world. Indeed, anything that's worth learning is worth passing on, but this is all the more the case with the Christian message, a message that Jesus' followers have been entrusted with and commissioned to share with all the world. So we conclude with some advice on how to start doing apologetics. The first thing needed to do apologetics is prayer. We are under no illusions that good arguments are the silver bullet in ministry. In fact, we have seen how good arguments can be misconstrued, misapplied, and ignored by people who are not yet ready to accept them. Prayer is vital here, for it reminds us that the power to change lives is solely in God's hands. Prayer is effective too. As James has reminded us, "The prayer of a righteous person is powerful and effective" (James 5:16). We pray before, during, and after our apologetic teaching. We pray for those in our lives who need to hear arguments for the truth of the Christian worldview. Our studying has given us confidence in what we say, but only God's power, to which we appeal when we pray, has ever made our apologetic endeavors successful. This is all the more important when one has a conviction of God's sovereignty, as we do. As my (Ike's) childhood pastor, Alan Eastland, often would say, "The sovereign God has sovereignly willed to accomplish his sovereign purposes through people who pray." Are there people in your life with whom you would like to share the good news? Are there people around you who have honest questions about Christianity? Are there Christians in your life who need a boost to their confidence that Christianity is true, rational, and pertinent to every aspect of life? Start praying now, and do not give up. God may use you as you share what you have learned in this book, but you will be effective only through his power, which you call on when you pray.

Second, the people in your sphere of influence are a key place to start as you think about how to do apologetics. God places his servants strategically to do his will. Of course, God calls us to go out into the world, seeking opportunities to preach the gospel and to teach, but going can also apply to one's immediate sphere of influence, those in your workplace, church, family, school, and neighborhood. As missiologist John Amstutz asserts, "More people come to Christ through existing relationships with family, friends, acquaintances, and neighbors than any other way. Such existing spheres of influence are the primary 'fishing ponds' in winning people to Christ."[8] When you do go into your immediate context, be extra aware of people who seem eager and open to you and your message. Jesus seemed to identify "someone who promotes peace" as one who is more open to receiving his followers and their message. He instructed, "When you enter a house, first say, 'Peace to this house.' If someone who promotes peace is there, your peace will rest on them; if not, it will return to you" (Luke 10:5–6). These kinds of people are those in our lives who are interested in engaging in conversations about spirituality or new acquaintances who seem extra eager to receive us as friends. This leads to a general guideline: as you bring apologetics to people around you, always be asking God if there are others, whether near or far, who need to hear the message of Christ through you. Keep your eyes open to opportunities for cross-cultural and international ministry (if only to partner, support, and pray, though also to go) just as much as you attend to your immediate context.

Third, you need to think about the art and science of persuasion. A great way to take a normal conversation and make it an opportunity to love someone through the sharing of apologetics is to be a good listener and a good questioner. Apologist Greg Koukl calls this "the Columbo Method," named after the bumbling but brilliant television detective. Imagine you're in a conversation where someone says something like, "All religions are basically the same." Koukl recommends asking something like, "What do you mean by that?"[9] Specifically, you might want to ask,

---

8. John L. Amstutz, *Disciples of All Nations: Continuous Mission until He Comes* (Los Angeles: Foursquare Media, 2009), 45.

9. Gregory Koukl, *Tactics: A Game Plan for Discussing Your Christian Convictions*, 10th Anniversary ed. (Grand Rapids: Zondervan, 2019), 65.

"How are they all the same?" Or, "Are you saying they are all the same in what they believe about God, the same in what they prescribe as a solution to our problems, or something else?" Starting off an apologetic encounter this way has a number of advantages: showing genuine, friendly interest in another's point of view; learning about which apologetic line of evidence makes a difference in the person's life; avoiding the appearance of being pushy; giving you time to think about how to engage the person with the truth of Jesus; and helping you to control where the discussion goes without sacrificing genuine interest in the views of the other.[10] Good questions can help you to show someone where there may be a contradiction in their presuppositions or where they have been misinformed. Good questions help you to expose their mistakes without shaming them and to avoid appearing as if you are interested in winning an argument.

Now, when you're in an apologetic endeavor, you also need to think about how you might winsomely persuade someone else to embrace the Christian worldview. There is no one-size-fits-all method for this. As Os Guinness instructs us, "Creative persuasion is the art of truth, the art that truth inspires."[11] This means lovingly addressing the heart and the mind with sensitivity to the unbeliever's predisposition against the truth. "We assume the biblical understanding of the human resistance to truth and hatred of God. And . . . we assume the biblical understanding of the conscious and unconscious desire for God that is fulfilled only in the knowledge of God who is love."[12] The person with whom we do apologetics may be resistant to the truth, but through creatively attempting to persuade them, we may reach their heart and mind with the very spiritual nourishment for which they have been longing. We have seen this work through succinct recitation of logical arguments for the existence of God, the use of poetry and other forms of literature, classical rhetoric, good storytelling, and the sharing of one's personal testimony. Again, there is no single way to do this. How someone might be persuaded is, in some ways, person-relative, but we need to think about how we communicate as much as what we communicate.

---

10. Koukl, 58–60.

11. Os Guinness, *Fool's Talk: Recovering the Art of Christian Persuasion* (Downers Grove, IL: InterVarsity, 2015), 34.

12. Guinness, 41.

Fourth, we need to think about how we live our lives as much as the reasons for our belief. Hypocrites and charlatans abound, unfortunately even among apologists. We need to attend to the condition of our souls even as we attempt to outthink the world for Christ. Nonbelievers are right to show us where we fail, so we should be people of humility, willing to own our sin, especially as we point to the Savior who is restoring our lives. But holy living, especially embodied in love for other Christians, gives more credibility to our message, just as Jesus said, "By this everyone will know that you are my disciples, if you love one another" (John 13:35). If we fail to live lives of love and holiness, those around us will notice, and it will discredit us and our message. As Christopher Wright warns us, "The world will see no reason to pay any attention to our claims about our invisible God if it sees no visible difference between the lives of those who make such claims and those who don't."[13] So make sure you are in relationships of accountability, that you confess your sins and receive God's forgiveness, that you are generous with those in need, and that you are doing all of these things for the glory of God. Most importantly, lean into God's grace. The Christian life is not about being good, but receiving God's grace, which is God's power made perfect in your weakness (2 Cor. 12:9).

Fifth, pray for boldness. It's okay if you are a naturally timid person. God has special blessing for those of us who are meek (Matt. 5:5). All the same, though, pray that God makes you bold to take advantage of the opportunities to share the good news with those around you. Remember the early church who, when under threat and fear of persecution, prayed, "Enable your servants to speak your word with great boldness. Stretch out your hand to heal and perform signs and wonders through the name of your holy servant Jesus" (Acts 4:29–30).

Sixth, pray for the power of the Holy Spirit. The Holy Spirit came into your life at your conversion, and you can ask Jesus for the Spirit's power in your ministry, as Jesus promised. "You will receive power when the Holy Spirit comes on you; and you will be my witnesses in Jerusalem, and in all Judea and Samaria, and to the ends of the earth" (Acts 1:8).

---

13. Christopher J. H. Wright, *The Mission of God's People: A Biblical Theology of the Church's Mission* (Grand Rapids: Zondervan, 2010), 132.

Finally, be sure to share the good news and invite those with whom you speak to receive Jesus. Simply explaining why you think Christianity is true can be easy, but it is necessary to lovingly invite others to accept the truth. Be gentle and kind but clear. "Jesus is real, he loves you, and he wants to be your Master and Savior. Would you be willing to welcome Jesus into your life? I'd be happy to show you how." Of course, what you say and how you say it will depend on the situation, but never be afraid to share the gospel and to invite others to receive it.

CONCLUSION

We hope that the end of this book is just the beginning of your journey of boldly sharing the good news of Jesus with Christian apologetics in your tool belt. We have covered a lot of ground, but it is inspiring and awesome ground. We welcomed you into the discipline of classical apologetics, explaining the basic but flexible method of establishing God's existence and the truth of God's revelation in Christ, particularly as given in the Bible. We answered objections to apologetics and established it as a biblical and helpful way of showing the truth of Christianity. We explained ontological arguments with their emphasis on logical *a priori* proof for God's existence. We established that the origins of the cosmos show that there is a Creator. We showed how objective moral values and duties require a divine lawgiver. We showed how features of the natural world give evidence of a designer. We explained how the Bible is historically reliable and a trustworthy source of knowledge. We showed how Jesus' life and ministry, his death and resurrection are facts that everyone needs to confront at some point. Most importantly, we have learned that God has spoken in the world and in the Word. Whatever truth we speak is just a rehearsal of his glorious revelation, the revelation in which God has spoken "at many times and in various ways" (Heb. 1:1), the revelation of his glory that we have seen, "the glory of the one and only Son, who came from the Father, full of grace and truth" (John 1:14). May God the Father, Son, and Holy Spirit be glorified in you as you speak the truth in love.

STUDY QUESTIONS

1. How is apologetics related to evangelism?
2. How is apologetics related to discipleship?
3. In what ways can a Christian start to do apologetics?

SUGGESTED READING

Amstutz, John L. *Disciples of All Nations: Continuous Mission until He Comes.* Los Angeles: Foursquare Media, 2009.

Craig, William Lane. *The Kalām Cosmological Argument.* Eugene, OR: Wipf and Stock, 2000.

Guinness, Os. *Fool's Talk: Recovering the Art of Christian Persuasion.* Downers Grove, IL: InterVarsity, 2015.

_____. *God in the Dark: The Assurance of Faith beyond a Shadow of Doubt.* Wheaton, IL: Crossway, 1996.

Henry, Carl F. H. *God, Revelation, and Authority.* 6 vols. Wheaton, IL: Crossway, 1976–83.

Koukl, Gregory. *Tactics: A Game Plan for Discussing Your Christian Convictions.* 10th Anniversary ed. Grand Rapids: Zondervan, 2019.

Little, Paul E. *How to Give Away Your Faith.* Downers Grove, IL: InterVarsity, 2018.

Moreland, J. P. *Kingdom Triangle: Recover the Christian Mind, Renovate the Soul, Restore the Spirit's Power.* Grand Rapids: Zondervan, 2007.

_____. *Scaling the Secular City: A Defense of Christianity.* Grand Rapids: Baker, 1987.

Shepardson, Andrew I. "The Spirit of Truth and the Unmoved Mover: The Presence of the Holy Spirit in Natural Theology." *Quadrum* 2, no. 1 (July 2019): 44–59.

_____. *Who's Afraid of the Unmoved Mover?* Eugene, OR: Pickwick, 2019.

Wright, Christopher J. H. *The Mission of God's People: A Biblical Theology of the Church's Mission.* Grand Rapids: Zondervan, 2010.

Ya'qub ibn Ishaq al-Kindi. *Al-Kindi's Metaphysics: A Translation of Ya'qub ibn Ishaq al-Kindi's Treatise "On First Philosophy" (fī al-Falsafah al-Ūlā).* Albany: State University of New York Press, 1974.

GLOSSARY

Chapter 1

1. **Special revelation.** A class or type of God's self-revelation that includes the Bible, the person and work of Jesus Christ, and the Holy Spirit. Special revelation is the primary and definitive material from which we understand the truth about God, humanity, the good life, the world, and any other topic it addresses.

2. **General revelation.** A class or type of God's self-revelation that includes the natural world, in logic, and in the human conscience, given generally or universally to all humanity. This revelation does not determine Christian doctrine and practice, but it does confirm special revelation. This forms the primary source material for arguments for the existence of God.

3. **Apologetics.** The ministry of defending and commending the knowledge of God that is revealed in the Bible and in the world around us. Apologetics shows how Christianity is true, rational, and pertinent to every area of life.

4. **Natural theology.** Rational reflection on God's general revelation. Natural theology employs deductive and inductive argumentation and inferences to the best explanation. In particular, natural theology develops arguments for God's existence, including ontological arguments, moral arguments, design arguments, and cosmological arguments.

5. *Reductio ad absurdum.* A Latin phrase meaning "reduction to absurdity." This is an argument form that takes a claim and shows that this claim leads to an absurd conclusion, which must be false. Therefore,

the initial claim is false. For example, if atheism leads to nihilism, and nihilism is absurd, then atheism is false. Formally: If P, then Q. Q (which is absurd). Therefore, not-P. This is a form of *modus tollens* reasoning. It is also called *denying the consequent.*

6. **Negative apologetics.** The activity of showing that non-Christian worldviews are illogical or do not fit the facts.

Chapter 2

1. **Fideism.** The idea that true faith is contrary to or, in the least, makes no reference to reason.

2. **Justification.** This is a necessary condition for knowledge. It is the idea that one must have good reasons for a belief. Along with the truth of the belief (for example, that your belief is the case), justification is necessary to have knowledge.

3. **Epistemology.** The branch of philosophy that is concerned with knowledge and truth.

4. *Modus tollens.* This is an argument type that means, in Latin, "in the method of denying." Formally it denies the consequent in a logical argument. If P, then Q. Not-Q. Therefore, not-P.

5. **Common ground.** Any beliefs that Christians hold with those who are outside of the Christian faith that can serve as a way to help those outside the faith to embrace the gospel. For example, belief in one God, belief in objective morality, or belief in logic are kinds of common ground that Christians can discover and build on to help others to embrace the gospel.

6. *Reductio ad absurdum.* A Latin phrase meaning "reduction to absurdity." This is an argument form that takes a claim and shows that this claim leads to an absurd conclusion, which must be false. Therefore, the initial claim is false. For example, if atheism leads to nihilism, and nihilism is absurd, then atheism is false. Formally: If P, then Q. Q (which is absurd). Therefore, not-P. This is a form of *modus tollens* reasoning. It is also called *denying the consequent.*

7. **Theological liberalism.** The general tendency to deny the truth and sufficiency of the Bible and the uniqueness and divinity of Jesus Christ. This is not typically related to political liberalism or classical liberalism.

8. **Particularism.** The perspective that Christian truth claims are uniquely true and that the truth claims of other religions that conflict with Christian truth claims are false.

9. **Law of noncontradiction.** This is the logical principle that two conflicting truth claims cannot both be true at the same time and in the same respect. This also refers to the principle that something cannot both be and not be at the same time and in the same respect.

10. **Ontotheology.** The sin of using philosophy to attempt to control and manipulate the concept of God. Christians who hold to the ontotheology objection claim that the god of natural theology is not the God of Abraham, Isaac, and Jacob.

Chapter 3

1. **Category mistake.** A logical fallacy in which the wrong category is used to assess a truth claim. To ask who created a being defined as uncreated is, thus, a category mistake.

2. *Ex nihilo.* A Latin phrase meaning "out of nothing." This applies to the biblical doctrine that God created the cosmos out of nothing. That is, he did not use preexisting materials, nor is the cosmos an extension of his own being (as in panentheism). See especially Genesis 1:1; Psalm 90:2; John 1:1–2; and Revelation 4:11.

3. **Methodological naturalism.** A way of approaching questions in which the very possibility of a nonnaturalistic explanation is ruled out in principle. This approach is used by Darwinists in biology to foreclose the possibility of intelligent design by an immaterial agent as the best explanation for some features of nature, such as molecular machines.

4. **Presuppositionalism.** An apologetic approach that presupposed the truth and rationality of the Christian worldview instead of seeking outside evidence from reason, history, and science to confirm the truth of Christianity. Presuppositions focus on negative apologetics, not natural theology, evidence for the resurrection, and so on.

5. **Red herring.** A logical fallacy that diverts attention from the real issue by injecting something having only a superficial relationship to the matters at hand and which is argumentatively moot. If an apologist gives an argument for creation *ex nihilo* and an atheist responds by saying that Christians cannot agree on the age of the universe,

this fallacy has been committed. This is because the dispute among Christians about the age of the universe has nothing to do with whether or not it came into being a finite time ago.

Chapter 4

1. **Actual infinite.** A completed totality that is unlimited. The kalam cosmological argument argues that an actual infinite is logically impossible or that it cannot exist in actuality.

2. *Ad infinitum.* A Latin phrase meaning "and so on forever"; that is, it continues without an end.

3. **Big bang cosmology.** A colloquial name for "the standard model" in cosmology that claims that the universe began to exist a finite time ago. At this point, space, time, matter, and energy all began to exist.

4. **Contingent truth.** A statement that corresponds to reality, but which might not have been true, such as my dog's name is Sunny. I might have named him Coltrane, or I might not have had a dog at all.

5. **Kalam cosmological argument.** A particular version of the cosmological argument that is deductive in form and argues that if the universe began to exist, it must have a cause outside of itself, and that cause is God.

6. **Necessary truth.** A statement that corresponds to reality and which must be true, such as the basic laws of logic and the validity of deductive argument forms, such as: If P, then Q. P. Therefore, Q.

7. **Potential infinite.** A series that ever increases but never reaches a terminal limit, such as the set of all positive numbers.

8. **Principle of sufficient reason (PSR).** A logical principle that holds that for any positive state there must be an explanation (known or unknown) for why it exists. Atheists who believe the universe is just there without any explanation deny this principle as having universal scope.

Chapter 5

1. *A priori.* A Latin phrase that refers to knowledge gained through internal rational reflection.

2. *A posteriori.* A Latin phrase that refers to knowledge gained by observing or experiencing something in the external world.

3. **Scientism.** The philosophical idea that knowledge is gained only through the sciences.

4. **Possible world.** A concept used by philosophers to consider a complete set of states of affairs that could all exist in a coherent reality.

5. **Methodological naturalism.** A way of approaching questions in which the very possibility of a nonnaturalistic explanation is ruled out in principle. This approach is used by Darwinists in biology to foreclose the possibility of intelligent design by an immaterial agent as the best explanation for some features of nature, such as molecular machines.

6. *Reductio ad absurdum.* A Latin phrase meaning "reduction to absurdity." This is an argument form that takes a claim and shows that this claim leads to an absurd conclusion, which must be false. Therefore, the initial claim is false. For example, if atheism leads to nihilism, and nihilism is absurd, then atheism is false. Formally: If P, then Q. Q (which is absurd). Therefore, not-P. This is a form of *modus tollens* reasoning. It is also called *denying the consequent.*

7. **Necessary and contingent truths.** A necessary truth is one that could not have been otherwise. A contingent truth is one that so happens to be the case but could have been otherwise.

Chapter 6

1. *Modus tollens.* This is an argument type that means, in Latin, "in the method of denying." Formally it denies the consequent in a logical argument. If P, then Q. Not-Q. Therefore, not-P.

2. **Objective moral values and duties.** Objective moral values are things that are good or bad regardless of people's opinions about them. Objective moral duties are actions that are right or wrong regardless of people's opinions of them.

3. **Moral subjectivism.** The idea that what is moral differs from person to person.

4. **Cultural relativism.** The idea that what is moral differs from culture to culture.

5. **Nihilism.** From the Latin *nihil*, meaning "nothing." Nihilism is the idea that there are no such things as moral values, and that our moral choices have no objective meaning.

6. **Reductive naturalistic moral realism.** This phrase means that only naturalistic or physical explanations are necessary to describe and justify belief in objective moral values and duties.

7. **Godless normative realism.** The belief that there are real and objective moral values and duties that do not require a divine foundation. These values and duties simply exist and do not have an explanation.

8. **Occam's razor.** A philosophical virtue in which, all things being equal, one should prefer simpler explanations over more complicated ones. It is also known as parsimony.

Chapter 7

1. **The two books of nature.** A concept developed in Christian philosophy to indicate that the same God is the author of the Bible and the author of nature (or his creation). Both books, when properly interpreted, reveal God.

2. **Irreducible complexity.** A phrase coined by biochemist Michael Behe to refer to a system in which each part is required for the whole to operate in a biologically successful manner. If anything is irreducibly complex, it cannot be formed in a slow, purposeless, and incremental fashion, as Darwinism claimed is the only explanation for any living organism (except the first, which Darwinism did not address as a theory). Behe takes the bacterial flagellum to be irreducibly complex.

Chapter 8

1. **Minimalist view.** The view that Jews living in Palestine in the fifth through the third centuries BCE compiled an imagined history of their past in the lands of Palestine that legitimized their claims to the land and their particularities as a people unique from their neighbors. They cobbled together what eventually took shape as the Hebrew Bible (what Christians refer to as the Old Testament), with its origin stories of the children of Israel, its wisdom writings, and its prophetic literature. It entails that the Hebrew Bible is primarily a fiction, an imagined national history used to legitimize the status of a people over and against their powerful neighbors.

2. **The bibliographic test.** This method of evaluation helps us to determine how closely the text that we have today matches with the

original text that ancient peoples read and heard. It tends to examine the number and age of manuscripts and variants of passages within the manuscripts.

Chapter 9

1. **Truth.** An indicative statement is true if and only if it corresponds or matches the reality to which it refers. Thus, the statement "Jesus is Lord" is true only if, in fact, he is Lord in reality.
2. **Propitiation.** To make peace or to atone through an action wherein two parties are reconciled. In relation to the work of Jesus, it means that he atoned for our sins through his sacrificial death on the cross, taking our punishment and thus giving us peace with God. The atonement involves more aspects than propitiation (such as adoption, reconciliation, deliverance from the devil, etc.), but propitiation is at the center of the atonement.

Chapter 10

1. **Karma.** The teaching that one's deeds determine one's fate in the next lifetime (reincarnation). Held by Hinduism and Buddhism.
2. **Miracle.** In the biblical sense, an event that cannot be explained by natural means alone but requires a supernatural cause. The pivotal miracle in the Bible is the resurrection of Jesus from the dead in space-time history.
3. **Reincarnation.** The idea that living things die and return to life in another living form over and over until they ascend to liberation beyond this karmic cycle. This is contrasted with the biblical teaching of final judgment and resurrection (1 Cor. 15; Heb. 9:27).

INDEX

The Knowledge of God in the World and the Word Workbook

An Introduction to Classical Apologetics

Douglas Groothuis and
Andrew I. Shepardson

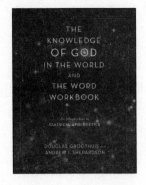

In the *Knowledge of God in the World and the Word Workbook*, designed to be used alongside the *Knowledge of God in the World and the Word* textbook by authors Douglas Groothuis and Andrew I. Shepardson, students are guided through learning exercises that introduce them to classical apologetics and to innovative defenses of natural theology.

Available in stores and online!

Believing Philosophy

A Guide to Becoming a Christian Philosopher

Dolores G. Morris

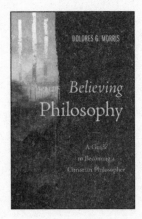

Philosophy has been a part of Christianity since its earliest days, and theistic philosophy predates Christianity by thousands of years. But Christians today often don't realize or are skeptical of all that philosophy can offer them.

In part 1, author Dolores G. Morris explains why Christians should read and study philosophy. She begins with a historical overview of Christian philosophy from the church fathers to contemporary philosophers and then introduces the basic resources of philosophical reasoning: the role and aim of reason, distinctions between truth and reason and provability, and learning to read like a philosopher. These chapters address three foundational questions:

- *What* is philosophy?
- *Why* should a Christian study philosophy?
- *How* should a Christian study philosophy?

In part 2, Morris introduces students to philosophical arguments and questions relevant to Christians. She presents arguments by three key branches of philosophy: metaphysics, epistemology, and practical philosophy. Building on concepts introduced in part 1, she explains what philosophical arguments are and how they ought to be evaluated from a philosophical and Christian perspective. The following chapters examine specific questions most pressing for Christians today:

- The problem of evil
- Rationality and faith
- Free will
- Skeptical theism
- The moral argument for the existence of God
- Reformed epistemology

Each chapter introduces the problem, explains Christian responses, discusses the strengths and weaknesses of each response, and leaves the final verdict to the reader. Finally, each chapter concludes with a list of recommended further readings.

Cultural Apologetics

Renewing the Christian Voice, Conscience, and Imagination in a Disenchanted World

Paul M. Gould

Christianity has an image problem. While the culture we inhabit presents us with an increasingly anti-Christian and disenchanted position, the church in the West has not helped its case by becoming anti-intellectual, fragmented, and out of touch with the relevancy of Jesus to all aspects of contemporary life.

The muting of the Christian voice, its imagination, and its collective conscience have diminished the prospect of having a genuine missionary encounter with others today.

Cultural apologetics attempts to demonstrate not only the truth of the Gospel but also its desirability by reestablishing Christianity as the answer that satisfies our three universal human longings—truth, goodness, and beauty.

In *Cultural Apologetics*, philosopher and professor Paul Gould sets forth a fresh and uplifting model for cultural engagement—rooted in the biblical account of Paul's speech in Athens—which details practical steps for establishing Christianity as both true and beautiful, reasonable and satisfying.

Available in stores and online!

ZONDERVAN ACADEMIC

The History of Apologetics

A Biographical and Methodological Introduction

Benjamin K. Forrest, Josh Chatraw, and Alister E. McGrath, editors

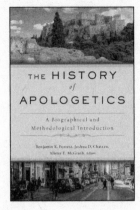

The History of Apologetics follows the great apologists in the history of the church to understand how they approached the task of apologetics in their own cultural and theological context. Each chapter looks at the life of a well-known apologist from history, unpacks their methodology, and details how they approached the task of defending the faith.

Available in stores and online!

Apologetics at the Cross

An Introduction for Christian Witness

Josh Chatraw and Mark D. Allen

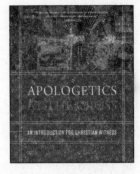

This is a guidebook for how to defend Christianity with Christlike gentleness and respect toward those who persecute the faith, making you a stronger witness to the good news of the gospel than many other apologetics books that focus on crafting unbreachable arguments.

Joshua D. Chatraw and Mark D. Allen first provide an introduction to the rich field of apologetics and Christian witness, acquainting students and lay learners with the rich history, biblical foundation, and ongoing relevance of apologetics. Unique in its approach, *Apologetics at the Cross*:

- Presents the biblical and historical foundations for apologetics
- Explores various contemporary methods for approaching apologetics
- Gives practical guidance in "how to" chapters that feature many real-life illustrations

But their approach pays special attention to the attitude and posture of the apologist, outlining instructions for the Christian community centered on reasoned answers, a humble spirit, and joy rather than anger, arrogance, and aggression. Chatraw and Allen equip Christians to engage skeptics with the heart as well as the mind.

Conversational in tone and balanced in approach, *Apologetics at the Cross* provides a readable introduction to the field of apologetics. You'll be informed and equipped for engaging a wide range of contemporary challenges with the best in Christian thought.

Available in stores and online!